BIG BUSINESS IN RUSSIA

PITT SERIES IN RUSSIAN AND EAST EUROPEAN STUDIES

Jonathan Harris, *Editor*

BIG BUSINESS IN RUSSIA

THE PUTILOV COMPANY
IN LATE IMPERIAL RUSSIA
1868–1917

Jonathan A. Grant

UNIVERSITY OF PITTSBURGH PRESS

Library of Congress Cataloging-in-Publication Data

Grant, Jonathan A., 1963–
    Big business in Russia : the Putilov Company in late Imperial
Russia, 1868–1917 / Jonathan A. Grant.
      p. cm. — (Pitt series in Russian and East European studies)
  Includes bibliographical references and index.
  ISBN 0-8229-4110-4 (acid-free paper)
    1. Krasnyi putilovets—History. 2. Firearms industry and
trade—Russia—History. I. Title. II. Series.
  HD9744.F554 Ky34 1999
  338.7'6234'0947—dc21

                         99-6562
                          CIP

Published by the University of Pittsburgh Press, Pittsburgh, Pa. 15261
Copyright © 1999, University of Pittsburgh Press
All rights reserved
Manufactured in the United States of America
Printed on acid-free paper
10 9 8 7 6 5 4 3 2 1

A CIP catalog record for this book is available from the British Library.

CONTENTS

Acknowledgments

This work is dedicated to the many people who have contributed to my intellectual growth over the long years of my higher education, and without whom I would not have been able to undertake the task, let alone complete it. First I would like to thank David McDonald for all his support and encouragement. He has been my mentor in the fullest sense of the word as a scholar, a teacher, and a friend. He was the reason I first came to study at Madison, and under his guidance I came to appreciate the full richness of the field of Russian history. I also express my thanks to Alfred Senn and Colleen Dunlavy for expanding my conceptions of history as a discipline and showing me how to be more imaginative and rigorous in my approach to research. In addition, from my days at Indiana University I owe a debt of gratitude to Ben Eklof, who first introduced me to Russian history. I would also like to thank Thomas C. Owen for his generous help in suggesting additional source materials and for his willingness to offer critical advice on this project at various stages in its development. Also, Yevgenia Borisova of the *St. Petersburg Times* very graciously allowed me to use some of her notes regarding the Kirovsky Zavod.

Since my arrival at Florida State in 1995, I have received tremendous moral and intellectual support from my colleagues in the History Department. Richard Greaves, Ed Wynot, Neil Betten, and Peter Garretson deserve special thanks for welcoming me so warmly to Tallahassee and encouraging me to grow as a member of the department. I would also like to thank the undergraduate and graduate students at FSU for their enthusiasm and their friendship. Amy Cores, Llew Cook, Karen Darden, Kevin McCranie, and Yamile Regalado have all inspired me in the classroom and in my research. In addition, Emily Weber and the members of the Catholic Student Union have provided me with inspiration outside the classroom, and I thank them for the special relationships they have given me.

Finally, and most important, I owe most to my family. My parents, Edward and Sydelle Grant, and my sister, Robyn, and my brother, Marshall, have all supported me generously with their love. In truth, I could not have made it without them.

INTRODUCTION

As Russia emerges from the legacy of the Soviet command economy in the late twentieth century, it is worth remembering that this is not the first time that Russians have struggled to adapt to the complexities of contemporary capitalism. From the late nineteenth century to 1917, entrepreneurs and government officials confronted comparable challenges as they attempted to integrate private enterprise, foreign investment, and the latest foreign production techniques into the Russian environment. To shed light on the tsarist experience, this study examines the history of the Putilov Company in the late imperial period. It offers a perspective generally lacking in previous works on the tsarist economy, namely, that of the Russian businessmen themselves.

The question of Russia's relation to the rest of the world, and to the West in particular, remains a fundamental issue in Russian historiography. Conventionally, historians have taken Russian development to be backward or an exceptional deviation from Western norms, and these scholars have suggested that Russian businessmen operated according to a different understanding from their Western counterparts. In this view, tsarist autocracy and Russian uniqueness conditioned these differences. My study seeks to answer the questions regarding the exceptionalism of Russian business development by posing the question: Did Russian businessmen conduct their affairs in a unique way based on an essentially different understanding of the market and the state, or did they pursue strategies for growth that would have been intelligible to their contemporaries in Britain, France, Germany, and the United States? This study eschews grand theory in favor of straightforward comparison. In posing this question I do not argue for a convergence toward a single path of development, but in answering it I do point out the strong parallels between the development of the Putilov Company in Russia and its cohorts in Europe and the United States. In making those comparisons, this study relies on the secondary literature in American and European business history.

The main thesis of this work is that contrary to long-held historiographical assumptions, Russian business development was not deviant; indeed, the Putilov Company's board of directors followed strategies for growth that were consistent with the decisions of contemporary firms in Europe and the United States. By 1900, the Putilov Company was already the largest private factory and the most important defense firm in tsarist Russia. Putilov's market behavior was not essentially different from that of its Western counterparts such as Krupp, Schneider-Creusot, Vickers, and Skoda. Putilov's directors made decisions to abandon old product lines and undertook new ones based on their reading of the markets, and they considered state agencies to be long-term customers in those markets.

However, contradicting the assumptions about its dependency on the state, by 1900 Putilov was no longer a creature of state indulgence, but enjoyed a healthy private market share as well. Moreover, the private market share remained the more substantial portion even as the company embarked on its career as a defense enterprise. Thus, an overview of Putilov's growth and development calls for a reevaluation of the strength of the Russian domestic markets for industrial goods and the direct role of the state in industrializing Russia.

Currently the subfield of business history in Russia is virtually nonexistent. Although a few specialists have delved into various areas of business activity in Russia, by and large these works deal either with companies established in Russia by foreigners or with nonindustrial firms such as banking, insurance, or publishing.[1] No one has yet created any detailed studies of a native Russian metalworking enterprise. Russian business history has not attracted much scholarly attention for a variety of reasons. First, in tsarist society itself few among the educated social groups had any interest in commercial activities, and if they gave much thought at all to businessmen, their attitudes were usually negative or hostile. The revolutionary intelligentsia, liberal urban professionals, and members of the old nobility all evinced a strong distaste for Russian businessmen, and to some extent this dislike had roots in an older negative image of the merchant.[2]

The intelligentsia, both liberal and revolutionary, played a particularly significant role in writing businessmen out of the picture because they were preoccupied with their own struggle against the autocratic regime. Consequently, the intelligentsia tended to view everything through the lens of an irreconcilable conflict between state and society. The seeming political apathy of businessmen was taken to mean that they were either irrelevant to the vital struggle or that they were too cozy with the state.[3] If it is true that the winners write the history, then the Russian Revolution in 1917 served as yet another reason to ignore business history. The Bolsheviks consciously swept aside the remnants of capitalism, and later Soviet scholars emphasized the heroic struggle of workers and party members to vanquish the exploiting class. The industrialists appeared as little more than background scenery to the real historical drama of proletarian revolution.

Even had they had the inclination, scholars faced serious obstacles to pursuing business history while the Soviet Union still existed. Soviet historians were not free to investigate any topic, and their interpretations were subject to official ideological constraints and censorship. In this respect, there were domestic political and career considerations at stake if one deviated from the guidelines. In addition, both Soviet and foreign researchers enjoyed only limited access to archival materials, and those materials were themselves reduced by the tendency of businesses not to maintain their records or by the destruction of records during the First World War and the Russian Civil War.

Studies of industrialization in Russia have tended to play down the role of Russian industrialists, and the few works written on Russian businessmen do not express much interest in their business activities. Even the most recent works by Thomas Owen and Susan McCaffray are less concerned with Russian business behavior than with capitalism as a system.[4] To rectify this imbalance and to answer the questions regarding the exceptional character of Russian business development, it is necessary to analyze business activity at the level of the firm. That is to say, it is the individual firm that integrates new technology into production, reacts to market forces, and develops strategies for growth. Therefore, it is important to understand Russian industrial history at the micro level.

Can we generalize from the history of a single firm? The Putilov Company offers several advantages for this analysis. First, the Putilov works had been under state and private ownership at different times and retained close connections to the War and Naval Ministries. In this way it resembled other metalworking enterprises established in St. Petersburg after the Crimean War. Indeed, the company's founder, Nikolai Ivanovich Putilov, had served in the Naval Ministry prior to purchasing the plant in 1868. Moreover, virtually all of the metalworking enterprises experienced financial hardship, even though they received significant government contracts and ultimately had to sell out to foreign investors or the Naval Ministry. For example, Putilov sold out to foreigners, while Thomson and Obukhov were bought out by the Naval Ministry because of financial collapse. As a result, the state took over the Russo-Baltic Iron-Working and Mechanical Company, the Obukhov plant, and the Nevskii Shipbuilding plant.[5] Thus, the experience of the Putilov factory was typical of all the major Petersburg industrial enterprises. Second, the company's evolution from a personally owned factory into a joint-stock company with a diversified product mix ranging from metallurgical goods to locomotives, rolling stock, and defense items paralleled the development of other engineering firms in imperial Russia—thus illuminating that development. Putilov was not unique in its early reliance on the state, its early hardships, or its development strategies.

However, the company's specific characteristics were also significant. In physical size and capacity, Putilov held pride of place in Russia. Ultimately, the Putilov works became the largest factory employer in Russia, and by the early twentieth century it had become the largest supplier of light artillery for the tsarist government. Thus, Putilov occupied an important place in Russia's heavy industry sector and in the Petersburg region. Putilov was also the largest joint-stock engineering company in Russia in terms of output. Although the view has been refuted that the state had a driving role in the Russian economy as a whole, assumptions about state-driven industrial development continue to hold sway in discussions of the Russian heavy industry sector generally, and of the industrial enterprises of St. Petersburg in particular. Therefore, the Putilov Company seems a useful choice as a critical case study for testing the limits of state dependency.[6] If Putilov, the most important defense supplier, was not dependent on the state, then who was? Given both its commonalities with other Russian firms and its own specific characteristics, Putilov can serve as an important case. This study will show that the state's role has been overstated even for such a presumed state-dependent enterprise as the Putilov Company.

The Problem of Russian Exceptionalism

Since Peter Chaadaev penned his philosophical letters in the 1820s and 1830s, his assertions about the exceptional nature of Russia's historical development and the idea of Russian backwardness in comparison to Western civilization have been central to discussions of Russian identity. In 1829 Chaadaev declared, "We have never moved in concert with other peoples; we do not belong to any of the great families of mankind. We are not part of the Occident, nor are we part of the Orient." Further, he wrote in 1835:

> What did we discover, invent, or create? It is not a question of running after them; it is a question of an honest appraisal of ourselves. . . . After that we shall advance more rapidly than the others because we have come after them, because we have all their experience and all the work of the centuries which precede us.

In his later thinking, Chaadaev also devised the concept of the advantages of backwardness: Russia, unburdened by the weight of history that has impeded the West, could actually skip a stage of historical development and overtake the West. Although Chaadaev cast his ideas in terms of moral and spiritual development, later generations of Russian thinkers translated them into materialistic and economic terms.[7] In this way, Alexander Gerschenkron's mid-twentieth-century thesis about the advantages of backwardness for industrializing countries was rooted in a much deeper Russian intellectual tradition.[8] Gerschenkron placed Chaadaev's old question of whether Russia was a Western or an Eastern country in an economic context.

Gerschenkron's achievement was to universalize the question of Russian exceptionalism; in so doing, he contributed to the emerging school of modernization theory.[9] The modernization model is based on two assumptions: first, that all societies are ultimately headed toward the same destination, even though they have different points of departure; and second, that success is assured. Hence the model assumes the convergence of social development: all industrial societies are becoming more alike.[10] Gerschenkron argued that in more "backward" or less developed countries the state takes on the role played by private initiative in earlier industrializing nations. Russia enjoyed the advantages of backwardness in that it could simply import the latest techniques and technology for its industrial advancement; meanwhile, the state would intervene to supply the missing elements, primarily by providing a market for heavy industrial goods, especially railway equipment. Through fiscal policy, Gerschenkron noted, the government encouraged the influx of foreign capital from Europe, which laid the basis for large-scale industry. Once the process of industrialization was initiated, the government could play a less active role, and by 1912, in Gerschenkron's view, Russia was on its way to self-sustaining growth. This, in turn, signified that Russia had arrived on the path of "normal" development for modern industrial economies.[11] Thus, rather than being exceptional, Russia was simply one example of a backward industrializer.

Subsequent scholarship on Russian economic history has seriously questioned Gerschenkron's propositions. In macroeconomic terms, several works, especially those of Peter Gatrell and Paul Gregory, decisively demonstrate that in terms of fostering investment and pursuing a conscious industrial policy, Gerschenkron overstated the role of the state in Russian industrial development.[12] Additionally, John McKay's work shows that foreign capital and foreign expertise made important contributions to Russian industrial development, but that high interest returns on private foreign portfolio investments played more of a role than state efforts in attracting foreign capital. This was especially true in the iron and steel industry of South Russia.[13] Taken together, these studies challenge Gerschenkron's model.[14]

Yet the issue of Russia's modernization remains. Indeed, although modernization theory has generally fallen into disuse, it still has a firm grip on Russian history. In fact, it has received a second wind in the 1980s and 1990s and is still central to discussions of Russian development in the late imperial period. Perhaps this quirk can be explained by the fact that historical studies are shaped by contemporary economic conditions in the country under study. Therefore, the difficulties experienced by newly independent countries in Africa since the late 1960s in fulfilling the promises of economic modernization, coupled with the continuing frustrations of industrialization in Latin America, have created a skeptical pessimism that rejects modernization theory in those areas.[15] Meanwhile, perhaps modernization theory has held on so long in the Russian field because of the Soviet Union's relative success as an atomic superpower with a large heavy industry base and a successful space program.

In the field of Russian studies, the main line of division runs between those who consider modernization to be essentially a material or technological process and those who view it as an abstract or institutional one. For scholars in the first group, the long-term secular trends in Russian economic performance since the emancipation of the serfs in 1861 conform to the pattern of a modernizing economy and society, and they generally regard Russia as modern. They point to urbanization, improved literacy, high annual rates of growth, and a declining share for agriculture combined with a rising share for industry in the national economy as evidence for Russia's modernization.[16] Historians in the second group suggest that Russian businessmen operated according to a different understanding from their modern Western counterparts—differences attributed to autocracy and Russia's unique history. Along these lines, Fred Carstensen and Gregory Guroff argue that in terms of entrepreneurship Russia did not modernize. As they see it,

> The use of the terms modernization and industrialization requires some reflection. For these purposes industrialization is but one possible component of the broad process of modernization. It is useful to distinguish between the terms because the thrust of our argument is that Russia failed to modernize even though it industrialized. To put the matter in somewhat different form, Russia wanted, and to a significant degree acquired, the industrial brawn of the West, but not the "brain" of Western development, the complex matrix of institutional arrangements that created a polycentric society which tended to devalue tradition, to emphasize functional specialization, to separate spheres of activity, and to promote individualistic behavior.[17]

Joseph Bradley's detailed study of the tsarist small arms arsenals supports this view. He presents specific examples of the failure to modernize in state arsenals through their inability to innovate. Thus, the arsenals were trapped in a continuing cycle of borrowing new technology and production techniques because cultural factors inhibited product development and retarded technological diffusion. Specifically, Bradley argues that technological change in Russia has come from above or outside— that is, from the state or from foreigners—and that consequently market forces played no role. As a result, the arsenals did not internalize the innovations they benefited from because they had no financial motivation to do so; hence the small arms industry failed to reproduce even native technology, much less domesticate foreign ones.[18] In effect, Bradley too argues that Russians were unsuccessful in obtaining the "brain" of the West. In addition, the second group of scholars consider tsarist autocracy to have been the impeding force. The implication is that entrepreneurship among Russians was fundamentally different or exceptional because it was conditioned by the strict limits imposed by the autocratic state.

Both groups share an assumption that there is a clear standard against which to measure modernity or modernization. Usually that standard is the West or, more specifically, the industrial experience of Britain. By framing the discussion in this way, they assume that there is a single model for development and that Russia either moves toward it to become modern or deviates from it to remain exceptional. In the absence of any single universal model, the whole concept of modernization has received considerable criticism.[19] Therefore, let us lay aside the term *modern* and the intellectual baggage it carries with it.

Since Russian business history is a veritable blank slate, it is useful to place it in the context of the more established field of business history in the West. In particular, Alfred Chandler's concepts provide a means of comparing the managerial mentality of Putilov's board of directors with the patterns established by their counterparts in Britain, Germany, and the United States. Chandler posits a connection between corporate strategies for growth and structural change in company administration on the one hand, and the emergence of *managerial capitalism* on the other. By this term he means that salaried professional managers came to make the firm's decisions.[20] In Chandler's terms, the modern industrial enterprise emerged as the result of entrepreneurs pursuing an interrelated set of investments in large production facilities, distribution, and management.[21] If we again remove the *modern* label and concentrate on the behavior of firms as Chandler describes them, then we can find some use in comparing his patterns of investment with Russian business behavior. From the standpoint of Chandler's work, the Russian experience at Putilov seems to resemble most closely the German case.

There are dangers, of course, in trying to make Russia conform to analytical models devised for Western Europe and North America. Just because Russian businessmen adopted institutional forms similar to those of the West does not mean they employed them in the same way. Carstensen and Guroff argue, for example, that St. Petersburg firms "adopted a Western form devoid of much of its Western content"[22] as part of their contention that Russian entrepreneurs organized joint-stock companies but did not manage them as they were managed in the West. However, since prior to this study no one had researched any one Russian corporation in detail, Carstensen and Guroff's position cannot be substantiated.

In terms of the firm's performance, a strong case can be made for the appropriateness of measuring Putilov against the standards for big business in Europe. In his comprehensive survey of enterprises in Britain, France, and Germany, Youssef Cassis devises an effective and tangible set of quantitative benchmarks for European big business in terms of the size of the work force, capitalization, and profits. For the pre-1914 era, he suggests as criteria 5,000 employees and 2 million pounds sterling for paid-up capital. While profits will vary most with size, Cassis noted that for the big armaments firms the profits in the years 1911–1913 ranged from 639,000 pounds sterling for Armstrong to 1,762,000 pounds sterling for Krupp. On all these counts, Putilov deserves to be considered a big business firm as well. The plant employed 12,000 workers by 1901; by 1914 it was capitalized at roughly 2.5 million pounds sterling; and from 1911 to 1913 Putilov earned profits equivalent to 724,490 pounds sterling, putting it ahead of Armstrong but below Vickers and Krupp.[23]

The role of the firm and of industrialists in imperial Russia remains terra incognita. Soviet historians produced a number of excellent statistical studies of military and naval production in the nineteenth and early twentieth centuries[24] and on the banking links to arms production.[25]

These authors, however, did not give much attention to the firms themselves or to their directors, although they assumed close connections between arms suppliers and state officials involved in the process. A recent exception is A. N. Bokhanov's work, which fleshes out some of the connections between Russia's business elite and the bureaucracy in general, although Bokhanov is not especially concerned with the arms business.[26] Meanwhile, Soviet histories of individual military and naval factories are preoccupied with the development of the workers' movement and Bolshevik organization and pay only scant attention to the industrialists.[27] The Soviet works provide comprehensive statistical descriptions of military and naval production and a thorough accounting of the financial arrangements involved in weapons contracts, but they do not move on to analyze who made the decisions that accounted for that production.

Western scholars have exhibited a similar lack of interest in the industrialists generally. In the last decade this situation has begun to change, however; a number of studies have appeared that discuss the role of industrialists in imperial Russia, and most of these concentrate on Moscow industrialists. In part, the greater attention to the Moscow group reflects the available source base.[28] On this score, the business elite in Moscow is unquestionably better represented than any other group in the empire. Additionally, the prominence of Moscow in Russian and Soviet historiography can be seen as the result of the Slavophile legacy. Although it is usually acknowledged that St. Petersburg was economically important, the imperial capital is often omitted from Russian business histories because there international trade, foreign investment, and the bureaucracy reigned. The Slavophiles loathed all those elements and saw them as contributing to the artificiality of St. Petersburg. It is testimony to the pervasiveness of the Slavophile ideology that present-day historians echo the same themes.

The limited number of studies on Russian businessmen have focused on their collective failure as a bourgeoisie rather than the business practices of their individual firms. The fixation with the historical "problem" of the bourgeoisie itself results from a reading of tsarist history with an eye toward the coming Bolshevik revolution. Western studies have taken the Moscow industrialists as models for the native Russian bourgeoisie for two reasons. First, researchers have reproduced the intelligentsia's Slavophile view that Moscow was the "natural" center of Russia, as opposed to the "artificial" capital in St. Petersburg. Beginning in the 1850s, the Moscow business elite were closely associated with Slavophile intellectuals, and that collaboration colored the Moscow businessmen's view of themselves in relation to St. Petersburg. This attitude on the part of Moscow industrialists has seeped into recent research. Without a doubt, Moscow businessmen conceived of themselves as qualitatively different from the "other" industrialists in St. Petersburg against whom they defined themselves. However, the "Slavic capitalism" of the Muscovites, as described by Owen, was more a myth of romantic self-conception than a real statement about actual business practices.[29] Just because some Moscow industrialists imagined themselves to be morally superior and less mercenary did not make them so. Second, a small number of Moscow industrialists did attempt to organize politically after 1905. Historians have interpreted the political activities of Moscow leaders as proof of the existence of a bourgeoisie and have contrasted these events with the lack of such activity among the St. Petersburg group.

This scholarly quest for a Russian bourgeoisie in Moscow has seriously warped our conceptions of Russian business history generally. By taking Moscow as the "natural" or legitimate center of a national bourgeoisie, this paradigm excludes St. Petersburg industrialists as somehow unnatural creatures of the state. If we set aside Moscow and take St. Petersburg on its own terms, we may better understand the complexities of business-state relations in the late imperial era, regardless of whether or not a bourgeoisie existed in Russia. Because it was the empire's corporate and financial capital as well as the political capital, historians should give more attention to business developments in St. Petersburg. However, with the exception of Ruth Roosa's study of the Association of Industry and Trade in St. Petersburg, the few studies that are concerned with Petersburg are primarily devoted to the labor question and the problem of workers' class consciousness, although these works do address management's collective role.[30]

Western historians who have studied business development in the Russian armaments sector focus on the role of foreign firms.[31] Among the few works available in English that directly address the topic of foreign arms suppliers in Russia, Goldstein concentrates solely on the English firm Vickers, while Bradley examines the technology transfer in small arms production from the United States to the three state arsenals during the 1860s and 1870s.[32] In addition, Jacob Kipp looks at foreign ties to Russian naval production during the 1860s and Peter Gatrell deals with naval procurement after 1905.[33]

The one notable exception to this pattern is Gatrell's monograph on tsarist rearmament in the 1900–1914 period. Because Gatrell considers the tsarist defense sector as a whole, he is therefore more concerned with macroeconomic trends than a detailed analysis of any one firm. Moreover, the state-owned defense works occupy most of his attention. Regarding private industry, Gatrell relies heavily on Soviet secondary works for his information. As a result, he has little to add to our understanding of the private firms. This is especially true of his specific discussion of the Putilov Company.[34]

Sources

The potential source base for Russian business history poses certain problems. To some degree, historical accident always determines what sources are available to scholars. As Gatrell observes with regard to the Petersburg industrialists,

> It is difficult to uncover evidence of their personal opinions and aspirations. Unlike politicians, they tended to leave no track in the memoir literature. Unlike full-time officials, their deliberations do not figure in the public record. Many business archives, which might shed light on their ideology and policies, failed to survive the war and revolution.[35]

Not to leave the impression that Russia is also exceptional in lacking adequate sources for business history, I should note that Gatrell's observations could just as easily apply to industrialists in the United States or Western Europe. Generally, business historians do not enjoy the rich variety of sources that usually aid the study of political leaders. Nevertheless, for this study, another historical accident has determined the availability of sources. The Central State Historical Archive of St. Petersburg, which holds the records for the Putilov Company's board of directors, was unfortunately closed for repair work during my research trip in 1994 and then was closed indefinitely. Owing to the relative scarcity of primary sources, the Putilov Company's special publication commemorating the centen-

nial of the founding offers a doubly valuable glimpse into the firm's operations.[36] Even though the inner workings of the company are difficult to
fathom, they may be explored indirectly.

The external relations of the company can be reconstructed through
a close reading of the firm's correspondence with various banks and government offices, which is preserved in the Russian State Historical
Archive (RGIA) in St. Petersburg. These collections of bank records have
been used before by historians, but the inherent bias in these sources
toward the role of the banks has not been adequately considered. One
reason for privileging the role of the banks lies in the operating assumptions of the liberal and Marxist schools of interpretation. In the liberal
interpretation of Russian industrialization, as exemplified by Gerschenkron's work, the economic historian adopts a version of the state-
versus-society paradigm whereby an emerging autonomous market serves
the function of civil society in casting off the heavy hand of state tutelage.
The Marxist version, taking the cue from Lenin's *Imperialism: The Highest
Stage of Capitalism,* attempts to lay the groundwork for 1917 by tracing the
evolutionary stages of capitalism from cartels through syndicates, arriving
finally at monopoly capitalism. In this scheme, the driving force becomes
the banks, whereas in the liberal version the banks replace the bureaucracy as the guiding hand of economic coordination.[37] One reason that
historians may overestimate the profile of the big banks in industrial
affairs is that they rely on bank correspondence, and bank involvement
naturally looms large in those documents. When viewed from the perspective of a single firm, however, the role of the banks rapidly dimin-
ishes.

In addition, the company's dealings with the tsarist army and navy
may be probed in the collections of the Russian State Archive of the Navy
(RGAV-MF) in St. Petersburg and of the Russian State Military-Historical
Archive (RGVIA) in Moscow. The records of the Main Artillery Administration (GAU), especially the contracts concluded between GAU and the
Putilov Company, yielded a great deal of information about Putilov's venture into armaments production. The value of these documents is that
they reveal how the firm competed with the state arsenals for orders and
how state officials responded. Besides these Russian archival sources, a
small volume of very insightful material assessing Putilov's growing armaments and naval production in an international perspective is available

from the British Admiralty intelligence reports of the British Public Record Office (PRO) in Kew.

Given the paucity of narrative sources left behind by the businessmen themselves, one must turn to other means to uncover their behavior and the operation of the firm. Here the problem is similar to that faced by social historians who are forced to rely on various forms of quantitative analysis in lieu of more traditional documentary sources. In the case of the Putilov Company, a useful source is the company's published annual account books, which cover the years 1873–1879, 1883–1902, and 1911–1914 and are available in the Lenin Library in Moscow. Corporations in Russia were required to publish annual accounts, and although these books are almost completely devoid of text, the financial information that they contain helps to illuminate the workings of the company and its implementation of various business strategies. How the board chose to allocate funds for new construction certainly is one gauge of corporate behavior. Nothing indicates the importance of a particular aspect of the firm's production better than the board's willingness to invest in it. More important, though, the balance sheets, dividends, working capital, and departmental production figures define and reflect the parameters of the business world in which Putilov's directors lived and worked, and therefore this information can also provide a glimpse into how they understood and functioned in that world.

However, without a way to corroborate the annual accounts with internal documents, one must use published account books with care. Soviet scholar I. F. Gindin questions the reliability of published account books generally, and the Putilov account books specifically. In 1913, according to Gindin, the company's president, A. I. Putilov, ordered the chief bookkeeper of the company to falsify the books in order to cover a loss of 1,137,000 rubles for the year and to create a profit that would allow for dividends. According to Gindin, the accountant complied and created a profit of 2,875,000 rubles on the books.[38] The origin of this accusation can be traced to M. Mitel'man's history of the Putilov factory in which Mitel'man states that the company kept two sets of books, one for publication and one for the board members. He presents as evidence a conversation between A. I. Putilov and the accountant, whom Mitel'man identified as Egor Egorovich Ioganson.[39] But Mitel'man's assertion is highly suspect for two reasons. First, he provides no citation at all for the conversation. Second, Ioganson did not hold the position of chief accountant in 1913; in fact, he did not become chief accountant until 1917, by which time A. I. Putilov had already been removed from the board when the state sequestered the firm in 1916. The chief accountant for the Putilov Company at the time of this alleged conversation was actually V. Breitigam.[40] Therefore, the specific case against the reliability of Putilov's published account books has no real foundation. It seems reasonable to accept them as valid sources and not outright fabrications, just as such published accounts and balance sheets should not be dismissed out of hand for business history in the West.[41]

A final useful source base for this project is the Russian business press of the era. In particular the *Trade-Industry Newspaper (Torgovo-Promyshlennaia Gazeta)*, 1893–1914, is invaluable for reconstructing the narrative of Putilov's development. The newspaper regularly reported on the annual shareholders' meetings of the major Russian enterprises including the Putilov Company and the large joint-stock banks. For the 1870s and 1880s, the business coverage is not as helpful, but tidbits of information can be found in the *Exchange News (Birzhevyia Vedomosti)* and the *Government Herald (Pravitel'stvennyi Vestnik)*.

What do these source materials indicate about the market strategies chosen by the company's board of directors and how they pursued their orders? How dependent was the Putilov Company on the state for its well-being, and how did the company's directors construct and market the firm's image? By analyzing the firm's perception of the market, its behavior in the market, and its use of the state as a market, one may answer these questions and shed some light on the functioning and conception of the market as understood by business decision makers in late imperial Russia.

It becomes clear that the Putilov Company in late imperial Russia developed atop an intersection of overlapping sets of states and markets. This may sound odd at first because Russian economic historians are accustomed to regarding the tsarist state as a monolithic body. Nevertheless, students of tsarist bureaucracy have recognized for some time that the different ministries pursued their own distinct policies, which often came into conflict.[42] For the Putilov Company the "state" customer was actually comprised of three different ministries: the Ministry of Transport, the War Ministry, and the Naval Ministry. Each ministry had its own procurement and payment policies, and each functioned as a distinct customer for a different set of products. Along with these bureaucratic clients, the Putilov Company also participated in multiple private domestic markets including the markets for railroad equipment, construction equipment, industrial machine building, and steel implements. In practical terms, the company's board identified segments in the state apparatus and the domestic market and generated product lines to fit. Therefore, in the Putilov board room, the state and the market interacted.

This interaction of state and market raises the issue of the compatibility of autocracy and capitalism yet again. We must distinguish between capitalism as an abstract social and legal system and capitalism as actual business behavior. One might expect capitalism in tsarist Russia to be very different from the Western variety because of the great differences between Russia's legal and political systems and those of the West. The common operative assumption, based on Weberian notions about capitalism as a system, is that Russia lacked the rational-legal order requisite for corporate capitalism because autocracy preempted property rights and other legal protections seen as necessary for predictability and long-term investment. On the surface this proposition is easy to accept. However, when we examine the actual business behavior of the Putilov Company we find that it mirrors exactly the behavior of comparable Western firms, even though Western firms operated in a different, nonautocratic environment. If autocracy and corporate business were so incompatible, how are we to account for the striking similarities in business behavior between the Russian businessmen at Putilov and their Western counterparts? The market strategies, long-term investment choices, and cartel behaviors were virtually identical, even though the legal and political structures were quite different in Russia.

The key point is that *autocratic* does not have to mean *unpredictable,* and in fact the Putilov Company's interactions with the state reveal that there was an increasing sense of routine and predictability that made it possible for businessmen to make long-term plans. This growing predictability and routinization meant that the Putilov board members could reasonably expect certain outcomes and act accordingly, even though they did not have the same legal guarantees as in the West. Under autocracy it was possible to have both personal predictability through the person of a patron and systemic predictability through the routine operation of the proper bureaucratic channels. Thus, it was possible to work the person or to work the system to achieve the desired results. Whether it was in the process of renewing the corporate charter or expecting business contracts to be arranged and executed in a certain way, the businessmen understood the rules of the game and were able to adapt to those rules. The Putilov Company's weakest business performance coincided with the period of its strongest personal support from the government. Later, in the 1885–1914 period, the company experienced its greatest corporate successes as the state's bureaucratic behavior became more routinized and therefore more predictable. In working the system, the Putilov Company could expect to be able to renew and modify its corporate charters and expand long-term capital investment in its diversification plans without any obvious concern or anxiety that those outcomes would not occur as a matter of course, even though Russia was an autocracy. Such matters had truly become routine. This is part of the reason why Putilov's business behavior had so much in common with its Western cohorts. The other part of the explanation lies in the fact that the market proved to be more important than the state for the company's prosperity.

The basic arguments of this book are organized chronologically. Chapter 1 traces the rise and fall of the Putilov Company under N. I. Putilov from 1868 to 1880. The state facilitated Putilov's rise as Russia's largest rail producer but could not prevent his fall. The company clearly enjoyed the indulgence of state officials, and in its formative stage the company owed much to the state. Chapter 2 examines the strategies for growth pursued by the company's board of directors under president N. N. Antsyforov (1885–1900). In this period the company reacted to a contracting rail market by diversifying its product line. Here I argue that the Putilov board's search for long-term growth led to development choices consistent with the strategies of European armaments firms. These choices did not result from immediate response to the economic downturn of 1899–1902, but were in fact the result of development strategies originating in 1885–1895. The expansion of the artillery business between 1900 and 1907 is treated in detail in chapter 3. The multiyear artillery contract of 1903–1907 proved to be pivotal for the fate of the firm. As the company committed greater and greater resources to artillery production runs, it fell victim to War Ministry payment policies that prevented the firm from receiving pay until the conclusion of the entire order. This resulted in cash flow problems that served as an incentive to recruit more active bank involvement.

Chapter 4 looks at the role of banks in financing and controlling the company from 1907 to 1914 as the company expanded into naval construction. I contend that the role of the banks in determining the direction of the Putilov enterprise has been grossly exaggerated and that the firm actually maintained its autonomy. Chapter 5 follows the fate of the company during the First World War and up to the revolutions of 1917. The state sequestered the company in 1916 as the result of a condominium of interests between Duma members, who supported Moscow suppliers, the War Ministry which wanted the factory under its control, and State Council members who feared labor unrest at the plant could spark a revolution in the capital. The company was vulnerable because of financial overextension during the years 1912–1914. Chapter 6 assesses the company's participation in cartels and draws conclusions about the position of Putilov between state and market in the tsarist era.

Because of its comparative dimensions, this Putilov case study should be of interest to a variety of scholarly audiences. Besides addressing issues of concern to Russian historians and historians of Western business, the Putilov experience speaks to those who are concerned with privatization and business in post-Soviet Russia as well. The company still exists as the newly privatized joint stock company Kirovsky Zavod in St. Petersburg, and today it is in the process of adjusting to the new market conditions in post-Soviet Russia by adopting strategies that are very similar to those of the old Putilov Company. Kirovsky's development since 1992 and its similarities to the Czech firm Skoda are the subject of the epilogue. Thus, a comparative study of Putilov/Kirovsky serves to illuminate a usable past for Russian business history.

1

THE RISE AND FALL OF A
RAIL MANUFACTURING GIANT

N. I. PUTILOV AND THE PUTILOV COMPANY,
1868–1885

Nikolai Ivanovich Putilov harbored a grandiose entrepreneurial vision. Perceiving opportunites in Russia's generally weak metalworking industry, Putilov embarked on a course of development in which he attempted to integrate rail production into an elaborate transportation network. Starting with a rail factory, Putilov sought to establish a series of enterprises including rail production, a railroad, and a huge commercial port. These rather frenetic plans called for large amounts of capital and ultimately resulted in bankruptcy by the time of Putilov's death in 1880. At first glance, it is difficult to find a coherent growth strategy in Putilov's various enterprises. However, if we look at his industrial and commercial enterprises as part of a whole, rather than individually, then an underlying logic does emerge. In the short term, a desperate situation for the Nicholas Railroad gave Putilov the opportunity to acquire the rail factory. Once he had this factory, it became the center of his plans to create the commercial port and the railroad line. With the creation of these projects, the factory would be linked both to the port and to the other main railroad lines of the empire, and additionally the transport costs for the factory's imported raw materials would be reduced.

The story of N. I. Putilov's meteoric rise and then financial collapse was by no means uncommon among metalworking enterprises in the St. Petersburg region in the 1860s and 1870s. Like the other St. Petersburg enterprises founded after the Crimean War, the Putilov rail factory suffered through financial hardship and change of ownership. Until the

1850s, most factories involved in heavy industry were state-owned because of the military importance of those fields. However, after the Crimean War the government turned to private enterprise because of financial difficulties. The tsarist government employed a number of methods to shift the financial burden of maintaining these plants onto the private sector, such as guaranteeing returns on loans to attract foreign capital, leasing state plants to private firms, setting up protective tariffs, and sanctioning the creation of joint-stock companies.

Nevertheless, virtually all of the new private metalworking companies in St. Petersburg experienced financial hardship, even though they received significant government contracts, and they ultimately had to sell out to foreign investors or the Naval Ministry. For example, the Baltic Works belonged in 1856 to Carr and Macpherson and was one of the first private works that undertook building ships of war of large dimensions, the hulls having been built at Admiralty or Nevskii, and the machinery at Baird's or Kolpino. In 1877 they reverted to the Admiralty's ownership. All these works depended entirely on government orders, and private firms seldom applied to them for any work except repairs.[1] Thus, the fate of the Putilov factory was typical of all major industrial enterprises in St. Petersburg.

Even though the end results may resemble those of other Petersburg firms, Putilov's experience was not necessarily typical. Why did Putilov rise and fall? How was his path similar to that of others and how was it unique? These are important questions because, at the very least, an analysis of Putilov's experience calls into question the standard explanation that the European depression of 1873 caused all these industrial failures.[2] The Putilov factory became the most important rail producer in Russia through a combination of state indulgence, private initiative, and luck. Putilov himself was remarkably adept at obtaining support through the personal intervention of particular state officials. The state aided N. I. Putilov's rise but ultimately could not prevent his fall, although state officials did try to cushion the blow as much as possible.

Therefore, Putilov's story reveals both the extent and the limits of state involvement on the Petersburg industrial scene, as well as the importance of the individual entrepreneur. In 1854 Russia had 29 mechanical workshops with 3,000 workmen, representing a production of 2 million rubles a year. By 1865 the number had increased to 126 workshops employing 18,000 workers and producing 12 million rubles' worth of

goods annually. In 1870 some 198 workshops with 30,000 workers averaged 29 million rubles of production per year. Commenting on Russia's
industrial expansion, a British consular commercial report observed,
"This increase is mostly in St. Petersburg and is attributable to Government orders."[3]

The factory that would become known as the Putilov works began as
a state iron foundry built on Kotlin Island in 1789. In 1801 this operation
was moved to the outskirts of St. Petersburg because the island location
seemed too vulnerable to coastal attack. By March 1801, the new iron
works was already making shells for the army and navy. Until 1803 the factory manufactured only shells, and it remained primarily a shell producer,
although later it began to produce other iron goods for both the state and
private customers. In 1842 the state sold the factory to the Vladel'tsev
Mining Company, and in 1844 this private firm attempted to introduce
rail production but went bankrupt in 1845. Given its importance as a shell
producer, the factory returned to state ownership. Three years later, the
state leased the factory to Colonel Ogarev. By that time, the factory was
quite large and employed approximately 800 workers. Ogarev proved to
be no more successful than the previous private owners, and the enterprise again failed. After being sold to yet another private firm and subsequently floundering again, the factory returned to state hands once
more. Eventually, N. I. Putilov bought the plant in 1868, and the works
bore his name until the end of the imperial period.[4]

Nikolai Ivanovich Putilov embarked on his industrial career by way of
state service in the Naval Ministry. Born in 1817 into a noble family in
Novgorod, Putilov entered the navy in 1830. After serving on various
ships on the Gulf of Finland and the Baltic, he became a lieutenant in
1841. He left the navy in 1844, but four years later joined the Naval Ministry, where he was attached to the shipbuilding department as a junior officer with a special commission. Trained in naval mathematics, he taught
at the Naval Academy until the early 1850s. During the Crimean War,
Putilov rose through the administrative ranks of the shipbuilding department and gained experience overseeing both private machine factories
and the repair works in Kronstadt. His contributions to the development
of Russia's steam-powered gunboats and Petersburg's shipbuilding and
munitions industries brought him to the attention of Grand Duke Konstantin, who later became an important patron. His accomplishments in

economizing the construction operations earned him the Order of St. Vladimir, fourth class, but after the war Putilov left the Naval Ministry and turned his attention to developing the metalworking industry in northern Russia and Finland.

By the mid-1860s, Putilov had leased several factories in St. Petersburg to bolster Russian military production, including the Samsonievskii (formerly Nobel) machine works and the duke of Leuchtenberg's foundry. At the time, the government's concern about a possible European war over the Polish crisis of 1863 enabled Putilov to arrange the leases with state support. Having undertaken the first production of iron railroads in Finland, Putilov built three factories on Lake Saima to make boiler iron for the Russian fleet. Then, with Obukhov and Kudriavtsev, Putilov created the first steel cannon factory in Russia (Obukhov) and experimented with preparing tempered iron shells to eliminate Russia's dependence on foreign suppliers. Putilov's enterprises had put him in debt by 1866, and only the state's renewed interest in subsidizing the military and railroad industries in 1867 saved his financial fortunes by opening the way for him to acquire the Ogarev factory. Along with the plant, Putilov landed a huge government contract for manufacturing rails.[5]

Putilov's career background shares some important similarities with others from the generation of Petersburg industrialists who emerged in this post–Crimean War environment. Generally, these entrepreneurs came from foreign or noble backgrounds and usually founded and managed their own factories. The few natives who established their own firms (Putilov, Poletika, Semiannikov) had all received training in the state's technical institutes. Vasilii Poletika, a Ukrainian nobleman and the new owner of Nevskii foundry, had retired from the army as a colonel in 1856. Like Putilov, Poletika had used his state contacts to receive orders for locomotive and railroad equipment from the Ministry of Transport.[6]

In turn, the managers in charge of the state naval factories also shared similar backgrounds. Typically, these factory commanders, contemporaries of the first generation of private Petersburg industrialists, began their careers in the Naval Cadet Corps. Then, like Putilov, after duty aboard ship they worked for a time in some administrative capacity, either in the commercial sector or in a government ministry before moving into factory administration. For example, L. F. Gadd, director of the Izhorsk naval yard from 1872 to 1887, served on commercial ships and as director-administrator of the Society of the Volga-Don Railroad and Steamship Line. N. A. Bykov served in the Ministry of Transport as an inspector of navigation along the Don before becoming the commander of Izhorsk (1892–1894).[7]

The similarities in the backgrounds of state and private industrialists in Petersburg offers a clue as to why N. I. Putilov rose so quickly in the iron and steel sector. As a member of the service nobility and having had a distin-guished career in the naval establishment, Putilov possessed the requisite background to earn the trust of state officials. State works continued to predominate in tsarist metalworking. When faced with a choice between saving a private enterprise or protecting a government operation, state officials usually chose to preserve suppliers under their own control. In a pinch, though, the state would turn to private enterprise to help carry the burden of maintaining existing plants.

The history of the state armories provides another good example of this relationship. Confronted by severe budgetary restrictions following the Crimean War, the War Ministry recognized that it had to attract private capital in order to save the three state small arms factories. However, the War Ministry sought to avoid becoming completely dependent on private manufacturers and did not want to relinquish the armories to private persons, whether Russian or foreign. So the ministry offered to lease the armories to their commanders. Under the conditions of leasehold management, the armories remained as the property of the War Ministry and the leaseholder had to be an officer in government service.[8] We have already seen this pattern in the history of the rail and shell factory prior to Putilov's acquisition of it. In this context, the fact that Putilov had a background in the armed forces undoubtedly helped his cause. It is hard to imagine the state handing over the Ogarev factory to someone without a background in the armed forces.

N. I. Putilov's background and experience were therefore important to his entry into Petersburg metalworking, but more significant in explaining his rapid rise was the fact that he fulfilled his promises regarding rail production very impressively between 1867 and 1870. On 15 June 1867, N. I. Putilov had already concluded a contract with the state Railroad Administration to supply 2.8 million poods of rails over seven years beginning in 1870 (one ton equals 55.5 poods). In fall 1867, however, the state-owned Nicholas Railroad was experiencing supply difficulties because an early freeze prevented overseas rail deliveries from Belgium and England. Seeing an opportunity, Putilov offered to provide 600,000 poods of rails if he were allowed to acquire the Ogarev factory to fill the order for the Nicholas Railroad. On 20 January 1868, Putilov's newly acquired rail factory began rolling rails and after eighteen days had produced 5,000 poods. Soon production reached 2 million poods per year.[9]

Beginning in 1869, Putilov devoted his efforts to building a commercial port in St. Petersburg and a railroad to connect the port to his rail factory. However, according to Baron A. I. Del'vig, a former head of the Ministry of Transport and later one of Putilov's business associates, "Putilov, by his nature, could not be content with this factory activity: a big dreamer and optimist in his own affairs, he intended to construct a port by the side of his own factory to attract all incoming and outgoing Petersburg trade."[10] Without the canal, only light-draught ships could travel up the Neva, and larger ships had to stop at Kronstadt and discharge there. The freight costs from Kronstadt to the city of St. Petersburg itself significantly added to the expense. From Newcastle to Kronstadt, shipping cost 6 shillings 6 pence per ton, yet it cost another 2 shillings per ton for the 30 kilometers from Kronstadt to St. Petersburg. In addition, traversing the final leg to the city often required two weeks, sometimes longer.[11] Putilov's proposal was one of a number of projects for developing a deeper St. Petersburg commercial port that had been floating around for years. Putilov proposed building a canal from Kronstadt alongside his rail factory to a deep-water port that would unite with the Nicholas Railroad along the Neva River, thus linking the Nicholas, Baltic, and Warsaw railroad lines. The charters of these new companies called for at least 18 million rubles of capital simply to construct the port near the Putilov rail factory and another 2 million rubles for the linking railroad. Del'vig observed,

> Neither of these enterprises was guaranteed by the government, and only Putilov and similar optimists could believe in the possibility to amass so much capital. . . . Putilov himself believed in their realization and, hoping that it would come about more quickly if part of his enterprises was already initiated, set about purchasing a large amount of land for the port and the construction of his railroad, spending on this money and deposits received from contracts for supplying rails.[12]

Putilov formed his railroad company on 27 March 1870 and initiated the construction of a railway network to connect the southwestern side of St. Petersburg with the southeastern part of the Neva, thereby linking the Warsaw and Moscow rail lines and tying them to the Putilov factory.[13]

We must be cautious about accepting Del'vig's assessment of Putilov's plans. Del'vig wrote his memoirs after these events, and no doubt the fact that he lived through the Putilov Company's bankruptcy, and suffered financially as a result, colored his recollections. Nevertheless, in this instance Del'vig identified accurately what proved to be the crack in N. I. Putilov's financial foundation that brought the whole edifice down. In order to generate the enormous capital necessary for his rail company and his port company, Putilov tapped the advances paid to his rail factory. In effect, Putilov treated these three separate enterprises as one big pocket from which he could draw money as he saw fit. In this way, he deprived the Putilov rail factory of its potential profits by redirecting its deposits and cash advances for rail orders into the Putilov Railroad Company and the port construction project, but this anticipates the outcome.

At the time, Putilov had every reason to be confident about his ability to realize his plans. In 1870 his reputation as an industrialist and his business fortunes had reached their zenith. Putilov basked in the glory of his rail factory's superior achievement. On 13 June 1870, Putilov hosted a parade and dinner at his rail factory to celebrate the completion of the four millionth pood of rails. Approximately 250 guests attended, including many engineers and representatives from the War Ministry. At the dinner Putilov toasted the working people of Russia, and especially those of his factory who were present at the festivities. Putilov could justifiably take pride in his accomplishments. The factory had provided about two-thirds of Russia's total rail production and had gained public attention as an enterprise to which the government ascribed great importance.[14]

Since Putilov was spending large sums for work on the construction of the port and linking railroad, he did not have adequate working capital at the rail factory in 1871 and 1872. As a result of his siphoning money from the rail factory to finance the port and railway companies, the factory's production fell off and the quality of its steel-headed rails suffered. From 1868 to 1870, rail production had steadily increased from approximately 1 million poods to 1.6 million poods. However, production declined by almost half over the following three years, from 1.4 million poods in 1871 to 700,000 poods by 1873. This in turn reduced confidence in Putilov in St. Petersburg financial circles. From other quarters, some criticized Putilov's success as a mirage based entirely on government orders. As evidence of the state's overindulgence of Putilov, they cited its sale of 5 million poods of used rails to the factory at an extremely low price and then buying back the finished product at a price considerably higher than the cost of imported rails.[15]

To line up support, Putilov approached Baron Andrei I. Del'vig in 1873, explaining that his factories were not functioning because of a lack of working capital. Moreover, he could not arrange any credit in Petersburg because of hostility to his enterprises on the part of the St. Petersburg Stock Exchange, expediters, and bankers. Local investors preferred to build the port in Oranienbaum, since they owned shares in the adjacent Baltic Railroad. Therefore, Putilov perceived that his only salvation would be found among the Moscow bankers—over whom, in his opinion, Fedor V. Chizhov had unlimited influence. Chizhov was a Slavophile writer and banker on the board of the Moscow Merchant Mutual Credit Society. Putilov therefore asked Del'vig to write to Chizhov urging support for his plans. Putilov added that he needed capital for the formation of the Putilov Manufacturing Company (chartered on 24 October 1872), since he would have to transfer the sums received for advances on rail contracts from the newly chartered company to other enterprises. Del'vig accordingly wrote the letter and gave it to Putilov.[16]

Upon his return from meetings with bankers in Moscow, Putilov declared to Del'vig that the Moscow Merchant Mutual Credit Society, the Moscow Commercial Credit Society, and the Trade Bank were prepared to loan him the necessary capital on condition that Del'vig serve on the council of the company. At first Del'vig refused on the grounds that the proposed company would be a fiction, since all the shares would belong to a single owner—that is, Putilov. Putilov eventually managed to persuade Del'vig, and in May 1873 the Moscow banks decided to loan Putilov 1.5 million rubles on the security of his 32,000 shares in the Putilov Company. Del'vig's concerns were justified. Putilov gave 100 shares each to various acquaintances, including Del'vig, so that they could be selected as members of the council and board of the company. Putilov then convened the general meeting of shareholders in early 1873—at which, of course, members were chosen according to Putilov's direction.[17]

The Moscow group's support of Putilov in establishing his company requires some comment because it seems to fly in the face of the Moscow businessmen's recognized antipathy toward St. Petersburg and the state bureaucracy. Undoubtedly, Moscow bankers and industrialists resented Petersburg officialdom, but they also had their own connections to the state. The Moscow group considered Del'vig their man in St. Petersburg, and he reciprocated the sentiment. Del'vig held Slavophile views himself and was on very close terms with Chizhov. It seems, then, that Putilov knew exactly what he was doing when he approached Del'vig in order to connect with Chizhov. Moreover, the Moscow group, including Del'vig, wanted to prove that a native Russian could construct railroads without state guarantees or foreign engineers. In their eyes, Putilov had earned a reputation as the first Russian to accomplish the large-scale manufacture of rails, and he had shown himself to be a technological innovator.[18] Putilov had played an important part in the strides taken by Russian heavy industry since its feeble beginnings after the Crimean War, and his rail factory acted as the core of the initial development of a domestic rail industry. The Putilov factory's position within Russia's rail industry can be seen from the data on rail production published in the journal of the Ministry of Transport. (See table 1.1.) In helping Putilov, the Moscow backers considered themselves to be furthering Russian business development in a useful enterprise. With financing from Moscow, the actual account year for the Putilov Company commenced on 1 September 1873.

The tsarist state set the legal confines for corporate activity in imper-

Table 1.1

Steel Rail Production by the Putilov Company, 1868–1874 (in poods)

	Russian Total	Putilov Company	(%)
1868	1,442,510	1,001,410	69.0
1869	2,580,104	1,599,787	62.0
1870	2,483,433	1,658,355	67.0
1871	2,352,278	1,416,022	60.0
1872	1,860,529	949,434	51.0
1873	1,602,970	713,720	45.0
1874	2,986,049	1,313,073	44.0

Source: Keppen, *Materialy dlia istorii rel'sovogo proizvodstv*, 118–21.

ial Russia under the law of corporations of 1836. This law combined an interest in fostering corporate capitalism, as in Western Europe, with the tsarist state's penchant for bureaucratic control of any potentially autonomous activity. These different impulses resulted in a guarantee for limited liability, as was common in Western Europe, along with stronger state oversight of incorporation, in keeping with tsarist proclivities. On the regulatory side, all charters for incorporation had to be reviewed by the ministerial bureaucracy and then signed by the tsar.[19]

The 1836 law established the operating rules for the relationship between the board of directors (*pravlenie*) and the shareholders. By law, the company actually came into existence at the first general assembly of shareholders at which the stockholders elected a board of at least three directors. The board was required to operate by majority rule, while at the annual meeting the shareholders were to set general policy and elect the directors by a three-fourths' vote of those present, with votes determined by the number of shares owned. In addition, an audit commission (*revizionnaia komissia*) had to oversee the company's books and present its audit to the shareholders at the annual meeting. To protect against potential abuses, members of the audit commission could not serve on the board simultaneously.[20]

The law did not outline a specific formula for corporate charters; however, certain items typically recurred. These included a stated purpose for the foundation of the company, along with its privileges and responsibilities, and the capital formation of the company in terms of stock capital, bonds, and the obligations of the owners. Corporate charters also usually described the company's board of directors and its duties, and specified the distribution of profits and dividends. In addition, charters established the role for shareholders and stated the means for disbanding the company.[21]

The charter for the Putilov Company conformed to this general pattern. According to the founding charter for the Putilov corporation (*Obshchestvo Putilovskikh Zavodov*) in 1873, the company consisted of five factories: the rail and mechanical factory in Petersburg, the Arkadiia factory in Petersburg, and three smaller ironworks in Finland. The administration of the business was to be divided between the board of directors and the council. The board consisted of four directors selected at the general shareholders' meeting. Each director was obliged upon entering the position to own no less than 100 shares of Putilov stock, which was to be kept in the cash account of the board of directors during his tenure. Two years after the first four directors were selected, one position would be up for election every year.[22]

Responsibility for the operation of the company rested with the Putilov board. The obligations of the board included maintaining records and accounts, and overseeing proper payment of interest for bonds and their liquidation. The board was also required to compose a plan of activity and estimates for the coming year no later than 15 November of each year, and equally to inform the council of the means for developing the enterprise for the council's examination. The board selected its administrative office, the bookkeeper, the administrators, and other divisional staff of the factories and presented them to the council for reward out of the company's profits. Additionally, the board had to present to the council any proposals for purchase or lease of immovable property and composed a semiannual account for the preceding year no later than 15 March. The board decided all issues by a majority vote. In case of a split on any question, the matter was transferred to the council. No fewer than three directors were required to sign requests for disbursements.[23]

The corporate charter clearly defined the rules and obligations for stockholders' meetings. The board had to call a general shareholders' meeting no later than May of each year. In addition, an extraordinary meeting could be called at the request of ten shareholders with voting rights. To have voting rights, a shareholder had to own at least 50 shares. Those holding 100 shares received two votes, 200 shares conferred three votes, and 300 or more shares four votes. Stockholders with fewer than 50 shares could attend the general meeting but could not vote. Shareholders could be represented by proxy, but in any event no individual could have more than eight votes at a meeting. For a general meeting to take place, at least one-third of the total number of shares had to be represented.[24]

The Putilov Company's charter spelled out the tasks that could be executed at the general meeting and included fairly precise formulas for the distribution of profits. For example, annual accounts were examined, and dividends, reserve capital, and pensions were determined at the meeting. It was also to be the forum for considering proposals for expanding or increasing the enterprise, for discussing motions to supplement or change the charter, and for electing directors and members of the council. As specified in the charter, no less than 10 percent of the gross profit had to be allocated for reserve capital. The remainder of the profit, if it did not exceed 8 percent of the stock capital, was converted into dividends for the shareholders. If the remainder amounted to more than 8 percent of the stock capital, then 12 percent went to the council, 8 percent to the directors, 10 percent to the division heads, 5 percent to the employees, and the remainder to the shareholders.[25]

In September 1873 the Putilov Company became active, but after a promising start the firm began to falter. Initially the infusion of new money from its incorporation as a joint-stock company buoyed the flagging rail production, and output practically doubled, returning briefly to 1871 levels (about 1.3 million poods). Soon after, however, the firm encountered financial difficulties. In particular, raw material costs increased. The prices for imported English coal and iron jumped 50 percent, and because materials were acquired so late in the year, freight was very expensive and a significant amount had to be moved by horse-drawn vehicles from Kronstadt in winter. These higher costs created financial difficulties because, according to contracts concluded with the Department of Railroads, the factories should have manufactured simple iron rails, not ones with steel heads. The price for a pood of the first was set at 1 ruble 47 kopeks, but the latter at 1 ruble 80 kopeks. Because of the high cost of raw materials, the preparation of simple iron rails would have caused losses to the factories.[26]

Putilov managed to avoid this problem by changing the contract. He began negotiations with the Ministry of Transport to convert the contracts for iron rails with steel heads into ones for rails made completely of steel in June 1873. After two years, in April 1875, the ministry approved a converted contract for 4 million poods of steel rails over five years. Under the new terms, iron rails would be accepted only through 1875. The price per pood of steel rails was 2 rubles 37 kopeks, and the total order amounted to 10,540,120 rubles after rail ties had been factored in. The company received an advance of 1 million rubles for the newly converted contract. Along with this, the company had to build new plant for the manufacture of steel and rolling steel rails. When steel-headed rail production concluded in July 1875, the company was completely tapped out financially. Minister of Transport K. N. Pos'et sought the agreement of Finance Minister M. Kh. Reutern to give the company advances for a million rubles for the assembly of rails in the second account year. The beneficence of the state in renegotiating the contract and providing advances enabled the Putilov Company to post a profit of 622,000 rubles in its first sixteen months.[27]

Why were the ministries so obliging toward Putilov? Although specific details are lacking, it is possible to speculate on two possible reasons. First, Putilov was taking advantage of the fact that Reutern generally placed military and political considerations above economic ones when it came to railroad construction. In this context, as long as domestic production capacity was expected to increase and improve, it was considered worth the additional expenditure. Second, from the perspective of the Ministry of Transport, Putilov was the only producer offering all-steel rails. Also, no Russian factory had undertaken the manufacture of railway parts such as bearings, nuts, bolts, and the like before Putilov did in 1868, and Putilov served as one of the very few Russian enterprises that made wheels and springs for locomotives.[28] In practical terms, this meant that the Putilov factory was a vital part of Russia's rail industry, and it would receive generous terms because of its unique position.

Putilov's practice of converting old contracts into new ones that offered fresh cash advances was not limited to rail production. Before the formation of the corporation, N. I. Putilov had also concluded a contract with the Department of Railroads for the assembly of locomotives and had received 300,000 rubles as an advance. At that time, he did not even have a workshop capable of manufacturing locomotives, since construction and equipment would cost enormous sums. As with the steel rails, Putilov found a way to convert this contract as well. With the aim of doubling Russian domestic production for railroads, the Ministry of Transport in 1874 ordered cars from many factory owners for high prices, demanding that all parts should be Russian-made from Russian materials. Since a railroad car workshop would cost much less than a locomotive workshop, the board of the Putilov Company decided to request a change from a contract for the assembly of locomotives to a contract for railcars. Putilov obtained an agreement to change the contract. Railroad car construction still required a new, special workshop, and the company did build one well and at significant cost. Yet production proceeded very slowly in part because of the cost of raw materials. Imported supplies of coal and iron cost the company about 350,000 rubles in 1876. These costs and the lack of working capital compelled the company to incur new debts, including 500,000 rubles from one of the members of company's council, Vasilii Pavlovich Aleksandrovskii, and a loan from the Moscow banks for 400,000 rubles.[29]

The advent of steel rail production did not deliver the company from its financial woes. The steel-rolling workshop made possible the production of all-steel rails at the factory beginning in 1875. In 1876, however, the company experienced losses totaling almost 1 million rubles, of which the rail factory itself accounted for one-third. The chief causes for the factory's losses were production delays; the rail factory had to pay over 200,000 rubles in late fines.[30] In 1877 the Putilov factory produced 643,000 poods of steel rails, and by 1879 this figure had grown to 3 million poods. However, at the same time the company suffered a series of losses owing to the high costs for imported raw materials and the large interest from the debt burden.

Despite ongoing losses and mounting debt, Putilov continued to pursue the development of the port and railroad companies simultaneously. For the construction of the canal, Putilov had managed to enlist contractors from England, Edwin Clark and William Ponchard and Company. Because Minister of Transport Pos'et preferred to give the contract to a Russian, Putilov stepped forward as the sole contractor, while the Englishmen served as silent partners. At that time, Putilov was still convinced that the construction of the port would bring huge profits. By lobbying Pos'et, Putilov got 4 million rubles in advance by rechartering the United Putilov Railroad Company in December 1875, even though the company charter was not approved by the Committee of Ministers until 12 October 1876. This reincorporation of the railroad company was designed to finish and supply a railroad from the Neva River to the sea canal, with links to the Nicholas, Warsaw, Tsarskoe Selo, and Baltic railroads. It would also have a continuation along the northern side of the canal. Meanwhile, in order to keep the rail factory solvent, Putilov was negotiating with a French company about leasing it. On 16 August 1876, construction work actually commenced for the St. Petersburg canal. Grand Prince Konstantin Nikolaevich, Minister of Transport Pos'et, and Naval Ministry representative

Stepan Stepanovich Lesovskii attended the ceremony. Unfortunately, Putilov never completed his grand plans for the canal. The government took over the canal project and finished it in the 1880s.[31]

Along with reincorporating and renegotiating contracts, Putilov continually reshuffled his loans in an attempt to slow the financial hemorrhage. Three Moscow banks loaned Putilov capital on their terms for only six months, after which time Putilov had to pay interest and arrange a new loan letter. Unable to pay all the interest, Putilov agreed with one bank in Moscow to pay off the interest on the other two. Then Putilov partially paid that bank and took a new loan for six months. In this way, Putilov got into a pattern of taking a new loan every half year. Each time, he assured the Moscow banks that he would pay all the capital early, then repawned his own shares to other banks and the State Bank.

In 1875 Putilov quickly formed the Port Company and repawned his stock yet again. This time, though, he did not manage to renegotiate the credit notes for a six-month term. Instead, the term was only three months. In January 1876, Putilov failed to make the interest payment to the Moscow banks, and they sent notes out for collection. Somehow Putilov found some money, but the constant shuffling of loans and stock threatened to ruin not just Putilov, but the banks as well. The potential collapse of the Moscow banks prompted the State Bank to step in and stabilize the situation. With great relief, Chizhov and the Moscow banks ceded their Putilov shares to the State Bank at a loss of more than 300,000 rubles in order to free themselves from any further entanglements with N. I. Putilov. As a result, beginning in 1877 a significant majority of company shares went into the hands of the State Bank, which from that time on became an actual owner of the factory with its own representatives on the board of directors.[32]

By the time Putilov died in 1880, he had managed to direct his enterprises into complete financial disarray. In 1881 the remaining board of directors considered selling off two of the company's factories in Finland and decided to close the Putilov factory itself for an extended Easter holiday, dismissing the workers because there were no new orders. The effects of N. I. Putilov's bankruptcy lingered until the early 1890s. The final meeting of his creditors took place in 1893, at which time almost 2.8 million rubles of the 6-million-ruble debt had been paid out by the administration responsible for its liquidation. The final payment represented about 10 kopeks per ruble of dividend held by the creditors.[33]

It is tempting to explain Putilov's financial collapse as a specific example of the general problem of Russia's weak industrial and financial development in the context of a European financial crisis. For example, Heather Hogan argues that by the mid-1870s the European depression tightened credit in Russia, and this adversely affected Putilov's strategy directly. His joint-stock company "soon faltered as well due to the financial crisis sweeping Europe," she writes. "Putilov was forced to curtail production and fire a third of his work force. His attempt to relieve the financial pressure by entering into the production of rolling stock also failed, and through the end of the decade the factory's debt continued to grow."[34]

Although Putilov certainly experienced chronic financial difficulties, Hogan's argument places too much emphasis on a systemic explanation and not enough on Putilov's contributions to his own problems. All told, from 1867 to 1879 the government paid out more than 131 million rubles for rails, locomotives, and wagons, of which Putilov received orders worth 32 million. These orders should have sufficed to keep the factory going. The problem, as we have seen, lay with Putilov's grandiose plans. Instead of reinvesting and providing his rail factory with sufficient capital reserves, Putilov used the factory's orders and cash advances in a financial shell game to develop his separate port and railroad companies. This extremely short-sighted policy brought down the whole operation because there was no way the port or railroad companies could possibly generate revenues in the immediate future.

Yes, Putilov felt financial pressures, but they were largely of his own making. His rail factory actually operated with a profit of 350,000 rubles in 1877 and 548,000 rubles in 1878, even as the company itself showed overall losses in those years. The fact that a rail factory could survive in Russia during the European financial crisis is proved by the example of the Briansk rail factory. In 1880, when the Putilov factory was heading for bankruptcy and state ownership, Briansk reported a profit of 1,911,521 rubles, and two other producers, Kolomna and Lilpop, were paying dividends of 12–20 percent.[35] Moreover, N. I. Putilov repeatedly managed to find financial backers within Russia. So lack of capital did not pose insurmountable difficulties. Given his poor performance record, one wonders why Putilov did not have more trouble finding capital.

His repeated success in arranging financial deals suggests that N. I. Putilov's personality must have played a significant role in attracting supporters. He was nothing if not persistent. Putilov continually hounded Del'vig. At first he wanted Del'vig to use his influence in Moscow, and then he pressured him to join the company. It is a testimony to Putilov's persuasiveness that Del'vig relented and joined the project despite strong misgivings. Also, Putilov's restless energy and hands-on approach seemed to fit the spirit of the times in postemancipation Russia. His early achievements were significant, and they fed his enthusiasm to achieve still greater projects. His supporters in Moscow were won over by his optimism for Russia's future and his genuine patriotism. By 1875, though, Chizhov had serious doubts about Putilov's entrepreneurial abilities. He had come to consider Putilov an incompetent entrepreneur who was consciously trying to drag as many people as possible into his enterprises in the hopes that somehow they would bail him out. Although Chizhov viewed the enterprises themselves as useful, he regarded Putilov as nothing more than a dishonest pretender and con man. When Putilov finally overreached himself, it was characteristically in grand style.[36]

Although Nikolai Putilov's attempts to combine a steel rail plant, a railroad company, and a port facility ultimately failed, his strategic thinking should not be readily dismissed as eccentric or uniquely Russian. Putilov's plans seem quite typical in comparison with the experience of American steel manufacturers in the 1870s. In the United States the same groups of corporations often owned and controlled both railroads and steel mills. For example, the Pennsylvania Railroad combined the roles of user and producer—common practice for this industrial sector. The Pennsylvania Railroad Company formed the Pennsylvania Steel Company and awarded it a $200,000 contract for steel rails.

In this regard, Nikolai Putilov's strategy would have been readily comprehensible to Andrew Carnegie. The Bethlehem Steel Company also started off in 1861 as a captive enterprise of a railroad company. In another similarity, steelmaking in the United States was initially created for a single product: Bessemer steel rails. Railroad officials had a stake in developing the early Bessemer steel plants, since the railroads consumed almost all of their steel.[37]

Yet N. I. Putilov did bequeath another lasting legacy to the Putilov Company besides debt. He had overseen the creation of a physical plant large enough to allow for economies of scale. Alfred Chandler observes, "The critical entrepreneurial act was not the invention—or even the initial commercialization—of a new or greatly improved product or process. Instead it was the construction of a plant of the optimal size required to exploit fully the economies of scale or those of scope, or both."[38] This observation certainly holds true in Putilov's case. His technological pioneering in Russia's rail industry did not save the company from collapse. However, he left behind a production facility that could dominate Russia's industrial scene by the scale of its output. Part of the reason for the State Bank's involvement was that the Putilov factory had already become too large to be allowed to fail. The Committee of Ministers noted in August 1881 that if the factory were to close, many workers would be left without any means of support.[39] Putilov's substantial contribution to Russian steel rail production is evident from table 1.2.

In October 1882 the government picked up the question of how to dispose of the Putilov Company. At that point, the State Bank owned seven-eighths of the company's shares and participated in the direction of the business. The State Bank also made large outlays to support the activity of the factory in view of the loans for the factory's materials and goods and itself took part in the administration of the company's business. The termination of this relationship could be attained by the sale of the stock belonging to the bank or the liquidation of the Putilov Company. Representatives of the Briansk and Warsaw factories proposed to acquire the shares, but the minister of finance rejected the offer, citing the potential

Table 1.2

Steel Rail Production by the Putilov Company, 1875–1880 (in poods)

	Russian Total	Putilov Company	(%)
1875	800,000	800,000	(100)
1876	800,000	800,000	(100)
1877	1,362,485	643,725	(47)
1878	3,332,513	1,045,466	(31)
1879	8,739,809	3,020,759	(35)
1880	11,977,542	2,992,351	(25)

Source: Keppen, Materialy dlia istorii rel'sovogo proizvodstva, 118–21.

loss to the bank of 4.8 million rubles. Therefore, Minister of Finance N. Kh. Bunge proposed that the activity of the Putilov factories should continue under state ownership until the working of the current materials and goods was completed. Then the factory should be closed if it had not received any new orders that could sustain it without state support or should be sold for less of a loss than currently proposed. If neither of those options appeared, then the company was to be dissolved in accordance with the firm's charter.

The following year, the state did sell the shares to the Briansk and Warsaw factories. As of 1885, the Putilov Company was able to buy out the Briansk and Warsaw steel syndicate by paying off the outstanding State Bank loans and regaining the 34,000 shares held in state hands. From that point, the board of the Putilov Company was headed by N. N. Antsyforov, former president of the company's council.[40] Bunge's sell-off of the Putilov plant was consistent with his belief that material aid for Russian industry was less important than legal reforms and factory legislation.[41]

The early history of the Putilov Company bore the imprint of the state's hand. The state had physically created the plant, encouraged and supported its product line, and come to its aid repeatedly with advances and orders. In the end, the factory returned to state hands. In spite of the pervasive presence of the state, however, Putilov's experience also illustrated the limits of state control over free enterprise and its tolerance of illegal activities. N. I. Putilov flouted the restrictions and principles of the corporate charter in any number of ways. He freely disposed of the company's shares and capital, and through reincorporations and renegotiations of state contracts he obtained multiple cash advances.

If anything, Putilov showed how much wheeling and dealing was possible within autocratic Russia. It was not difficult for him to obtain approval for his corporate charters. If an industrialist could gain the confidence of powerful officials and patrons such as Minister of Transport Pos'et, he could accomplish much. So even if autocracy could impede free enterprise through a stifling control over business activity, it could also potentially permit business a very wide latitude indeed. N. I. Putilov succeeded brilliantly in securing personal support from high state officials, thereby working the individual official within the autocratic system. Yet he ended in business failure and bankruptcy because his fortunes rested on the extremely narrow base of these few personal connections.

Finally, the story of Putilov's rise and fall has much in common with the experience of other Petersburg industrialists. His social background and career path fit the profile of the other plant directors and owners in Petersburg heavy industry, and this no doubt aided his rise by affording him the very important state connections that he used so well. Also, his enterprise ended in failure, as with most of the others in his generation. However, we need more detailed studies of the other firms before we can safely generalize about the reasons for their business failures. While it may be true that these other firms collapsed because of the strains of the European depression, the Putilov case raises doubts about ascribing that general cause as the explanation for specific failures.

2

ENGINEERING GROWTH

LOCOMOTIVES, ARTILLERY, AND
DIVERSIFICATION STRATEGIES
1885–1900

The Putilov Company emerged as Russia's leading defense producer by the beginning of the twentieth century; however, that outcome was hardly predetermined. The factory had initially operated simply as a steel rail producer. Its rise to preeminence resulted from the strategies of the company's board of directors in the 1880s. In shaping their strategies, board members sought solutions to the long-term problems that confronted the factory. Chief among those concerns were the high costs of raw materials and fuel, and the related high cost of importing these items. The company's founder, N. I. Putilov, unsuccessfully sought to solve these difficulties in elaborate schemes to create a railroad and commercial port in St. Petersburg. The succeeding board of directors under president Nikolai Nikolaevich Antsyforov (1885–1900) resolved these problems by directing the company's product line away from metallurgy and rails into technically sophisticated mechanical goods. By choosing this option, the Putilov Company headed down a path very similar to that taken by its contemporaries in Europe and the United States. The leading European defense producers—Krupp, Schneider, and Vickers—all pursued parallel strategies and developed into the premier suppliers in their respective countries. Therefore, the Putilov board's approach would have been completely intelligible to contemporary Western industrialists and should not be considered in any way exceptional or eccentric.

Before we turn to the formulation and implementation of the Putilov Company's growth strategies in detail, it would be useful first to consider the backgrounds and profiles of the strategy makers themselves. The men who directed the Putilov enterprise from the 1880s on had considerable business and private factory experience before joining the Putilov board, and this gave them a very different perspective from that of N. I. Putilov. These men had strong connections to banking and metal factories, and their corresponding knowledge and experience made them highly competent businessmen. Unfortunately, little information is available about business managers and directors in Russia. Nevertheless, a collective portrait of the Putilov Company's strategy makers can be pieced together from the tidbits gleaned from the contemporary business press and the company's contracts and correspondence.

As part of the resurrection of the Putilov Company as an independent enterprise, the firm had to be reincorporated under an entirely new charter. The second charter, issued in 1884, increased the number of directors to five, each serving a five-year term, and created positions for five candidate directors who served in the absence of the full directors. The shareholders then elected one director and one candidate annually. The formal structure of the board of directors changed very little over the years. In 1912 the number of directors increased to seven, along with seven candidates.[1]

Of the five directors, limited biographical information is available for four. Starting at the top, Nikolai Antsyforov, the company's president from 1885 until 1900, had served on the board of directors of the Petersburg International Commercial Bank since 1876 and continued at the bank after becoming a member of the Putilov board. Additionally, Antsyforov held the post of president of the council in the Nevskii Shipbuilding plant in 1880 and served as a delegate from the Stroganov Ural plant at the Congress of Iron Producers in 1885. V. A. Chatskin, another Putilov board member, acted as a delegate for the Briansk rail plant at the same Congress in 1885. One of Antsyforov's colleagues on the board of the International Bank, A. Laski, also held a directorship at Putilov (1885–1898). Working under Antsyforov was Aleksandr Karlovich Voigt, a retired lieutenant and director of the Putilov factory in 1883. Voigt had held the position of candidate on the Briansk board in 1873 and had been designated head of the Putilov plant when Briansk purchased the Putilov works as part of the syndicate with Warsaw Steel.[2] Voigt served on the Putilov board briefly in 1885–1886 and then from 1889 to 1900.

Although the board positions were not officially differentiated, it would seem that the board functioned according to a professionally specialized division of labor. The Antsyforov team of directors consisted of financial experts and engineering specialists. In terms of active involvement, Antsyforov and Laski handled the financial dealings, while Voigt and subordinate engineers dealt with the contracts concerning railroad products and military goods. This arrangement is evident from the pattern of signatures on contracts and correspondence. If we bear in mind that the company's charter allowed for any board director to sign on behalf of the company on any contracts, it is striking that only three of the five directors regularly signed the relevant documents: Antsyforov, Voigt, and Laski. Furthermore, among these three by far the most frequent signers were Anstyforov and Voigt. Before 1893 Antsyforov's signature always appeared first, followed by Voigt's, on all documents. However, beginning in 1893 Voigt's signature usually appeared first on contracts for engineering materials, while Anstyforov or Laski signed first on documents pertaining to payments or financing agreements.[3] This emerging differentiation and specialization among board directors was most likely connected to the expanding scope of engineering products, since the new locomotive department initiated production in 1893 and the increasing activity for locomotives, wagons, and defense contracts probably required greater attention from the board.

While at the top of the company sat the board of directors and candidates, the plant itself was headed by a director and two assistants. The first assistant was mainly an administrative officer, while the second dealt with aspects of production such as overseeing orders and their execution. The general administration consisted of a secretariat for correspondence, bookkeeping, the registration office, the receiving office, supervisors, the central store, and the orders office. As of 1902, some 118 people worked in the general administration of the Putilov factory. Of a total of 467 employees, 350 served in various aspects of technical administration.[4]

This generation of factory directors at the Putilov Company benefited from an increasing degree of technical training. Ignacy Jasjukowicz, who served as the Putilov plant director between 1884 and 1888, graduated from the St. Petersburg Technical Institute. After leaving Putilov, Jasjukowicz became an important participant in the steel business and the Southern Association of Coal and Steel Producers in the 1890s. The succeeding plant director, Nikolai Ivanovich Danilevskii, began his career at Putilov as the plant mechanic in 1886. He was promoted to plant director in 1888 and continued in that capacity until 1895. During that time, the daily workings of the plant fell to Danilevskii because of his expertise in steam engineering. He was company president from 1910 to 1913. Thanks to Danilevskii, the Putilov works became the largest steam engine producer in Russia by 1898 and successfully expanded production for the Trans-Siberian Railway without turning to state loans or government aid.[5]

The picture of Putilov's directors and managers that emerges from these sources suggests that the changes at Putilov fit into a broader process of increasing professionalization and specialization taking place throughout Russian society in this period. For example, at the Izhorsk naval plant Fedor Khristoforovich Gross replaced Bykov as factory commander, and this transition marked a generational shift as well. Unlike factory commanders of the previous generation, Gross had not started in the Naval Cadet Corps but instead received his education at the Naval Engineering School. Gross's career reflected a more specialized technical path. In 1876 he was promoted to the corps of engineer-mechanics; the following year, he achieved the rank of master in the Kronstadt masters of self-propelled mines; and during 1880–1882 he taught at the Nicholas Naval Academy. After serving as port mechanic in Baku, he began his service at Izhorsk in 1888 in the capacity of main mechanic and in 1895 became the factory director.[6]

It should come as no surprise that the career profiles of the managers in both state and private enterprises followed parallel paths. Like the other professional groups developing at this time, the managerial elite who also possessed the requisite technical skills emerged from a small but expanding base.[7] Most came from the select group of Russians or Russified foreigners who received their education in the few universities or technical institutes within the empire. The administrators at the Putilov Company certainly fit this mold. Around the turn of the twentieth century, the technical administration at Putilov numbered 350 people, including 100 engineers and technicians who had received their education at the St. Petersburg Imperial Technological Institute, the Mining Institute, the Institute of Civil Engineers, the Nikolas Engineering Academy, and the Riga Polytechnical Institute. Given the lack of a body of highly qualified managers from the free professions or the merchant class, large corporations had few options but to recruit personnel from the bureaucracy and the armed forces as well.[8]

The Putilov Company's increasing preference for technical specialists among its staff had implications for the firm itself and, more broadly, for Russian business as well. For the Putilov Company, the growing number of technical specialists in house allowed for greater attention to the firm's technical development and enabled the company to integrate new production techniques into the factories. In turn, the technical talents of the firm consistently raised Putilov to the top of the field in each new product line it engineered. As the enterprise became more and more complex, the need for technically trained professionals also increased. This process at Putilov and other companies created not only an industrial demand for engineers, but also a demand for business professionals such as accountants and other white-collar employees. In this way, Putilov's technical professionalism increased the educational demand for more technical and professional business training within Russia and offered employment opportunities for newly trained professionals.[9]

Having sketched a collective portrait of the Putilov Company's strategy makers, I will now turn to the strategy itself. Antsyforov effectively conceded rail production to the factories of South Russia, which enjoyed a comparative advantage in price of raw materials and transportation costs because they were located near the coal and iron fields of the Donets basin region. Instead, he urged the company to opt for a product line that could generate greater profit with less output so that the cost of raw materials would be less burdensome. Thus the machine shop became the crucial element in the factory's development, and a diversified product line that included railroad cars, locomotives, and artillery yielded the profits.

By and large, these strategies were not short-term responses to the stimuli of economic crisis or depression. Rather, the board foresaw these options and began to implement them before the economic downturn of 1899–1902. A close examination of the articulation and timing of the board's strategies shows that Antsyforov and other directors did not seek a quick fix, but a long-range path for growth and steady orders based on an assessment of the potential markets for diverse products. As a result, company strategy played a more significant role than macroeconomic trends in shaping the development of the Putilov Company.

The years 1887–1889 were the most difficult account years for the company for a variety of reasons. In 1887–1888 the Putilov factory was almost exclusively a metallurgical factory that produced railroad cars and mechanical items in relatively small numbers. In fact, 58.3 percent of total production went to rails and rail ties. The oldest existing section of the plant was the metallurgical department, which was responsible for iron and steel processing. Unfortunately, the company experienced a rapid decline in rail orders. Besides decreasing rail orders, the introduction of an import duty for foreign iron in 1887 increased company expenses. Finally, the 1887 bond issues for 2.5 million rubles realized only 500,000 rubles.[10]

In a report presented to the general shareholders' meeting of 7 November 1887, Antsyforov laid out the company's present difficulties and charted a new course for its development. The proposed new path partially resembled N. I. Putilov's attempts to expand into railcar production. Since the factory still faced many of the same difficulties that had vexed its founder, one might expect a certain resemblance in the search for a solution to the old problems. The direction was the same, but the new board's plan avoided the financial overextension that had plagued the company's founder. Besides being more cautious, the new plans broke away from Putilov's one-dimensional reliance on a single state customer, namely, the Ministry of Transport. The directors of the new Putilov Company sought to expand by manufacturing new products that were related to the firm's existing technologies but would appeal to a variety of state and private customers. As a general rule, product diversification led to the creation of additional production departments and separate workshops between 1885 and 1900. In this way, the metallurgical, locomotive, wagon, machine-building, and artillery departments all developed into distinct divisions with their own specialized workshops.

Antsyforov's vision was very practical. He explained to the shareholders,

> Until recently the main and most profitable branch of production of the Putilov factory, as you could surmise from the annual accounts presented to you, has been the production of rails; however, currently, owing to the absence of indigenous iron and fuel in the local region and of the assessment of almost prohibitive duty of iron imported from England, the production of rails

should be completely removed from the activity of our factory, since due to such a high cost of imported raw materials, we are not in position to compete with the three southern and one western factories, which work on their own local iron and coal which of course comes to them much cheaper.[11]

Antsyforov noted that the company had prospected for iron ore in the Olonetsk region, but prospectors concluded that these iron pits would be insufficient to cover all the factory's demands. In addition, it would be necessary to use comparatively expensive foreign coke, since there was no local fuel. Therefore, that option would add to the expense of producing both iron and fuel. Under such conditions, the company could not hope for further production of rails at the Putilov factory. Furthermore, Antsyforov observed, with the curtailment of railroad construction, the demand had sharply decreased and did not provide enough work even for the four factories that could manufacture rails significantly more cheaply than Putilov. The immediate consequence would be the cessation of mass production of rails at Putilov and curtailment of output by at least 50 percent, with a corresponding decrease in annual profit.[12]

Such a cutback in production would make it very difficult for the enterprise to meet its obligations and to satisfy the shareholders. To compensate, the board of directors proposed that certain measures should be taken so that as rail production decreased, profits would not suffer. To achieve such an outcome, the company would have to increase sales of goods for which the cost of raw materials was of secondary importance—that is, goods of higher value. Therefore, Antsyforov proposed to develop certain branches of factory production and introduce several entirely new lines as a way to increase profits.[13]

To that end, the new plans demonstrated the directors' greater appreciation for separating the state and the market into discrete units that would be consumers of different steel goods. The board urged upgrading the factory's furnaces to accommodate the production of higher-quality steel, but in smaller quantities. Crucible furnaces had to be constructed for the manufacture of steel shells, which the board identified as one of the more profitable branches of the metallurgical business. Crucible furnaces would also enable the factory to manufacture significant quantities of instrumental steel, which could be sold in large quantities on the private market and would yield very high prices. Moreover, up to this time not a single Russian plant had branched out into this product area; the Russian market was exclusively supplied by English factories. These furnaces would also allow for the production of thick sheets of steel required for the army and the navy fleet.[14]

The board envisioned the machine workshop as a vital component in satisfying demands for the railroad car business and factory repairs. Therefore, the existing workshop had to be adapted for work exclusively on passenger and freight cars. As part of this specialization, the board proposed that painting and paper workshops (for railcar interiors) should be attached to the machine department, and also proposed the addition of a workshop for fine carpentry as well. Heretofore, the absence of these specialized departments for producing passenger railcars contributed to the expense and time required to complete orders.[15] Improvements in the machine shop would also permit the factory to branch out into specializations requiring greater technical competency. The board observed,

> At present the workshop is not in a position to cope with the orders we have for artillery machines and railroad switches . . . and denies us extremely profitable orders. The deficiencies of our mechanical workshops are well known to both the Naval and War Departments through their receiving agents.[16]

The expansion of work for the machine branch held out the possibility of manufacturing the extremely intricate and complex machinery for the naval and land artillery that could provide highly profitable orders in the near future. Moreover, the time was ripe for expanding into this field. The board observed in the report that "Demand for mechanical goods daily increases in Petersburg since the two factories of Krell and Lesner are so behind work that they are turning down orders three months in advance."[17] In this way, the improved machine shop could benefit the company by appealing to both civilian and military markets.

The 1887 company report marks an important transformation in the business mentality at Putilov and therefore deserves some comment. Overall, Antsyforov's report reveals a greater awareness of the potential markets in Russia than N. I. Putilov had shown. Nikolai Putilov had fixated on a single state customer as his target, with the result that the Ministry of Transport was the ultimate arbiter of the company's fate. Antsyforov perceived not only multiple state customers (the War, Naval, and Transport Ministries), but also private markets for steel and mechanical goods. Additionally, Antsyforov was more pragmatic regarding the factor endowments of the factory. Whereas N. I. Putilov had sought to lower the cost of raw materials by building a commercial port, Antsyforov resolved to get around that problem by expanding into engineering goods for which raw material costs were of secondary importance.

The divergent approaches of the two men reflect the very different backgrounds they brought to the enterprise. Given his experience in the navy, perhaps it was natural for N. I. Putilov to look to a port facility as a logical solution to his problems. By contrast, Antsyforov and the new directors sought less risky ways to maximize the assets they already had. The fact that the new directors also had connections to the Petersburg International Commercial Bank, the Briansk factory, and the Nevskii factory meant that they could more easily ascertain market conditions because they had access to more information. More important, the new board's banking ties probably inhibited the gambling streak that characterized N. I. Putilov's approach, while at the same time they strengthened the firm's ability to arrange financing for expansion.

The new strategy was already beginning to show promising results by 1890. In accordance with the plan, Antsyforov guided the factory out of rail production and into high-quality production for the market to the extent that Putilov's steel production increased from 4.4 percent of total output for 1883–1887 to 21.4 percent in 1887–1890. He also strengthened mechanical production, including bridge production in 1886–1887 and machine building in 1889, and initiated passenger railcar production in 1888. Also in 1888 the Putilov Company organized its crucible steel workshop. The expansion of this area made possible the large machinery needed to produce artillery shells, and by 1890–1891 output for the artillery department had already reached 591,000 rubles, or 11 percent of the factory's total production.[18]

The machine division of the factory began to grow rapidly starting in the early 1890s. Indeed, by January 1891 the Putilov Company was in a position to take on the preparation and assembly of a portion of the machine-building workshops for the Baltic Shipbuilding and Mechanical

Company. For 175,000 rubles it built the Baltic Company's machine shop, using Putlov's own materials and workers. Because the Baltic workshop had to meet the Naval Ministry's demand for steel construction appropriate for shipbuilding, Putilov's fine performance in this venture enhanced the firm's reputation in the eyes of state officials. The company completed the work on 31 May 1891.[19] The Baltic contract also shows the interconnectedness of the state and the market, since it represented a private contract for Putilov, but it was concluded to allow Baltic to complete state naval orders.

In 1889 Putilov won a contract for two torpedo boats, *Bierke* and *Rochensalm*, its first venture in the torpedo boat line. These resembled Schichau boats, but their bottoms were not so flat. The Putilov boats combined German and French components in that the engines were of the Schichau type, but the boilers followed the Du Temple pattern. Two of the boilers had been supplied by Du Temple, and the others were constructed at Putilov. The armament consisted of two 37mm Hotchkiss guns and one torpedo tube on each broadside. Up to this point, Putilov had produced plates for shipbuilding and manufactured projectiles and torpedo boats, and the plant was capable of considerable expansion because of its location near the Putilov Canal and rail connections. Along with the two torpedo boats, the company had in hand coastal defense mountings of the Krupp pattern, the mounting and hydraulic gear for the 12-inch gun of the *Gangut*, and chrome steel plates. Putilov also produced plates for commercial ships, although the company imported the cast iron and coal from England. By 1890, most of the machinery in the old fitting shop was somewhat obsolete and in need of modernization.[20] The firm finished work on the torpedo boats and delivered them on schedule to the navy in 1891. By now Putilov employed 3,500 workers, but most of the expansion was due to large orders for railway equipment and shells, rather than naval orders.

The robust health of the enterprise was reflected in the new physical plant. A new fitting shop had commenced operation, and another small one was on the way. Meanwhile, many of the old workshops underwent extensive repairs. The barbette for the *Gangut* was nearly finished. Putilov's successful completion of the pair of torpedo boats opened the way for more orders. By 1893, two new torpedo boats, *Tosna* and *Domesness*, were in the works, and prospects looked favorable for more orders upon their completion. Putilov was not only making Du Temple boilers for its own boats, but also building them for the torpedo boat *Aspe,* which was building at Kolpino.[21]

As the demands on the machine department increased, it became necessary to create other specialized departments; in this way, the machine shop generated whole new production departments. The expansion of the machine department was made possible by the good results attained by the factory in making shells and other items of artillery and also by the boom in railroad construction. Spurred by the railroad boom, Putilov began building locomotives in 1893 under the guidance of the director N. I. Danilevskii. The locomotive department got its start in 1892–1893. In January 1893, following the reception of an order for twenty-eight locomotives for a sum of approximately 1 million rubles, the company set about arranging a new department especially for locomotive production. Workshops that up to this time had performed locomotive repairs were expanded to make new departments. In this way the new, specialized locomotive department grew out of the old machine-building department and included newly constructed forge, mechanical, and assembly workshops, equipped with new machines.

Danilevskii also ordered machinery from abroad. Work at the new department was scheduled to start in the spring of 1893. By April, part of the machinery ordered from abroad had arrived, and the cost of constructing the new department reached about 300,000 rubles. The factory produced its first locomotive engine in 1894. By 1898 Putilov had manufactured 160 locomotives, and three years later this total had climbed to 964. At the same time, railcar construction developed into a special workshop. By 1897 the factory added a new machine shop to meet the factory's own needs, not for outside orders.[22]

Of all the new production departments created as a result of the board's strategy, none carried greater significance for the future of the company than the artillery branch. Although it had manufactured iron shells at the beginning of the nineteenth century, for many years the factory had not engaged in the production of artillery goods at all. Not until the 1870s under N. I. Putilov did it take a new order for shells, and at that time the company also received its first order for shells from the Naval Department. These orders were followed by various small orders for the repair of gun carriages and spare parts in the 1880s. However, as yet this work did not require any special equipment. Then, according to the Putilov Company's official history, "In 1886 the board of the Putilov Company made up its mind to manufacture objects for the defense of the country."[23]

To establish the new product line, the company enlisted the aid of foreign technology and expertise. Perhaps the most significant mechanism for the technology transfer was the license or co-production agreement through which the company acquired whole production methods. The Putilov Company's board employed this method when it initiated its foray into military production. Eight months after receiving an order for six 6-inch naval guns in 1887, the Putilov Company arranged the development of the crucible and tempering workshops through an agreement with the French firm Jacob Holtzer. By 1891 Putilov was manufacturing armor-piercing projectiles made on the Holtzer system under the direction of a French expert from that firm, but not in large lots. Production amounted to several thousand shells of all calibers.[24]

The advantages of foreign technical agreements appeared self-evident to Putilov's board. As the official history of the factory reports,

> The board of the Company, realizing that having assistants from abroad the factory will be richer with technical information and will always be found in the path of all the newest inventions and improvements, did not let slip this propitious moment and concluded in 1889 an agreement with one of the most prominent artillery engineers in Europe, Gustave Canet, by which the Putilov plant received all the plans, practical experience and technical personnel of his office.[25]

The continuing collaboration with Canet yielded orders for gun carriages for the 6-inch coastal quick-fire guns from the Main Artillery Administration (GAU) in 1895. Under the terms of the agreement between GAU and Canet, the first order for the carriages could be presented only to Putilov. In this way, the company benefited by being the sole Russian producer that possessed the Canet system. In return for this advantage, Putilov agreed not to export the system. The final contract, concluded on 29 November 1895, called for Putilov to produce thirteen 6-inch coastal gun carriages of the Canet system at 16,500 rubles apiece, for a total of

214,000 rubles. For its part, Putilov promised to produce the pieces within eighteen months from its own workshops and materials without any state assistance.[26]

The positive results obtained from foreign collaboration with Canet led to other such arrangements. Actual gun production for the army, as opposed to mere gun carriages, began with foreign help when the first light field artillery guns were produced in 1892. Production aid came from the French firm Schneider-Creusot, with whom the factory maintained ties. Thanks to the strong performance of this gun during testing, the factory earned its first order for seventy-five 57mm guns of the English Nordenfelt system in 1893. Along with the artillery production, the board also fostered production of other defense items using foreign experts. French expertise enabled the firm to manufacture shells and electric turrets for warships, while it also purchased designs for underwater mines from the British. In 1898 the company entered into an agreement with the English firm Armstrong and received the right to manufacture underwater mines of the Armstrong system.[27]

More significant for the future of the factory, the company's board oversaw artillery production and encouraged the development of defense production as an increasing share of Putilov's output. Up to 1890, the company manufactured artillery orders in the general machinery workshops. As the artillery business grew, in 1890 the administration found it necessary to construct a special workshop that was designated the gun carriage-shell department. This workshop subsequently developed specializations for large-caliber shells, mines, and shrapnel. Then, in 1893 the company purchased land upon which to build a workshop and a firing range for test-firing artillery pieces. The cannon workshop officially began in 1895 with the receipt of an order for light field artillery with carriages. Between 1895 and 1900, one-quarter of the resources in new construction at the factory went into the artillery masters and the manufacture of light field artillery for the army. Additionally, the company created an Artillery-Technical Office at the Putilov factory, which designed its own 3-inch light field gun.[28]

British naval intelligence reports gave Putilov's technical development high marks in the mid-1890s. Royal Navy Captain Wintz observed, after visiting the Putilov works in 1895 and 1896, "The very latest plant and tools are fitted up here, some of the smaller turning lathes were worked by electric motors; the castings had all been made in the works. Another new building is shortly to be added for the construction of Maxim-Nordenfelt machine and Q.F. [quick-fire] guns; the work was just being commenced." A new copper smithery and a large locomotive erecting shop had just been completed, and a new shop for turning out small guns for field service had also been added. The captain counted thirty 87mm guns on hand in the works. He found the gun carriage shop well employed in producing 10-inch land guns. No torpedo boats were building at that time, but Putilov could construct only two at once. The plant made both Siemens-Martin and Bessemer castings, and locomotive output averaged nine units per month, and twenty per month for carriages. Wintz concluded, "Everything here showed signs of increased activity; there was plenty of work in hand and plenty in prospect, and the workmanship was, I should say, excellent."[29] Putilov's technical modernization continued in the late 1890s. The factory was upgrading and improving the plant by replacing the old-pattern tools with the latest types of electric-powered machine tools. By 1898 the new installation of eighteen Babcock boilers and 2,000hp electrical machinery was nearly complete. The works could handle large castings up to thirty tons.[30]

The formative phase of Putilov's career as an artillery supplier culminated around 1898 with the development of the firm's own system for quick-fire 3-inch guns and gun carriages. In field tests of various new systems for the quick-fire field gun, the Putilov model outperformed those made by Schneider, Krupp, and Chamond, and therefore the tsarist army's Rearmament Commission determined that the Putilov gun was technically superior.[31] In light of this achievement, the Putilov board "proposed the strengthening of the activity of the artillery department in light of the forthcoming renovation of field artillery in connection with the excellent results attained in the competition of the model of the field gun carriage manufactured by the technicians of the Putilov factory."[32]

Putilov's predominant type of military production between 1885 and 1900 had been shell production. Prior to 1900, the company was in the process of completing defense contracts signed in the period 1895–1900 amounting to 2,555,840 rubles; 41 percent of those contracts involved gun carriages, while the rest consisted mostly of orders for shells and shrapnel.[33] With the success of its new field gun, though, Putilov had climbed to a higher level of specialization. The firm had become the sole private manufacturer of artillery pieces in tsarist Russia. Anticipating the state's upcoming modernization of its field artillery with quick-fire guns, the board felt certain that the factory would be given a significant order for artillery and gun carriages. Currently the Putilov factory could prepare up to 100 guns a year, which was not a significant portion of the factory's output, and therefore equipping the cannon department comformed with modest orders. In view of forthcoming long-term orders for artillery, the board planned to expand the workshops and their equipment, which demanded significant outlays of capital.[34] To cover the cost of expansion, the board proposed increasing the company's capital by issuing supplemental stock in the amount of 3 million rubles. The stockholders approved the proposal "in light of the expansion of the activity of the factory for the fulfilment of accepted artillery orders," and the stock capital increased to 12 million rubles in 1899.[35] In this way, the artillery department paved the way for the firm's capital expansion.

The development of Putilov's artillery department casts serious doubts on Joseph Bradley's negative assessment of Russian entrepreneurship. In his study of the state arsenals, Bradley concludes that Russians proved themselves unable to domesticate foreign technology and failed to generate their own technical innovations. Contrary to this view, at Putilov they not only kept abreast of the latest technology, but also adapted it in an innovative way. Yet, Bradley's broader point that the state impeded development seems to be borne out by the Putilov experience. Bradley pointed to the lack of market stimuli for profitability as causing the failure of the state arsenals.[36] In contrast, it was indeed the quest for profits in the market that drove the Putilov Company to adopt foreign technology and innovate its own.

Putilov's distinctiveness in Russia resulted from the directors' decision to develop the company as a military supplier. However, Putilov's development was similar to that of other Western defense firms. Like its counterparts in the United States, France, Britain, Germany, or Austria-Hungary, the Putilov Company originally moved toward a defense product line and away from rails and simple metallurgy because it could not compete with domestic rivals who paid less for raw materials and transport. As a result, these future military-industrial firms sought to offset these disadvantages by moving into more specialized engineering. What set Putilov apart from firms such as Krupp (in Germany) or Schneider (in

France) was that Putilov relied on technical support from those foreign firms. Thus, unlike the leading European arms manufacturers, Putilov never became an arms exporter because it was itself an importer of military technology, and according to the terms of the technical agreements it could not export its products.

Like the Putilov Company, Bethlehem Steel had been primarily a rail maker in 1870s, but in the early 1880s declining profits led the company to reconsider its dependency on the rail market and to contemplate diversification. In 1885 Bethlehem opted to move out of the rail business in the face of tough competition from Pittsburgh's high-volume rail producers. To compensate, the company positioned itself for large naval ordnance contracts by negotiating technical agreements for cutting-edge armor and for a heavy-forging plant. Working through U.S. naval officers with foreign contacts, Bethlehem arranged technology transfers with European ordnance companies. In 1885 Bethlehem secured a contract with the British firm Whitworth for heavy-forging technology, while at the same time Schneider approached Bethlehem for an entree into the American market. The Schneider negotiations yielded an agreement in 1887 through which the French firm provided Bethlehem with patent rights, drawings of machinery, and information on manufacturing methods and shop practices.[37]

Defense contracts became a vital component in the growth of both Bethlehem Steel and Carnegie Steel. Bethlehem secured its first naval armor contract in 1887, and Carnegie soon followed suit in 1890. Bethlehem derived more than half its profits from armor plate in the 1890s. Similarly, Andrew Carnegie noted in 1895, "Railroads too poor; . . . general trade may be better but there's no profit in that. Good thing we are to get more Armor this year."[38] With the help of technical information from naval insiders, both companies succeeded in divvying up the armor contracts between them by cooperating in their pricing into the new century. Thanks to the profits from defense contracts, Bethlehem managed to extricate itself from the rail market in the 1880s and further diversified. For Carnegie, military contracting generated enough retained profits for the firm to become America's most fully integrated steel producer without recourse to outside financing.[39]

Skoda, in the Czech city of Plzen, made its first strategic moves into the defense business in the 1890s. The Austrian navy accepted the Skoda pattern for quick-fire artillery in 1890. Skoda had designed the gun as a modified Hotchkiss piece. Around the same time, the Austro-Hungarian army adopted the Skoda 8mm machine gun. Although Skoda did not yet produce its own steel, the firm had begun to prepare for that task by setting up the necessary Siemens-Martin furnaces and other plant. Skoda already manufactured a considerable quantity of defense goods for the Austrian government, as well as commercial goods for both domestic and foreign markets.[40] By 1892 Skoda was gaining in importance as a defense supplier. Although railway plant still served as the main product line, Skoda's proficiency with war material was increasing. The firm had delivered to the Austrian government forty-four quick-fire guns (47mm) and eight quick-fire guns of 7cm calibers. Besides guns, the company made cast-iron turrets for land defenses.

Skoda also entered into the competition with other firms for the contract for armor plates for ships.[41] In 1896 Skoda erected new buildings and gun shops, and the new machine shop was capable of turning out machine guns and quick-fire guns of up to 15 cm. Production facilities employed electricity both for machines and cranes. Along with casting artillery, Skoda could make large castings with the Siemens-Martin process, including a 40-ton Lloyd steamer. This casting prowess had brought orders for heavy castings for new German cruisers and some for Italy. A report from British Naval Intelligence concluded, "It will be seen from above, and from the work carried out at the Skoda factory, that Austria is thus fast becoming independent of outside help for the supply of her war material."[42]

A brief comparison of the histories of the German firm Krupp, the French firm Schneider-Creusot, and the English firm Vickers with that of Putilov shows some remarkable parallels in strategy and timing. Krupp was distinguished from the other three by the fact that it had already moved out of rail and general steel production and into armaments in the 1860s. Even though the timing differed, Krupp also pursued a strategy of product diversification.[43] In 1886 Creusot gave up rail production entirely, thus ending its days as an ordinary steel company, and switched over to the business of war supplies. This conversion was due in part because the Loire enterprises faced stiff competition from steel producers in Lorraine and therefore the Loire firms sought a product line that deemphasized raw material costs. As a result, the Loire became the center of French arms manufacture.[44] By 1888 Schneider had created a separate gun founding department.[45] Similarly, in 1888 the English firm Vickers first turned to the manufacture of armaments as its rail and general steel trade fell away. As was the case with Putilov, Vickers opted to improve its furnaces as a necessary first step. In 1890 Vickers produced its first artillery piece. Vickers became the largest employer in Britain by the early twentieth century, and in this way held a position analogous to that of Putilov in Russia.[46]

Putilov's experience closely followed Vickers' not only in strategy, but also in the profile of the firm's strategy makers. In terms of professionalization, the board of directors at Vickers worked as a team of technical and financial experts and included retired military officers. In addition, board members were chosen on the basis of their professional qualifications for specific duties. Clive Trebilcock, in his detailed study of the Vickers enterprise, describes the major traits of the firm as "a capacity to meet pressures upon the firm, not with the all-too-familiar policies of retrenchment, but with consistently bold strokes of innovation or diversification, and equally important, a constant emphasis upon technical leadership of the market, whether it was civilian or military."[47] The same could be said about Putilov.

How then shall we assess the Putilov board's strategy? How successful was it? Almost a decade after Antsyforov and the board had charted the new course for the factory toward producing more high-value goods, the longer-term positive results of that decision had become clear. By the mid-1890s, the government was seeking to make the country independent of other states for all war material and was encouraging some orders for private works, mainly in St. Petersburg. Putilov, Aleksandr, and the Franco-Russian Company made some steel artillery matériel by 1894. The size of Putilov's work force had climbed from 3,500 in 1891 to 5,500 by 1894, and work in hand for 1893 included locomotives, railway matériel, torpedo boats, and artillery matérial. Among its defense orders, Putilov was finishing turntables for turrets of *George the Victorious* and *Poltava*, and the seventy-five 57mm quick-fire Nordenfelt guns. By 1894 the company was carrying out War Department orders worth 500,000–700,000 rubles yearly. Moreover, the War Ministry deemed the quality of Putilov shell to be so superior that in December 1893 the state-owned Obukhov plant ceased to manufacture shell—apparently because of its inferiority to

Putilov shell.[48] Addressing the shareholders in 1898, Antsyforov observed that the price of metallurgical goods had been dropping while material costs had remained the same. Meanwhile, the company's total manufactured goods had decreased from around 4.3 million to 3.3 million poods in the past year. Yet, the average actual value per pood was 5 rubles and 70.5 kopeks against 4 rubles and 32 kopeks the previous year. So the firm earned 1 ruble and 38 kopeks more per pood of output. The increase in prices was the result of the improved productivity of the locomotive, railroad car, and artillery departments.[49]

The extent to which Antsyforov and the other directors had transformed the company's product line between 1887 and 1900 is evident from changes in the value of goods produced by each department (see table 2.1). Production figures show that the factory did not really abandon metallurgy at all. In fact, after reaching bottom in 1888, the metallurgical department's output increased so much in value that by 1892 it was producing more than ever before. In 1888 the ruble value of the metallurgical department's output equaled about 2 million rubles, whereas in

Table 2.1

The Putilov Company's Production of Goods by Department, 1885–1899 (in rubles)

	Metallurgy	Locomotives	Railcars	Mechanical	Artillery
1885–86	4,668,060	—	490,907	695,753	206,605
1886	4,653,035	—	762,797	452,489	18,413
1887	3,311,720	—	233,739	584,749	186,058
1888	2,000,597	—	818,474	1,136,495	124,152
1889	2,839,668	—	585,482	1,002,662	268,461
1890	3,008,000	—	525,370	511,116	589,902
1891	4,599,908	—	635,618	942,591	747,362
1892	6,353,271	—	1,057,533	1,226,008	838,234
1893	6,865,313	—	2,503,875	1,095,343	1,481,011
1894	5,884,639	2,085,952	2,228,833	1,024,867	1,512,768
1895	7,027,069	3,304,783	3,407,610	884,160	654,326
1896	6,947,577	4,246,832	4,691,083	929,879	1,603,703
1897	5,224,550	5,318,408	5,838,211	459,713	1,952,730
1898	4,564,338	6,306,844	5,412,051	1,147,313	2,062,337
1899	5,178,279	5,609,348	4,670,153	1,008,879	2,823,309

Source: K stol., 26.

1892 it reached 6.4 million rubles. The real change appeared in the declining percentage of total output that metallurgy claimed (see table 3.2). As a percentage of total output, metallurgical department production dropped from 77 percent in 1887 to 27 percent by 1900. Antsyforov's achievement lay in adding on whole new production departments and creating a balance among the metallurgical, locomotive, and railcar departments. As a result, by 1900 locomotive production accounted for 29 percent of total ruble output, and railcars comprised 24 percent. Artillery production amounted to 15 percent at that time.[50]

Although Putilov had been the first to manufacture steel rails in Russia, stiff competition soon emerged from the south, and in fact that region became the center for Russian rail production. Facing a losing battle against southern steel producers that enjoyed cheaper raw material costs, Putilov and other factories switched into rolling stock and diversified into engineering product lines. The majority of Russian locomotives came from just three producers: Putilov, Kolomna, and Briansk. Putilov's

Table 2.2

The Putilov Company's Production of Goods by Department, 1885–1900 (in percentages)

	Metallurgy	Locomotives	Railcars	Mechanical	Artillery
1885–86	77	—	8	12	3
1886–87	79	—	13	8	<1
1887–88	77	—	5	14	4
1888–89	49	—	20	28	3
1889–90	60	—	13	21	6
1890–91	65	—	11	11	13
1891–92	66	—	9	14	11
1892–93	67	—	11	13	9
1893–94	57	—	21	10	12
1894–95	46	16	17	9	12
1895–96	46	22	22	6	4
1896–97	38	23	25	5	9
1897–98	28	28	31	3	10
1898–99	23	32	28	6	11
1899–1900	27	29	24	5	15

Source: K stol., 26.

prominence in Russian locomotive production is evident when we consider the firm's share in the Russian market (see table 2.3). From the time locomotive production commenced at Putilov in 1894 until 1898, the company manufactured 534 locomotives, or 22 percent of the Russian total. Furthermore, in 1898 Putilov led all other producers with its annual output of 172 locomotives.[51]

Russia's engineering companies rarely specialized in only one aspect of machine building. The largest enterprises usually had diversified into at least two areas from among the product groups of transport equipment, agricultural machinery, industrial equipment, electrical production, and shipbuilding. Thus, for example, Nevskii Shipbuilding in St. Petersburg made rails, locomotives, and ships, while Sormovo in Nizhnyi-Novgorod produced steamships, steam engines, boilers, shells, and locomotives. As a function of such strategic diversification, already by 1902 the Putilov Company had eight main departments: administration, artillery, locomotives, machine building, mechanical laboratory, metallurgy, railcars, and steam turbines. Each department also contained a number of specialized workshops, and the factory had thirty-eight in all. The metallurgical department was headed by a technical engineer, while the plant's chief mechanic managed the mechanical department. Additionally, the plant

Table 2.3

Steel Rail Production by the Putilov Company, 1885–1895 (in poods)

	Russian Total	Putilov Company	(%)
1885	5,782,151	1,803,829	31.0
1886	6,893,509	1,695,326	25.0
1887	5,368,616	1,002,615	19.0
1888	3,926,233	483,576	12.0
1889	5,839,771	242,599	4.0
1890	10,563,654	1,354,806	13.0
1891	10,442,831	944,862	9.0
1892	12,043,610	1,549,452	12.0
1893	14,486,823	2,593,618	18.0
1894	15,260,762	2,762,921	18.0
1895	18,448,122	2,786,393	15.0

Source: Keppen, *Materialy dlia istorii rel'sovogo proizvodstva*, 118–21.

had facilities for research and development, including a chemical laboratory for metallurgy and a testing range for artillery.[52]

Putilov's profit record compared favorably with those of other firms.
If we take annual profits as a percentage of stock capital, then for the
years 1893 to 1900 the Putilov Company averaged between 11 and 13
percent profit. The average for all enterprises in Russia was slightly higher
(12–15 percent). However, the average profit rate for metallurgical firms
was 8–9 percent.[53] Meanwhile, profits for Vickers in the same period hov-
ered around 15 percent.[54]

Thus, the board's strategy under Antsyforov and Voigt to guide production away from metallurgy and into mechanical goods allowed the
company to weather the general economic downturn of 1899–1902 with
large profits. The company's revision commission, assessing the progress
over recent years, observed that the factory had managed its conversion
into a mechanical enterprise. As a result, the general sum of output of
goods had not decreased, and in fact it rose. This had proved vital for the
factory's future, because "under current conditions the Putilov plant as
primarily a metallurgical factory could hardly have survived."[55] The company had not only survived, it had flourished. By the turn of the century,
Putilov had become the largest factory employer in Russia. In one decade
the factory had grown fourfold and employed 12,440 workers. The next
largest, Briansk, employed 10,500, while Sormovo had 8,700 workers and
Kolomna had 6,850 in 1901. In 1903 Putilov had become the single
largest artillery supplier in Russia and had full orders for locomotives.[56]

By 1901 the Putilov Company had positioned itself between state and
market, but markets held preeminence. At the turn of the twentieth century, the private share accounted for 72 percent of the firm's annual output, and the share would increase.[57] The Putilov Company's "centennial"
publication offers a rare glimpse into how the company marketed its own
image at the turn of the century. Several themes echo throughout the
company history. First, the plant was distinguished by its size. The author
compares Putilov's labor force with that of other Russian factories and
also places it in the same category as Krupp, Armstrong, and Cockerill.
Here he was exaggerating. Whereas Putilov was the largest factory
employer in Russia in 1901, it did not measure up in size to Krupp. In
1902 Krupp had 42,600 employees, of whom 24,109 worked at Essen
alone. Putilov employed 12,440.[58]

Another rhetorical strand in the official history is the longevity and stability of the factory:

> The ownership by private people and a company since 1848, that
> is a period of more than fifty years, itself serves as the first indica-
> tor of the stability of the enterprise. . . . In particular, the factory
> survived several unfavorable periods. (Not mentioning the sec-
> ond half of the activity of N. I. Putilov when the factory, after
> extremely rapid development, could not acquire satisfactory
> amounts of capital for the continuation of the business and had
> to be transferred to other hands.) In 1888 and 1889 because of
> the very unfavorable situation for all metallurgical and mechani-
> cal factories of Russia due to the temporary stagnation in rail-
> road construction, the Putilov factory even switched from sound
> profits to losses.
>
> Since that time the factory has become an enterprise of unin-
> terrupted profitability.[59]

To promote the perception of Putilov as a long-term survivor, the company claimed 1801 as its founding date and referred to itself as having
been a private company since 1848. However, legitimately the company
could not claim to have been in existence before 1873, and a more accurate date would be 1885.

The company also reinforced its image as a helpmate to the state, but
emphasized its own role as an agent of progress and innovation in Russia's
economic development. It was both a partner with the state—not a com-
petitor—and an autonomous private commercial enterprise. According
to the official company history published in 1902, Putilov "was the first
accomplice of state factories when the latter did not satisfy the accelerat-
ing demand."[60] The company also emphasized its innovative role as a private enterprise.

> Thus, the Putilov factory managed to be the first to establish the
> production of rails in Russia; it was the first of the rolling factories
> to establish in large measure the rolling of construction beams,
> significantly surpassing in number foreign factories, and one of
> the first private factories which began the rolling of ship steel; it

was the first to introduce the preparation of large steel castings
for battleships. Among private factories Putilov was the first to
organize on broad bases the manufacture of instrument steel of
the very highest type, and currently is arranging the manufacture
of cheap steel for handicraft (kustar) production. In the business
of making railcars and even in the factory's comparatively young
locomotive business, the Putilov factory produced for the country several new types. Still a more apparent role befell the Putilov
factory in the artillery business.[61]

Thus, the Putilov Company presented itself as Janus-faced, with one
face toward the market and the other toward the state. Overall, the company grounded its image in its identity as a commercial business and
emphasized the commercial side "which above all undoubtedly defines
the viability of the factory—the security of its further prosperity."[62] Yet, in
conclusion, the author looked to still brighter days ahead:

All the forementioned reasons call us to look to the future of the
factory with confidence in the durability of its existence and the
further successful development for the benefit of the fatherland
and profit for the shareholders and many thousands of workers
and employees of the factory, and along with this to hope indeed
for the attentive relationship to the factory by government organs
who make up its chief customers.[63]

Although little is known about this publication, one may speculate
about why it appeared when it did and the company image it presents. To
claim a centenary for an enterprise that did not become the Putilov factory until 1868 seems curious. Although the state factory was founded in
1801, probably a more important reason for claiming a hundred-year
heritage was the Putilov Company's situation in 1901–1902. Having taken
a loan from the State Bank in 1901, the company was undoubtedly engaging in a little self-promotion before an audience of state officials. By stress-
ing the company's endurance and usefulness for the state, it attempted to
establish creditworthiness.

Fundamentally, Putilov's evolution into a high-quality defense enterprise was the result of conscious policy to restructure the works into an

engineering firm. The origins of the policy were laid out in Antsyforov's 1887 proposal and carried on into the next century. The government's promotion of railroad construction in the 1890s certainly helped sustain Putilov, and large artillery orders likewise insulated the company from economic shocks during the depression of 1899–1902. However, the key point is that the company put itself in a position to take advantage of these opportunities before they came along. Thus, broader economic trends reinforced and supported the strategy, but the strategy appeared first. Moreover, that strategy was based on a reading of the market opportunities in Russia, and in its basic contours the Putilov board's program for growth paralleled the development strategies of comparable firms in Europe.

3

THE RUSSIAN KRUPP

PUTILOV AND THE ARTILLERY BUSINESS
1900–1907

Even as the state share of the company's annual output continued to decline after 1901, the artillery business took on greater significance, and in fact the Putilov Company turned into Russia's premier military supplier. This seemingly paradoxical situation can be explained by the company's manner of adjusting to the segmentation of the Russian market. The various segments had different rhythms of demand, payment, and turnover. In the end, the artillery segment of the market shaped the firm more dramatically than any other. Putilov obtained its first large artillery order in 1900. That order was a two-year contract calling for 750 guns. In 1903 the company earned an even larger order for 1,600 artillery pieces to be completed during 1904–1907.

In the history of the Putilov Company, the acceptance of the large 1903 artillery order stands out as a decisive turning point for the fate of the company in tsarist Russia. Prior to taking this order, Putilov operated primarily as a locomotive producer. After that point, the company was transformed into Russia's artillery producer par excellence, with all the advantages and disadvantages inherent in that position. The 1903 contract was pivotal because it served to define the working relationship between the state defense organs, primarily the Main Artillery Administration (GAU), and the company. GAU's practices regarding the procurement process, pricing, and payment for artillery orders had a direct impact on the company. In spite of the company's attempts to convince

GAU of the need for change, the officers in the artillery department refused to modify the procedures. Therefore, civil-military relations conditioned Putilov's business performance. In its disputes with GAU, the company had no consistent ministerial backing from any quarter. Occasionally a representative from the Ministry of Finance might voice support for sending an order to Putilov. However, the Ministry of Finance was more concerned with the government's fiscal interests than any private business. Based on its production, Putilov had attained a prime position in defense production, but it was hardly an undisputed master among artillery factories. As we shall see, the company could not dictate conditions in its relationship with the state, and on a variety of issues such as pricing, financing, and acquiring orders it failed to set the terms more often than it succeeded.

The 1903 contract also played a key role in shaping the firm's development because it was the all-important "follow-on" order for the factory. That is to say, receiving the 1903 contract confirmed Putilov's status as the logical choice for large-scale artillery production; from then on, Putilov had to be given orders to maintain capacity. Especially significant was the fact that the contract was a multiyear arrangement, thus satisfying one of the Putilov board's greatest desires—to execute long-term production runs with some sense of predictability. However, the period 1904–1907 actually brought a highly unpredictable and volatile series of events that placed some major obstacles in the way of the board's best-laid plans. How Putilov responded to the strains of genuine war production and the worker unrest from the time of the Russo-Japanese War through the Revolution of 1905, and what the company expected from the state reveals just how intimately bound up with artillery production the factory had become.

Invariably, in discussions of the armaments business in the nineteenth and early twentieth centuries, one company stands out: Krupp of Essen. The German giant served as the standard against which all other artillery producers were measured. Historians have often remarked that there was no "Russian Krupp." By this they mean that Russia lacked a specialized armaments manufacturer. This deficiency has been taken as further proof of the weakness of the Russian domestic market for industrial goods. Peter Gatrell sums up this position:

Russia possessed little in the way of a developed private armaments industry prior to 1910. . . . Several private firms engaged in
defence work, but they operated . . . without any conviction that
defence contracts could yield long-term rewards. No Russian firm
dominated the industry in the manner of the European giants,
such as Schneider, Vickers or Krupp. Russia lacked the equivalent
of these specialist suppliers of armaments. The relatively small
size of the Russian market compelled engineering firms to
engage in the manufacture of a broad range of products.[1]

In this view, Putilov was no Russian Krupp because it did not specialize solely in armaments. Yet if one uses this criterion to define a defense
enterprise, even Krupp could not be considered a "Krupp." A diverse
product line was not unusual for other European defense firms. Krupp,
by far the largest armaments concern in the world, only devoted 30 percent of its output to military goods. Similarly, Vickers manufactured a
whole range of products from heavy artillery to lamp holders, and by
1907 its armaments section provided roughly 23 percent of the firm's
total output by value.[2]

If we take Krupp's level of 30 percent annual defense output as the
measure of a specialized armaments firm, then a good case can be made
that Putilov belongs in that category. Putilov's artillery production averaged a little more than 30 percent of annual output in the period
1908–1912. What is more significant, Putilov had crossed that threshold
of defense production at the beginning of the twentieth century. By
1902–1903, artillery production as a percentage of annual output averaged 35.5 percent. In light of this information, Putilov's transformation
into a defense enterprise had already happened at the beginning of the
century and not, as Gatrell argues, as a result of Aleksei Ivanovich
Putilov's strategies in 1908–1914.[3]

By 1902–1903 Putilov had established itself as a vital player in Russia's
defense sector. British Naval Intelligence paid close attention to the firm's
growing capacity as an armaments supplier. After a visit to the plant on 20
August 1902 by one of its officers, Admiralty Intelligence representatives
noted that the factory constructed gun mountings for the largest types of
naval ordnance, fortress gun mountings, and complete field guns and carriages. In other shops Putilov made torpedo tubes for both above-water

and submerged discharge. The company arranged with the Canet Works to be kept informed of all recent improvements for guns and gun mountings, and also with Messrs. Sautter and Harle regarding electrical motors. The officer also reported, "The A.P. [armor piercing] projectiles are said to be so good that the Russian Admiralty have accepted them as the standard for testing all their armour plate." Turning to the gun works itself, he observed, "The field gun shop, which is a vast new structure, has the most elaborate plant. All the bigger lathes and tools have their separate motors; the smaller lathes are grouped together, and have motors to work each group."[4]

As of July 1903, Putilov was preparing to rationalize its shipbuilding operations to specialize in armor plate for naval orders. Since neither the government works at Obukhov nor Izhora could cope with the greatly increased demand for armor plate for use in the Russian navy, the Naval Ministry had no alternative but to order that material from abroad. With a view to keeping these orders at home, Putilov intended to turn out armor plate on the most improved modern system. Previously the Putilov Works had produced rolled steel and steel parts used in shipbuilding, but at a loss. However, that section of the works was about to be reorganized to specialize exclusively in armor plate.[5] While advancing its specialized defense production capabilities, Putilov continued to preserve its diversified product mix by manufacturing labor-saving machinery, railway plant, and a variety of boilers.

The absence of a specialized armaments producer has been taken to mean that the Russian domestic market for industrial goods was underdeveloped. This notion also does not stand up to scrutiny. If we accept this proposition, then we must conclude that the domestic markets in Britain, Germany, and France were likewise underdeveloped. The governments of Britain, Germany, and France all preferred to rely on state-run arsenals as their primary source of armaments supply. As a result, private manufacturers were compelled to diversify or export their war products to remain solvent. In Britain, free trading in arms exports began in 1862 because the government favored state arsenals exclusively until 1887, when state policy began to allow half of its procurement orders to go to private firms. The effect of the British policy was that exports figured prominently in the output shares of the private firms. For example, Vickers's exports of naval production in the period 1903–1912 accounted for 33.9 percent of its total output, and the firm became the preeminent international producer. Similarly, Krupp exhibited a reliance on arms exports. By 1877 Krupp had produced 24,576 cannon, of which the firm had exported 57 percent; 51 percent of Krupp's 53,000 cannon went to foreign customers by 1914. During 1875–1891, only 18 percent of the company's production remained in Germany.[6]

The French experience differed slightly from that of Britain and Germany. In France no private gun producers existed until 1870, and both military and naval guns were manufactured at state foundries. In 1885 the French government repealed the law against arms exports and as a result private exports jumped dramatically. With the backing of Parisian banks, Creusot created a syndicate for French naval exports that included the shipyards of La Seyne, Loire, and Gironde. These firms continued to compete with one another for domestic orders but cooperated internationally. From 1885 to 1914, half of the 90,000 artillery pieces manufactured by Schneider were sold abroad, and 44 percent of the military production at Forges et Chantiers de la Méditerranée was also exported. Nevertheless, exports as a total of all arms production in France stayed below 10 percent because the state arsenals did not export their products.[7]

Schneider, best known as an armaments firm, also followed a diversification strategy. An unidentified British naval officer who visited the works in March 1903 reported the following about Schneider's military output to Admiralty Intelligence: "The Schneider establishment (of which Le Creusot is the central and most important factory) is by far the largest mercantile firm of its kind in France, and its output of war material compares on almost equal terms with factories as renowned as those of Kolpino or Oboukof in Russia, Terni in Italy, or even Krupp in Germany."[8] As was the case with Putilov, Schneider's military output formed but a part of the firm's annual production. Certainly Schneider's annual production of guns, armor, shot, and shell was impressive, but for Le Creusot these constituted only a portion of the material manufactured in its shops. The 1903 Admiralty Intelligence report noted:

> Thus at Le Creusot, and at the affiliated factories . . . the dead weight of the annual output of iron and steel exceeds 146,000 tons, and includes products as diverse as armour plate, engines and boilers for ships of all sizes, locomotives, railway rolling-

stock, rails and material, bridge work of all descriptions, iron and steel girders, plates and ship building material of every grade and scantling, electrical machinery (a great and growing feature), as well as the renowned artillery material which we are accustomed to associate with the name of Schneider. Torpedo craft are built in considerable numbers at the Company's yard at Châlon on the Saône River.[9]

On the basis of this comparison, Putilov must be considered a first-class defense producer in its own right because it already was outproducing Obukhov and Kolpino in Russia.

The affinities between Schneider and Putilov deserve comment. Schneider had achieved the position of market leader and among French firms came closest to being a complete-cycle producer. In this regard, Putilov's place in Russia was analogous. After its purchase of the Canet workshops in Le Havre in 1897, Schneider acquired and preserved the existing technical links between Putilov and Canet. The two firms were thus in direct business contact before the turn of the century. Putilov and Schneider were also evenly matched in the size of their work force, each employing roughly 12,000 workers. Yet both were significantly smaller than Krupp in both physical size and capital investment.[10]

In its capacity and market niche, Skoda occupied an interesting middle position between Schneider and Putilov. With a work force of approximately 3,500 in 1905, Skoda was considerably smaller than the French and Russian enterprises. However, what it lacked in size it made up for in technical skills. The company had risen rapidly since the 1890s to become the main supplier for the Austrian naval and military forces. The Czech firm could completely arm two battleships a year and prided itself on having turned out the largest steel casting in the world, a piece of machinery shipped to the Niagara works in the United States. Thus, in notable contrast to Putilov, Skoda had already projected itself into export markets, which included gaining a foothold in the Russian defense market itself. Skoda delivered the stem and stern posts for a Russian warship in 1905.[11] Like the other European armaments firms, Skoda also appreciated the potential vastness of the tsarist defense market after the Russo-Japanese War. British Admiralty Intelligence reported that at the Skoda plant in 1905 "a large number of light and medium calibre guns were ready, waiting for purchasers. It is hoped that the visit of a Russian Commission, which spent some days at Pilsen during the summer, will lead to extensive orders from Russia. An important member of the firm has lately settled in St. Petersburg with the object of competing against Krupp whose influence there is said to be strong."[12]

In the context of the European arms trade, the Russian market does not seem unusually weak. Judging from the export figures discussed above, one could say that the home markets in Britain, Germany, and France were insufficient to support their respective private specialist firms. Vickers, Krupp, and Schneider relied on the international arms trade because their own governments did not offer a large enough market. Therefore, we should not take the existence of a defense supplier as the proof of the strength or weakness of an industrial market. Additionally, product diversification does not necessarily equal a weak market, either. All the major European armaments firms had diversified their product lines.

Before examining Putilov's career as an artillery supplier in detail, I should explain how the procurement process functioned generally. Any order from GAU had to be presented for permission and affirmation by the War Council prior to concluding agreements on the conditions for the order. Among its duties, the War Council oversaw the Coordination Committee, the Commission for Barracks Construction, and the Military-Sanitation Committee. The Main Artillery Administration was part of a different chain of command. The War Ministry was comprised of twelve departments, of which the Artillery Department was the sixth. The grand master, with a grade of general of artillery, headed the department and functioned as ex-officio chief of the GAU, as well as president of the Artillery Committee. He had supreme authority over all personnel and matériel. The Artillery Department itself had eight sections: (1) personnel, (2) arsenals, (3) fortresses, (4) armaments, (5) powder mills, (6) accounts, (7) experiments and reports, and (8) mobilization of artillery. Both the War Council and GAU were subordinated to the war minister's chancellery, which was directly under the war minister himself.[13]

The laborious procedures for initiating preliminary negotiations with manufacturers and determining conditions and technical specifications rested with the Rearmament Commission, which fell under GAU's jurisdiction. Once the Rearmament Commission had arranged the terms with

Putilov, it had to draw up papers for interdepartmental agreement with the War Council. Then the chancellery of the War Ministry examined GAU's papers and gave final approval. All these bureaucratic steps contributed to lengthy delays in assigning orders. It was not unheard of for manufacturers to wait several months while the War Council affirmed an order and then concluded a contract for production. These delays occurred even in cases where granting the order was already determined after competition. For example, the Putilov Company endured a one-year delay in concluding a contract with GAU for its first large-scale order of 3-inch caliber field guns even though its own design had already been accepted as the new model for the tsarist army.[14]

Despite the fact that all artillery orders came from a single customer, the artillery sector should be considered a market, albeit an unusual one, because there was in fact competition among sellers to secure contracts from GAU. Yet the sole customer, GAU, was itself a defense producer. For the Putilov Company, this meant that the tsarist armaments market was doubly competitive because the firm had to compete against other domestic and foreign private producers; moreover, it also faced competition from state enterprises that were not supposed to produce for a profit. Among potential sellers, the state enterprises figured prominently. Three state plants at St. Petersburg, Obukhov, and Perm produced artillery and shells.[15]

Procurement of quick-firing artillery became a priority for all the European powers at the beginning of the twentieth century. French officers engineered the technological breakthrough that opened up the quick-fire era in 1896 by designing a field gun that remained stationary during firing while the barrel itself moved backward. A piston cylinder mounted parallel to the barrel worked as a braking mechanism by absorbing the recoil shock and redirecting it to compress fluid. The fluid in turn reexpanded the brake and pushed the barrel back to its initial firing position. Prior to this innovation, the rate of fire for artillery had reached its limit, and even the use of partial recoil suppressors such as springs in the mountings or a shovel blade to dig the piece into the ground could not significantly compensate for the disturbance created by the recoil kick. The new technology dramatically improved the deadliness of artillery by quadrupling the rate of fire and improving direct-fire capabilities because quick-fire guns did not have to be repositioned after every shot. As a result, acquiring artillery with quick-fire mechanisms dominated army weapons budgets between 1900 and 1914.[16]

Naturally, the French sought to keep their technological advantage a secret, so other countries were forced to find their own solutions. The Putilov gun was a 3-inch (76.2mm) quick-firer that could fire either quickly or accurately, but not both, because of imperfections in the recoil system. The gun had a partial recoil buffer employing a stock of rubber rings inside the trail as shock absorbers. Nevertheless, the Putilov Model 1900 could fire over twenty rounds in a minute, and the gun proved technicaly superior to the Japanese Arisaka gun in its range for both shell and shrapnel. The Japanese considered the Putilov a superior weapon to their own during the Russo-Japanese War of 1904–1905.

Putilov managed to rectify the deficiencies in Model 1900 in the successor Model 1902, a 76.2mm piece with a hydro-pneumatic brake. The improved piece went into production at Putilov in 1904. On this score, the Russians were ahead of both Austria-Hungary and Germany. The Austro-Hungarian design for a quick-firing gun was still in the experimental stage in 1904, and even after the design was completed in 1905, lack of funding prevented its going into production. The Germans were unable to incorporate an absorption system into their gun production until 1905.[17]

In 1900 the Putilov Company made its bid to enter the tsarist artillery market in earnest and set out to establish a new niche for itself as a private supplier. The War Council announced that it would be seeking to rearm the army with a new quick-fire field artillery system and that the first order would be presented through the Rearmament Commission to firms based on projected quantities and price. Accordingly, the Putilov Company declared its estimated prices and delivery time for carriages, shrapnel, and other materials in quantities of 500, 750, 1,000, and 1,500 guns. Putilov's board offered a price of 1,892,000 rubles for 500 guns, but reduced the price to 1,121,000 rubles per 500 if GAU would order 1,500 guns. The order would be filled over the course of three years. Putilov's board proposed the following costs: 2,380 rubles for the 3-inch gun itself, 1,770 rubles for the carriage, 70 rubles for the wheels, and 7.85 rubles for shrapnel. GAU made a counteroffer for 750 guns and reduced its prices to 1,870 rubles per gun, 1,500 rubles per carriage, 65 rubles for the wheels, and 7 rubles for shrapnel. On 2 May 1900, the company agreed to

GAU's lower prices but only on condition that the order be increased to 1,000 guns, 1,200 carriages, 18,800 wheels, and 600,000 shrapnel and that Putilov should be paid a premium of 250,000 rubles. GAU did not find this acceptable because prices in state factories were lower. However, feeling the need to equip the field artillery of the western military districts quickly to match Germany and Austria, the commission placed an order for 1,500 guns to be filled in two years, but only 750 of these would be produced at Putilov. The remainder would come from the state factories at Obukhov and Perm.[18]

As with subsequent artillery orders, GAU insisted on prices that were in line with estimates from state factories. Putilov's proposed cost for the 750 pieces amounted to 10,240,450 rubles, whereas GAU's price tag was 9,032,750 rubles, or 11 percent lower. GAU estimates were based on the costs projected by the state works at Obukhov and Perm of 1,110 rubles and 850 rubles per gun, respectively. GAU had arrived at a counteroffer of 1,870 rubles per gun by presenting a base price of 1,650 rubles and then calculating a 13 percent profit margin for Putilov. As a frame of reference, the Commission for Rearmament of Field Artillery noted that in 1877 GAU had paid about 1,800 rubles per field piece of light artillery in an order for Krupp guns, and the Putilov 3-inch gun required significantly higher-quality metal than the Krupp order.[19] According to the final contract signed on 13 June 1900, GAU achieved the lower prices it desired.

In this instance, GAU demonstrated an unusual degree of indulgence toward the company. Putilov received a 3-million-ruble advance, which represented one-third of the total order, to enable the factory to proceed with the production run. However, because Putilov encountered a number of difficulties in the initial phase, in late November 1901 the board petitioned the Rearmament Commission for a two-month extension of the deadline for delivery of the first 200 quick-fire guns. The commission recognized Putilov's plight and saw the difficulties in organizing the extremely complex operation required for the first wholesale manufacture of the various parts necessary for the new system. It granted the extension. Under the terms of the extension, Putilov had to deliver 200 guns by 1 January 1902 and the remaining 550 pieces by January 1903. As it happened, gun number 750 was approved for service on 29 December 1903.[20]

Although Putilov had achieved an important success in winning the 1900 contract, the company was not yet secure as an artillery supplier. Even though its design was the accepted model for light field artillery in the tsarist army, Putilov did not automatically receive more artillery orders. The Rearmament Commission had originally considered the 1900 contract with a private firm as a short-term arrangement to supplement state factories, and in general GAU was wary of becoming dependent on any private supplier.[21] At that time, there was no guarantee that Putilov would receive any further orders after 1902. The Commission noted,

> Granting the order to Putilov for 750 quick-fire field guns does not infringe upon the interests of state factories and such an order addresses the actual need for the participation of private factories in furnishing the order in view of the possibility of terminating all preparations at the end of 1902.[22]

In 1902 the Rearmament Commission wanted to order another 987 gun carriages for the coming year. From that number, the commission determined that 587 should be produced by factories not belonging to the Artillery Department. To that end, GAU requested estimates from Obukhov, Putilov, St. Petersburg Metal Factory, Nobel, Aleksandr, Franco-Russian factory, and Briansk in 1902. Once again, speed was of the essence for the commission, so offers could be made only to those factories that already generally prepared gun carriages for the Artillery Department and thus were experienced in fulfilling orders with gun carriages. In this, Putilov appeared to have a distinct advantage. As noted in the commission's journal, "Since up to now the Putilov factory represents the only factory at which the business of preparing carriages for the 3-inch quick-fire goes completely successfully," it was proposed to increase the number of orders in inquiries to Putilov.[23]

In response to GAU's request, the factories submitted their prices. Their estimates were as follows: Nobel, 1,075 rubles but without wheels; St. Petersburg Metal, 900 rubles; Briansk, 900 rubles without wheels; Putilov, 1,180 rubles without wheels. Aleksandr declined and Franco-Russian failed to respond. Given these prices, the orders for 587 carriages should have been distributed between Briansk and St. Petersburg Metal because they proposed the lowest bids. Yet commission members were concerned that under these conditions all the supplies of quick-fire carriages for 1903 would be transferred to factories that did not yet actually manufacture these goods, whereas factories that already managed wholesale production of the carriages would be excluded.[24]

The commission had good cause for concern about using an entirely new set of suppliers. Having watched Putilov's delays in initiating the production run, the commission knew what to expect. Experience had taught that setting up wholesale production of these carriages required extra time. It took the Putilov plant nine months to begin making the first examples after receiving the order and devising the system for the carriages and guns. Obukhov and the steel processing factory and local arsenals started issuing carriages more than a year after the order was granted. Because time was of the essence, the commission did not want to let purely economic considerations determine the distribution of orders; there was a great risk that the army would not receive the needed items in 1903. Furthermore, the commission worried that Briansk and St. Petersburg Metal, and even Nobel, might have underestimated the price for gun carriages.[25]

The commission's skepticism regarding the bids also had a basis in recent experience. After the state plant at Obukhov received orders in 1901–1902 for 620 gun carriages at the price of 940 rubles per unit, it decided that the estimate was too low. In the second order, it increased its price to 1,200 rubles per carriage. The discrepancy was caused by miscalculations about the quantity of raw materials and labor costs. In preparing each carriage, Obukhov spent 426 rubles more than its first estimate, bringing the cost per unit to 1,366 rubles. Considering costs and time factors, the Rearmament Commission recommended granting orders for 100 carriages each to Briansk, St. Petersburg Metal, and Nobel, and the other 287 to Obukhov. GAU concluded contracts with the first three on 22 August 1902.[26]

The exclusion of Putilov from this order caught the attention of the Ministry of Finance. An unidentified ministry representative pointed out that not issuing a carriage order to Putilov for the coming year would bring a halt to carriage production at the factory. Putilov had established itself quite firmly in the first rearmament of field artillery, but the Finance Ministry representative observed that this circumstance would not last if the factory did not obtain additional orders for carriages. Additionally, he argued that since the factory would likely receive further orders for carriages for many years to come, closing the production line for carriages in 1903 could lead to higher prices in 1904. This problem would have to be seriously considered in light of the time constraints involved in filling the order. The Finance Ministry representative advocated awarding Nobel's order for 100 carriages to Putilov on condition that it be filled at the lower prices declared by St. Petersburg Metal or at the higher price proposed by Nobel.[27] The Rearmament Commission chose not to follow this advice and did not order any carriages from Putilov.

The attempt by the Finance Ministry to intervene in the procurement process raises two questions. First, why did the ministry feel free to intervene, and second, why was it ignored on this point? It seems likely that the Putilov board approached the Ministry of Finance to lobby on its behalf. The Finance representative's point about the impending shutdown of the Putilov production line sounded like a specific worry that the company would voice, not the ministry. In all probability, the Putilov board looked to Finance as an institutional counterweight to GAU, one that would be favorably disposed toward a private firm. For its part, Finance's willingness to serve as an advocate for Putilov did not reflect a predisposition to favor that firm in particular, but rather the general goal of holding down government expenditures. The Finance representative's action was rooted in a concern for keeping down costs: future contracts would cost the state more if the factory were forced to restart production. The Rearmament Commission may have rejected this intervention because it wished to assert its prerogative to determine procurement policy. In any case, Finance's failed intervention proves that the state was not a monolithic actor.

In 1903 GAU solicited estimates from Obukhov and Putilov for the modified 1902 model of the 3-inch quick-fire field gun. In this instance, Putilov's asking price of 3,300 rubles per piece turned out to be lower than Obukhov's price of 3,800 rubles, so the Rearmament Commission awarded the contract to Putilov for 1,600 guns and 1,800 carriages. The contract totaled 5,580,000 rubles and was to be completed over a four-year term from 1904 to 1907. Thereafter the system for the Putilov 1902 model field gun would become the property of the Russian government.[28]

Since Putilov had been excluded from the carriage orders in 1902, its future as an artillery supplier was in doubt. GAU had not viewed the original contract in 1900 as a long-term commitment to the company. In this light, the firm's success in securing another major artillery contract in 1903 was a watershed. Even though the new contract was for less than the first order in 1900, the 1903 order established Putilov as the premier artillery producer in Russia for two reasons. First, because it carried a four-year term, the contract of 1903 ensured that Putilov's artillery production line would be preserved. In this respect, the duration of the new contract was twice as long as the first one. Second, GAU had definitively decided on Putilov's 1902 model as standard issue for the tsarist army. This held out the prospect that when the order was finished Putilov would be able to continue in the artillery business.

Once again, the Putilov plant had difficulty in establishing the production run. In a letter dated 9 July 1904, the company's president, A. K. Voigt, informed the War Department that Putilov would not be able to begin issuing artillery until eight months after the contract signing date. Instead of producing 400 guns and 450 carriages by 1 January 1905, as stipulated in the original contract, the factory would not achieve that level of production until 1 March 1905. After production came on line, though, the factory quickly caught up with the original timetable. By 13 November 1906, only 194 guns remained to be manufactured, and the factory director informed the artillery inspector that the entire contract would be concluded by 1 February 1907. Thus, having started eight months behind schedule, Putilov finished one month behind schedule.[29]

As one would expect, the war with Japan in 1904 brought additional orders and extra pressure on artillery production. During 1904 the army needed an additional 250 guns. Putilov declared a price of 700 rubles per carriage, while the Petersburg Arsenal offered a price of 727 rubles. Even though the company had underbid the state arsenal, the Rearmament Commission proposed that Putilov lower its bid to 660 rubles. Putilov responded that a lower price was impossible since "the experience of the large-scale preparation of the 1902 model carriages for the current order gives the possibility in actuality to verify the preliminary pricing and lowest price at 700 rubles." The Rearmament Commission then turned to Briansk, but that factory proposed a price of 700 rubles per carriage, excluding wheels or compressors. Since apart from Putilov the Briansk

factory was the only private factory completely prepared to produce carriages for quick-fire guns, the commission decided to divide the order
equally between the two. To get part of this order, Briansk had to include
all the parts in its price of 700 rubles. If Briansk did not accept these
terms, then the entire order would go to Putilov. In the end, the two factories split the order.[30]

The pressures of wartime production ultimately worked to distinguish Putilov from all the state factories. On 11 March 1904, Putilov
accepted a supplemental order for 3-inch guns and carriages for the price
defined in the 1903 contract, namely, 1,800 rubles per gun and 1,500
rubles per carriage. The commission again considered Putilov's bid price
too high because the state factory at Perm could make guns for 1,700
rubles and carriages for 1,450 rubles. Putilov's board then offered to
lower its price. The Obukhov factory was already behind in its production
of regular orders, so it was in no position to manufacture additional guns.
Also, the state works at Perm declined to take the order. At this point, the
commission had no alternative but to turn to Putilov. Its situation was evident from the journal record:

> From the answers received, it is obvious that the Gun and
> Obukhov factories refused the fulfillment of the supplemental
> order in 1905 and only the Putilov factory agreed to take upon
> itself to supply in the given year 230 3-inch guns and 259 car-
> riages and according to the price of the Perm factory, which cur-
> rently presented the lowest price. Recognizing the extreme
> urgency to prepare the supplemental quantity of 3-inch guns and
> carriages in 1905, in light of the haste of rearmament of field
> artillery, the sole decision was to present the order of these guns
> and carriages to Putilov, the prices of which under the circum-
> stances should be recognized as moderate and acceptable.[31]

The main state plants' inability to meet the challenge was no secret. In
1904 British observers recognized that the gun factories at Obukhov and
Perm could hardly keep pace with the demand for guns,[32] and Putilov's
board was most likely cognizant of the situation when it agreed to lower its
contract price. The value of the order, to be completed in 1905, totaled
766,550 rubles.[33]

Thus far we have seen how Putilov had managed to obtain artillery orders. The firm entered into negotiatons with GAU, and in each instance GAU insisted on lower prices based on the cost estimates of the state factories. In every case when Putilov succeeded in securing an order, the company had either complied with GAU's demand that it lower its price or had already submitted a price below that of the state factories. From GAU's perspective, pricing primarily determined which factories gained the orders. There was little opportunity for lobbying or exerting outside pressure on the War Ministry, nor is there any evidence that the Putilov Company tried to lobby the bureaucracy. The one occasion on which the Ministry of Finance spoke on Putilov's behalf appears to be an isolated occurrence, and most likely Finance's motivation had more to do with keeping future production costs down than with benefiting Putilov.

The Artillery Department's success in driving down the contract price pressured the company to compensate by holding production costs down. Although raw materials were always the single highest component of the company's annual expenditures, the Putilov Company had little power to control those costs. Instead, labor appeared as the more flexible input. On a yearly basis, the company's labor costs invariably exceeded profits, but during the period 1900–1903 the firm managed to push down total labor expenditures while increasing profits. For example, in 1901 Putilov spent roughly 8.8 million rubles on workers' wages, but by 1903 these costs sharply decreased to about 5 million rubles. While wages and salaries as a percentage of total annual expenditures remained fairly constant at about 30 percent over the three years, the value of profits generated per ruble of labor rose dramatically. In 1901, for every ruble spent on labor the company made 18 kopeks, but by 1902 this rate increased to 28 kopeks. In 1903 the company generated 33 kopeks from each ruble paid for labor—a record high rate of return up to that time. In their annual report for 1903, the board explained the higher profits despite reduced output by pointing to improved plant equipment as the cause of lower labor costs.[34]

The squeeze on labor contributed to the dramatic change in strike activity at Putilov late in 1904, with the result that the plant was located at the epicenter of the 1905 Revolution. During the 1890s Petersburg's metalworking and engineering works had been relatively strike-free, and these few strikes were localized and brief. In December the dismissal of four workers from the woodworking shop on grounds of incompetence served as the immediate cause for worker unrest at Putilov; however, economic issues quickly came to the fore as well. Workers were prepared to push for their rights and economic improvements. On 2 January 1905, the Putilov workers voted to strike, and over the next two days they brought the factory to a halt. Their demands also extended beyond the rehiring of fired workers to include the establishment of a permament body of elected representatives to monitor wages and grievances and an eight-hour day. In addition, they called for freedom of speech and other civil rights.

The Putilov workers' demands served as a model for other workers, and Father Gapon, head of the Assembly of Russian Workers, drew them up into a petition to be presented to Tsar Nicholas II. The thousands of peaceful workers who joined the procession to deliver the petition to Nicholas on 9 January 1905, a Sunday, were met by gunfire as they approached the Winter Palace. The slaughter became known as "Bloody Sunday" and marked the beginning of the 1905 Revolution. By 17 January, over 100,000 workers were on strike affecting more than 300 enterprises. It was no longer a question of winning concessions from the Putilov directors. By now, resolving the strikes at Putilov would have been insufficient to contain the labor unrest that was erupting throughout the empire, swelling to include 2.7 million workers in 13,000 strikes, or roughly 60 percent of Russian workers and one-third of all factories.[35]

Putilov's management was willing to make concessions. On 27 January the plant's director, S. I. Smirnov, partially granted the workers' demands, but this did not satisfy the workers and the entire Putilov factory began a week-long strike the next day. On 6 February they submitted a new list of economic demands. In his reply on 10 February, Smirnov acceded to half the list of demands and compromised on others. The director refused outright the demand for an eight-hour day, payment for strike time, payment for allowances based on length of service, and the abolition of overtime or double pay for overtime. Workers responded to Smirnov's refusals by striking again on 11 February 1905.

Through the rest of 1905, Putilov's workers and management squared off in a series of conflicts. The workers would go on strike, and management would close down the plant and lay off the "troublemakers."

Smirnov, speaking before the shareholders in May 1905, reported that the vast majority of workers expressed a desire to work but were hindered by an insignificant militant minority. He also gave his opinion that shortening the working day to less than ten hours would unavoidably lead to decreases in production. The board wanted production to return to normal as quickly as possible and therefore proposed voting emergency funds to meet workers' demands. Under these conditions, orders would obviously be delayed and the company would have to pay late fines to the government. Already in November 1905 the company was experiencing financial difficulties, and in 1906 the board had to dip into the company's reserve capital to cover payment transfers for the strike days.[36]

Whether the Putilov plant remained closed due to workers' strikes or management's layoffs and lockouts, the net result was the same: the company was falling behind in its artillery contracts. As a result, the company not only faced financial losses from lack of production, but also added expenses because of the state fines for nondelivery, as stipulated in the contracts. Putilov's execution of the defense contracts brought to the fore two issues of great consequence for the future of the firm and for the tone of civil-military relations for the rest of the imperial era: late fines and payment schedules. By 1907 the Rearmament Commission was discussing charging Putilov 68,900 rubles in late fees for delays on the 1905 order. The Petersburg district artillery administration accused Putilov of noncompliance with the contract regarding delivery time. In turn, Putilov petitioned GAU for redress. The district administration had wanted an output of 19–20 guns and 21–22 carriages monthly, whereas the company insisted that it had met the total production requirement on time, although the particular monthly output did not conform to GAU's expectations. The commission found in favor of Putilov and ordered the repayment of 68,900 rubles to the factory.[37]

Putilov's delayed completion of the multiyear artillery order signed in 1903 would become a serious source of friction between the government and the company. Disagreements over the degree to which the Putilov Company was responsible for a breach of contract would continue to fester until 1909. The contentious issues included how to measure the delays and how much the company had to pay in late fines. More important, the tumultuous period 1904–1907 revealed how completely the company had been converted into an artillery supplier. Putilov emerged from the Russo-Japanese War and the 1905 Revolution as a bona fide defense enterprise.

During 1905 labor unrest gripped the factory, and the effects on production and timely fulfillment of defense contracts forced the company into a conflict with state offices over the degree of culpability imputed to the company. At the time of the great strike waves, Putilov was carrying sixteen different contracts with GAU for guns, carriages, and shells. Among the contracts adversely affected by the labor problems was the 1903 order. The board explained its position to the Rearmament Commission in a letter dated 28 January 1906: despite all the measures taken for the proper development of work, the factory was unable to avoid a whole series of misfortunes and difficulties, many of them beyond its control. First, foreign machinery arrived as much as six months late. Also, work in the machine shop developed very slowly on account of workers' inexperience and lack of preparation for such precise work as making artillery and carriages, since the factory had to dismiss the cadre of masters who had completed the 1900 order and then hire new people who had never done that kind of work. On this point, the board indirectly blamed GAU for the lack of work after the conclusion of the first large-scale order in 1902. The net results were delays in delivery and enormous new expenditures in comparison with proposed estimates. However, the successful performance during the last months of 1904 had given the board grounds to believe that the rest of the work would be completed and that the company's material sacrifices would be covered by improved productivity by the workers. In fact, by the end of 1904, production had reached a level of 50–60 guns and 60–75 carriages per month, and by 1 January 1905 the company had already presented 212 guns and 150 carriages for inspection.[38] Thus, although the factory started late, it showed its capacity to complete all orders even significantly earlier than the deadline.

Unfortunately, the promising circumstances at the beginning of the year turned out to be short-lived. The board asserted that beginning in January 1905 widespread workers' unrest utterly destroyed the normal course of work and made it completely impossible for the factory administration to execute its orders. Over the course of 1905, extended strikes completely interrupted the factory's activities. As a result, the factory worked only superficially and production dropped to a trickle. Artillery production should have reached the 7-million-ruble mark by December 1, but productivity amounted to only 2,366,059 rubles.[39]

The company pleaded extenuating circumstances before the War Council and sought to renegotiate the contracts in light of exceptional conditions.

> The Board of the company, when accepting this order in 1903 for a four-year term could not foresee the historic events of Russia which occurred in 1905. Already at present the factory cost of guns and carriages is higher than the sale and order for 3-inch quick-fire guns, and therefore unprofitable for the factory.[40]

Finding itself in this financial predicament, the company requested several changes in the terms of the contracts. First, the board hoped to be allowed to raise the price for guns and carriages of the 1902 model to 2,000 rubles per gun and 1,950 rubles per carriage in the contract of 17 July 1903 (for 1,600 guns and 1,800 carriages), in the contract of 16 July 1904 (for 230 guns and 259 carriages), and in another 1904 contract (for 60 guns and 60 carriages). Second, Putilov wanted to be relieved of the financial penalties for delays stipulated in the 1903 contract. Third, the board requested an extension of fourteen months for fulfillment of the 1903 order. Finally, the board suggested supplementing point 18 of the 1903 contract so that assessments for fines should be withheld from payments due the factory on conclusion of the entire delivery, only if the firm failed to demonstrate that it was not at fault in observing a contract deadline. To prove its innocence, Putilov submitted a copy of a report from the Ministry of Internal Affairs confirming the factory director's statement that strikes had caused delays of up to fifty-five days.[41]

The Rearmament Commission displayed little sympathy for Putilov's plight in this instance. It observed that labor unrest had not uniquely affected Putilov, since strikes had plagued all factories and branches of industry. Therefore, if the commission made an exception for Putilov, it would be opening the door for analagous claims by every factory in Russia that had any dealings with artillery production. Naturally, that prospect raised the possibility of very large additional expenditures, which the War

Ministry found unacceptable. On this point, the Ministry of Finance also declared its opposition to Putilov's petition because of the financial difficulties of the State Treasury, and (what is more important) because "the contract prices for objects cannot be changed post facto."[42] Once again, it seems that Finance's primary concern was based on fiscal interests; it was not an unreserved supporter of the Putilov Company. One bright spot for the company, however, was that the commission did grant the fourteen-month extension on the 1903 contract, and as a result the new due date became 1 March 1909. Nevertheless, the commission assessed a penalty of 273,000 rubles against Putilov based on GAU's audit on the account.[43]

Voigt, Putilov's president, complained about the payment process in a letter to the War Council dated 1 March 1907. He called attention to the importance of having sufficient working capital for any manufacturing enterprise. A vital concern of every enterprise was raising investment capital for production as quickly as possible. With that aim, both foreign and Russian practice had worked out a series of measures to facilitate capital flow. Voigt observed that the payment was usually disbursed as follows: one-third upon receipt of the order, one-third during its fulfillment (for example, the preparation of materials), and one-third after the delivery of the entire order. He stressed that such a practice was not alien to the War Ministry, either. He stated:

> This progression of accounts became so common that the War and Naval Ministries employed it when granting orders to foreign factories. The conditions of our manufacturing and our money market unavoidably force Russian factories also to strive for the consolidation of this means of disbursement which offers the possibility of more rapid turn around of capital invested in the enterprise, and also extends the productivity of the factory and its means while at the same time allowing the received orders to be completed with greater speed.[44]

Voigt added that several Russian state institutions already partially recognized this payment process. For example, several years previously the Naval Ministry had established partial payments for shipbuilding and ship assembly in the course of filling the order. The Ministry of Transport also introduced this system for locomotives, railcars, and bridges. Under this system, the factory received the remainder of the payment, usually between 15 and 30 percent of the total value, upon completing the order.[45]

Voigt protested the discrimination that Russian firms suffered in this regard. He argued that under the War Ministry's payment system the advantage should be given to Russian factories that were located in Russia, employing Russian workers, technicians, and engineers, and using Russian materials. Under these conditions, the completion of orders for state institutions would be more secure in Russian factories than in foreign ones. Yet the War Ministry gave out advances only to foreign firms. Private domestic firms, including Putilov, did not enjoy this advantage. State factories constituted the sole exception, where it was commonplace to give out advances up to 50 percent of the order.[46]

Putilov had made the enormous investments in specialized equipment in order to facilitate faster production for GAU but constantly had its working capital tied up in preparing orders for GAU. As Voigt pointed out,

> The payment for these orders, sometimes for very large sums, is received only after the final delivery of the items, without any kind of partial payment according to degrees of completion of the order. In such a situation, the plant's outlays of working capital for artillery orders reach a level of 60 percent of the annual output of the factory in this department alone. This cost does not include expenditures for work on the new systems of carriages and guns.[47]

In light of this, Putilov found itself in a significantly more difficult position than competing factories that did not work mainly for the artillery department, but for other departments and private customers who employed more contemporary business practices in making payments. Voigt further argued that Putilov's profit for War Department orders was lower than for other orders. It was also more conditional, since it depended on the results of controlled experiments for firing, which if not successful entailed the rejection of whole sections of the items. Due to the bureaucratic formalities connected with the registration and delivery of an order, the Putilov factory at any moment had prepared artillery goods worth no less than half a million rubles lying around as dead capital.[48]

Because artillery items demanded high-quality precision work and controlled test firing, it was often difficult to deliver goods on time; moreover, the company had to make extensive capital outlays before it finally received payment. Voigt complained that if one factored in the time de-manded for completing the formalities required to receive payment, delays permitted for inquiries about penalties, and assessments for nonobservance of time of delivery, it was necessary to invest considerable working capital that "could and should have been invested into the business under more normal conditions of payment for orders."[49]

Putilov often had to request payment even upon the timely delivery of an order. For example, in November 1907 the company's president wrote to GAU demanding the 127,000 rubles for the delivery on a contract from September 1904, three years earlier. The board was required to pay 10 percent of a bank loan taken out for this contract to cover wages. Noting that Putilov had not yet received this sum, the board requested the disbursement, since further delay would place the company in a difficult position with the bank.[50]

To establish the precedent for receiving advances, Voigt reminded the War Council that Putilov had been granted an advance of 2.5 million rubles as part of its 1900 artillery order. In Voigt's view, this advance had proved beneficial to both the factory and the War Ministry. The plant had the working capital to develop the enterprise during its expansion, thus avoiding an expensive loan, and could complete the order cheaper and faster. Voigt and the Putilov board requested 50 percent of the value of an order prior to completion.[51]

The Rearmament Commission rejected this line of reasoning. With respect to Putilov's 1900 order, it argued, the 2.5 million rubles had not been in the form of a secured advance, but was 1.2 million rubles' worth of iron and 1.3 million rubles in cash. Furthermore, the Artillery Department had decided to provide the 2.5 million rubles in order to establish production at the factory for the quick-fire gun Model 1900 and its materials because of the need for rapid rearmament of field artillery.[52] In other words, conditions in 1900 had been unique, and the War Department's response at that time would not become the norm.

Unable to convince GAU of the need for advances, the company next tried to renegotiate the terms of the 1903 contract after the fact. Voigt recognized that the company had contractual obligations to the state. However, artillery production often encountered cost overruns. In meeting the higher costs for small orders, the factory could readily cover these overruns with profits from other orders. While Voigt acknowledged this fact in general, he countered,

> But this process is obviously impossible in those enormous and extraordinarily important orders which the Putilov factory fills for the Artillery Department. Here one unprofitable order can decide the fate of the factory, bringing its activity to utter destruction, which can in turn no less adversely affect the interests of the customer. The magnitude of the order, swallowing up a significant portion of the productive force of the factory, along with the lack of profit for the given order, prohibits the factory from compensating the account from other orders.[53]

Therefore, Voigt maintained that every exceptionally large order should answer for itself and should contain within itself the means for maintaining the factory. So, in 1907 the board asked to be released from the contract without responsibility in order to protect the company from further losses.[54]

The company's inability to renegotiate the contracts demonstrated how much business conditions had changed since N. I. Putilov's time. Like Putilov, Voigt sought to change the terms when they became unprofitable, but the resolute refusal of the War Ministry and the Ministry of Finance to tolerate the company's suggested contractual modifications shows how standards of procedure had taken root among the bureaucracy. The ministries were not nearly as lenient with Voigt as they had been with Putilov in the 1870s. In part this was because the War Ministry simply lacked the friendly disposition toward private enterprise that had characterized the outlook of Finance and the Ministry of Transport in the 1870s. More significant, however, Voigt's attempts to change contracts after the fact offended the bureaucrats' increasing attention to proper procedure and routine.[55]

As a final gambit for state sympathy, the board suggested that without more support perhaps the company would have to abandon the artillery business completely. Although this might appear unpatriotic, the company saw little choice. The board observed, "Since the War Department still needs guns and carriages, it would probably turn to foreign firms that would undoubtedly cost significantly more, independent of the enormous losses which would result from the transfer of Russian money abroad."[56]

As late as 1908, the Rearmament Commission continued to fend off petitions from Putilov. In particular, the commission had grown quite weary of hearing about the company's lack of profitability on artillery orders. While reiterating its position that prices could not be changed after a contract was signed, the commission pointedly observed that the orders for 3-inch quick-fire guns of the 1902 model, which the company alleged caused losses, comprised less than 10 percent of its total annual production in the years 1904–1906. Consequently, "the losses from these orders, if they actually occurred, could not so adversely have affected the profits and losses of the general activity of the company in those years."[57] As its final retort, the commission presented evidence from the company's published accounts for the years 1904–1906 that demonstrated company profits as follows: 1.97 million rubles in 1904, 900,000 rubles in 1905, and 2 million rubles in 1906. On the basis of these figures, the commission concluded that Putilov suffered no losses due to artillery orders.[58]

Why did the company insist on the unprofitability of artillery orders, given the record profits for 1903–1906? Part of the answer can be found in the difficulties with the payment process. With so much of the company's production resources tied up in the large artillery orders, the long lag time between the start of the production run and the receipt of payment created a strain on the company's financial resources and cash flow. As a result of taking so many artillery orders, more than 40 percent of total factory output was geared for artillery production, and thus the company had to devote significant resources for labor, capital, and raw materials simply to fill the contracts. However, the company received payment only after completing the entire order. Therefore, any unprofitability in the artillery orders became manifest only later. It was not accidental that Putilov began to complain about its difficulties in 1907 because by then the strain had become visible. The reduction in both profits and factory output in 1907 reflected the financial problem. In turn, the board could see the approaching squeeze and sought to renegotiate the contract prices of the earlier orders in an attempt to ride it out.

A comparison of Putilov's profits and performance with other Russian engineering firms confirms Putilov's contention that artillery contracts yielded lower profits than other areas of production. The firms Sormovo and Kolomna were both diversified engineering companies, but unlike Putilov they did not engage in artillery production. If we compare the profits for all three firms as a percentage of stock capital, then it becomes evident that both the nondefense companies generated higher returns on investment than Putilov. For 1904–1907, Putilov's annual returns were 16.4 percent, 7.8 percent, 16.9 percent, and 6.1 percent. Sormovo's returns averaged around 32 percent in 1904–1906, then dropped to 8.9 percent in 1907. Kolomna did not perform as well as Sormovo but generated an average around 20 percent in 1904–1906 before declining to 12.2 percent in 1907. More telling was the fact that Sormovo and Kolomna achieved higher gross profits than Putilov, even though they were smaller enterprises. Sormovo's gross profits for 1904–1907 amounted to approximately 8.74 million rubles, as compared to 6.23 million rubles for Kolomna and 5.67 million for Putilov.[59] In an international comparison, Krupp was also generally less profitable than purely civilian steel and metalworking firms in Germany.[60] At the very least, we can say that the artillery business did not generate super profits for the Putilov Company.

Putilov's experience during 1903–1907 throws into relief the evolving relationship between the company and the state as the artillery component in the factory's production increased. Putilov established itself as a reliable partner of the state. During the war, the company performed for the state when no one else could. Furthermore, the company did not gouge the state on prices even when the opportunity clearly presented itself. Faced with a customer in desperate need for more field pieces and seemingly lacking alternative suppliers, the Putilov board passed up the chance to extract maximum profit in a high-demand situation. Rather than engaging in war profiteering, Putilov's board actually lowered its price to conform with the price offered by the state factories, even though no other factory wanted or was capable of accepting the order. After the war, Putilov wanted the state to return the favor by allowing the company to raise prices on old contracts that were about to be completed. This would have injected more capital into the enterprise. When the government refused, the company tried to raise the threat of giving up the artillery business altogether. This approach also brought no result.

In lobbying for state support, Voigt pointed to the unique position of the company in Russia: "Putilov cannot be compared with any one of the private Russian factories which manufacture these kind of goods, since it significantly set the standards for all factories in this regard, both by measure of production and in particular by technical merits of its product."[61] Clive Trebilcock's comment about the unconventional marketing characteristics in the case of the British armaments firm Vickers seems to apply equally to Putilov. Trebilcock observes, "Broadly speaking, the well-adjusted armament entrepreneur will tend to discount the skills of conventional marketing and distribution and to emphasize those of technological inquiry and market diplomacy; in the current jargon, R and D and PR are his forte."[62] The reason for such behavior is rooted in the reality that defense producers do not face a mass market but "the exact reverse, a market composed at best, of a score of customers, not infrequently of a single isolated client-state."[63]

The factory's increasing emphasis on defense orders continued into the post-1905 period. In 1910 the War Ministry ordered 214 new guns for mountain artillery. The new model, designated the "3-inch mountain gun, mark 1909," was one of Schneider-Creusot's designs, but the guns were being manufactured at the Putilov works.[64] By 1911 the amount of war production as a part of total output had increased to 43.3 percent (7.6 million rubles).[65] This growing percentage of military production for Putilov was due in part to the company's past success. Putilov was the sole private firm in Russia that prepared artillery, and its negotiations with Schneider and Krupp about technical assistance gave the company a virtual monopoly over the implementation of new foreign artillery systems within Russia. In all, Putilov provided 43 percent of all ordnance made for the Russian army in the years 1900–1914.[66]

The Putilov board now recognized the disadvantages of being a specialist defense enterprise. Realistically, the company could not renounce artillery production; yet the state showed no sign of relenting, nor could the state really afford to pay out more to Putilov, given its own fiscal weakness in the immediate postwar and revolutionary years. When the government foreclosed Putilov's option to receive advances for new orders or partial payments during production, the company faced a chronic weakness in its ability to finance artillery production. This led the company to turn toward the large Russian banks as the solution to the credit problem. As the banks became increasingly involved in finance issues, the opportunity arose for possible bank control of the Putilov Company.

4

BANKS, BOARDS, AND NAVAL EXPANSION

THE QUESTION OF BANK DOMINANCE

1907–1914

Russian historians have taken the appearance of bankers among company directorates as a manifestation of bank control. The traditional arguments for crediting the banks with the commanding roles in organizing the defense sector and for manipulating interlocking directorates do not adequately explain the Putilov Company's participation in these activities. When relations between banks and firms are analyzed from the perspective of the company itself, it becomes clear that the decision making and implementation of Putilov's business strategy resided with the Putilov Company board, not the large banks.

Scholars in European economic history and the subfield of Russian economic history have often assumed that the large joint-stock banks acted as a guiding force behind the concentration and coordination of large industrial sectors. On the basis of Rudolf Hilferding's work in 1910, observers have seen the relationship of the enterprises to the banks as a dependent one, so the fact that bankers or representatives of banking institutions served on the companies' boards of directors and councils indicated bank control. In Russian historiography, Lenin's reading of Hilferding and the Leninist idea of imperialism as the highest stage of capitalism (i.e., monopoly) were points of departure for Soviet scholars, who emphasized the rise of control by the banks beginning in 1910. These studies stressed the appearance of interlocking directorates in the metalworking branch as a product of monopolistic unions created by the large banking groups.[1]

Western scholars also have credited the Russian banks with playing a commanding role in industrial enterprises.[2] However, a recent wave of revisionism points in another direction. In European business history, questions about the role of banks have varied somewhat from country to country. In Britain and France, historians have concentrated on evaluating the extent to which banks and financial markets provided adequate funds to industry, whereas in Germany the degree of bank "control" or "dominance" over industry has been the central issue.[3] Detailed studies of French and German firms show that it is unwise to generalize about bank-industry relations not only for the economy as a whole, but also for whole sectors or branches of industry.[4]

The experience of the Putilov Company suggests that it is just as misleading to attempt to generalize about the bank-industry relationship even for an individual firm. Throughout its history, the Putilov Company's relationship with banking interests varied. The only constant was the fact that the company always turned to external financing, and the company's directors expressed no aversion to external financing or fear of bank dependency. This can undoubtedly be explained in part because the firm itself was never a family enterprise. Observers have assumed the dominance of banks in the planning and execution of mergers in the defense sector and in appointments to company boards so as to create interlocking directorates. However, one can safely say that mutual benefit, not bank dominance, is a more apt characterization of the relationship and that the decision making and implementation of Putilov's business strategy rested with the Putilov Company board.

What role did banks play in planning and executing mergers and coordinating business activities in the tsarist defense industry? The leading specialists offer two variations on the theme of bank dominance over the Putilov Company specifically. The first considers the activities of Aleksei Ivanovich Putilov, president of the Russo-Asiatic Bank, as part of a concerted effort to wrest control of the Putilov Company from the Petersburg International Commercial Bank (PICB). In this view, two main banking groups were vying for the Putilov Company, and the Russo-Asiatic Bank emerged victorious.[5] Another interpetation stresses interfirm cooperation in the defense sector. According to this line of argument, the banking groups carved out their own spheres of influence in the armaments industry, and the PICB chose to concede the Putilov Company to the

Russo-Asiatic Bank in exchange for a free hand in the Nikolaev docks on the Black Sea.[6] Both schools agree that the banks controlled the fate of the enterprise.

Most of the evidence for the "dueling banks" interpretation comes from correspondence between A. I. Putilov, president of the Russo-Asiatic Bank, and French bankers. Therefore, we need to consider A. I. Putilov's background in order to understand why historians have been predisposed to credit him and his bank with such an influential role in shaping the armaments sector. Aleksei Ivanovich Putilov (no direct relation to Nikolai Putilov) was born in 1866 and received his education at St. Petersburg University. After graduation, he entered the bureaucracy in 1893 where he served in the credit chancellery of the Ministry of Finance under Sergei Iu. Witte. As part of Witte's team, Putilov was able to establish ties with French banks. He rose to become the director of the general chancellery of the Ministry of Finance during 1902–1905. He administered the Gentry and Peasant Land Banks in 1905–1906 and directed the Russo-Chinese Bank after leaving the Ministry of Finance in 1905. In 1910 the Russo-Chinese Bank joined with the Northern Bank, and Putilov became the president of the newly amalgamated Russo-Asiatic Bank.[7] Because of these prominent state and foreign connections, historians have assumed that A. I. Putilov played a driving role in the Putilov Company.

In a letter to the French banker Louis Dorizon in December 1911, Putilov assessed the situation at the Putilov Company and prospects for taking it over. At that time, Putilov had already become a member of the Putilov Company's board. He remarked that the current equipment at the Putilov factory was insufficient for the manufacture of large-caliber artillery and that the company would need to install new plant under the direction of Schneider-Creusot. To this effect, the Putilov Company would have to augment its capital by 18–19 million rubles. Creusot had expressed the desire to participate for 25 percent in the new stock issues. However, the Putilov Company was not obligated to have a representative from Creusot on its board. According to A. I. Putilov,

There are two banks which are the masters of the enterprise, the International and Russo-Asiatic, the first represents up to a certain point German capital, ours French capital. The Putilov Company has contractual connections with Creusot, but it is equally connected and works from time to time with Krupp. Creusot desires to take the business in its hands and to have exclusive influence; our interest (the Russo-Asiatic Bank) is in supporting Creusot and, with its aid, weakening the influence of the International Bank on the Board of the Putilov Company (if not completely dispelling it). Currently we must share half the operations of the Company, active and passive. Until now the International Bank has had the dominant influence in the Putilov Board since for a long time this enterprise has been exclusively under its control. Only in the past year and a half have I succeeded in injecting our institution into this business, by means of the Russo-Chinese Bank. In order to achieve this result I had to enter the Putilov Board.[8]

The director of the Russo-Asiatic Bank was clearly trying to enlist the financial support of the French. If Putilov stock remained exclusively on the Russian exchange, Putilov stated, he would not be able to continue the struggle with the International Bank because on the Petersburg Exchange the International was stronger than the Russo-Asiatic Bank and, thanks to the outside brokers and the banking houses with which it worked, the International Bank could always have more stock. Putilov wrote:

> The struggle would not be possible for me unless our clients in Paris held a certain number of shares; then, with the help of Creusot, which expects to retain shares in its portfolio, and with the aid of the clients of the Russo-Asiatic Bank, I could have the upper hand over the International Bank in the shareholders' meeting.[9]

He went on to describe the International Bank as categorically opposed to French involvement, and to that end the International Bank was trying to arrange matters so that the French participated only for bonds and no stocks would be introduced on the Paris market. To outmaneuver the PICB, Putilov promised to act temporarily as the representative of French interests through the Russo-Asiatic Bank in the Putilov board. Then at the first general meeting after the stock issue, when he would have a majority, Aleksei Putilov could force the entry of the Creusot representative onto the Putilov board. However, for him to have this majority, the stocks had to be introduced on the Paris Exchange. Putilov closed his letter to Dorizon by pointing out that neither the International Bank nor the Russo-Asiatic Bank held enough Putilov shares to assure approval of the projected stock increases at the shareholders' meeting. Therefore, he had to combine the packets of shares and, with the aid of French bankers, purchase stocks in Paris. He concluded, "In a combination such as this we will be masters in the meeting."[10]

Superficially, the above evidence supports the interpretation that the machinations of Putilov and the Russo-Asiatic Bank functioned as a hostile takeover of the Putilov Company from the Petersburg International Bank. It appears that A. I. Putilov had outlined his bank's rivalry with the International Bank, organized his shareholding clientele, and prepared to gain control of the Putilov Company at the 1912 stockholders' meeting. Thus, the interpretation of "dueling banks" seems confirmed. However, upon closer examination the actual situation proves to be more complex and considerably less decisive. In fact, the Russo-Asiatic Bank did not gain direct control of the company, nor did the bank even acquire a majority of the stock. Before considering an alternative interpretation, let us critically evaluate the picture painted by the president of the Russo-Asiatic Bank in the above correspondence.

In order to appreciate the extent of bank involvement between 1910 and 1914, we must contextualize the role of banks throughout the life of the company. The Putilov Company's connections to banks and other enterprises predated the arrival of A. I. Putilov and the Russo-Asiatic Bank. So, the novelty attributed to the interlocking directorates and personal unions among Russian enterprises in the 1910–1914 period is misplaced. During its formative years under Nikolai I. Putilov, the company mainly relied on banks in Moscow for short-term loans, which were applied to working capital. After 1885 it was not uncommon for individual bankers to hold their own personal portfolios of Putilov shares and also to hold elected positions on the company's board of directors or revision commission. Antsyforov and Laski were examples of this phenomenon. As noted earlier, the Putilov board already had lateral ties to the Briansk and Nevskii firms at that point, and in fact the Putilov Company was in the process of paying off a loan received from the Briansk and Warsaw Steel syndicate.[11]

Greater bank involvement in the long-term capital expansion for the Putilov Company began in the 1890s. As part of the company's plant expansion, the Russian Bank, Junker and Company, and several other financiers subscribed a 6 percent Putilov bond issue worth 2.5 million credit rubles orchestrated by the Petersburg International Bank in 1894.[12] The following year the offices of three Petersburg joint-stock banks (Petersburg International Commercial Bank, Russian Bank for Foreign Trade, Petersburg Discount and Loan Bank) disbursed annual dividends for the Putilov Company.[13] The Petersburg International Commercial Bank solicited another bond package worth 8.5 million rubles to fund Putilov plant expansion from late 1897. The bonds bore 5 percent interest over a thirty-five-year term and were subscribed by the following banks:

> Diskontbank (Berlin), 10 percent;
> Volga-Kama Bank (St. Petersburg), 10 percent;
> Wawelberg banking firm (St. Petersburg), 10 percent;
> Moscow Kaufman Bank, 10 percent;
> Azov-Don Commercial Bank (St. Petersburg), 5 percent;
> Junker and Company (St. Petersburg), 5 percent;
> Lampe, 3 percent;
> G. Schereschwasky, 1 percent;
> Riga Bonsbank, 2 percent;
> Riga Stadt Diskontbank, 2 percent;
> miscellaneous others, 30 percent.[14]

What was unusual about the period after 1907 was that the banks changed from being financiers to owners of Putilov stock. The extent of the banks' growing involvement in the Putilov Company from 1907 to 1914 can be seen in the percentage of shares held by banks. The banking firms Junker and Company and Wawelberg did appear among the list of large shareholders in 1903.[15] However, in 1907 the joint-stock banks began holding Putilov stock as institutional shareowners. In that year the Azov-Don Bank and the Petersburg International Bank both owned 1,000 Putilov shares, and the Petersburg Discount and Loan Bank had 500 shares.[16]

If we limit the total number of shareholders only to those who actually attended the annual stockholders' meeting and then determine the percentage each member owned from the total number of shares represented at the meeting, we can focus on the active participants. Under these conditions, 105 shareholders held Putilov stock in 1907, and three of them were joint-stock banks representing 8.1 percent of the total shares. In 1910 three joint-stock banks held 6.2 percent of the shares, while four banking houses held 22.2 percent. However, the total number of shareholders had declined to eighty-one. Between 1912 and 1914, the proportion of shares held by banks rose dramatically. In 1912 joint-stock banks held 32 percent of Putilov's shares. Finally, by 1914 five joint-stock banks held 44.8 percent and two banking firms held another 7.4 percent. The major shareholders consisted of the Russo-Asiatic Bank (4,000 shares), Petersburg Trade Bank (3,332 shares), Azov-Don Bank (3,000 shares), Russian Trade and Industry Bank (2,200 shares), and the Siberian Trade Bank (1,000 shares). Additionally, A. I. Putilov, president of the Russo-Asiatic Bank since 1910 and the Putilov Company since 1913, held 2,200 shares personally, while Ignatii Porfir'evich Manus, president of the Russian Trade and Industry Bank and a member of the Putilov Company's revision commission since 1905, held 1,200 shares personally in 1914. As a result, by 1914 the majority of Putilov stock was held by banks.[17] As this information shows, the participation of banks as shareholders dramatically increased over the period, but most sharply in 1912–1914.

In that lengthy letter to Dorizon written in December 1911, A. I. Putilov had asserted that the Petersburg International Bank and the Russo-Asiatic Bank were masters of the Putilov Company. Although it was certainly true that both banks played important roles in financing the company's operations, in terms of stock ownership neither bank held a controlling interest. In a letter dated 4 August 1911, K. K. Spahn, a board member of the Petersburg International Bank, wrote to Schneider, "The Company works primarily with the St. Petersburg International Commercial Bank and the Russian Bank for Foreign Trade, its obligations are always put in order accurately and it enjoys credit always without limit."[18]

At Putilov's general shareholders' meeting in April 1911, the following banking firms held shares: G. Wawelberg, 3,100 shares; Kaftal', Handelmann and Company, 3,500 shares; M. Nölcken, 4,000 shares; and G.

Handelmann and St. Kaftal', 2,500 shares each. The Petersburg International Bank held approximately 1,000 shares of Putilov stock in 1910–1912, whereas the Russo-Asiatic Bank had obtained its 2,850 shares over the course of 1912. Yet the total number of Putilov shares increased from 40,477 in 1910 to 60,741 in 1912. So A. I. Putilov spoke accurately when he observed that individually neither bank had enough shares to pass the proposed capital increases. The two banks' shares combined did not surpass the 4,000 shares held by the banking firm Nölcken in 1911. Additionally, the Petersburg Trade Bank was the single largest shareholder, and that bank commanded a whopping 9,349 shares in 1912 at the time of the alleged takeover by the Russo-Asiatic Bank.[19]

In April 1912, A. I. Putilov mobilized his supporters in order to call a special shareholders' meeting of the Putilov Company to discuss the acquisition of the Nevskii Shipbuilding factory. A. I. Putilov identified his companions in this matter as the following:

Petersburg Private Commercial Bank, 1,000 shares;
Siberian Trade Bank, 1,000 shares;
I. P. Manus, 1,000 shares;
P. A. Vok, 900 shares;
S. V. Pennatsio, 500 shares;
L. K. Neumann, 300 shares;
V. O. Von Manteufel, 400 shares;
A. I. Friedberg, 800 shares;
A. T. Makasevich, 500 shares;
Iu. Iu. Busch, 500 shares;
R. Shantero, 900 shares.[20]

On 24 April 1912, the Russian Trade Industry Bank (Manus) obtained the right for the Russo-Asiatic Bank to vote in the Putilov Company's general shareholders' meeting representing 2,850 shares.[21] Among the issues on the agenda were the acquisition of all Nevskii's stock by the Putilov Company, the issue of new Putilov stock, with a nominal value of 9 million rubles, to facilitate the purchase of Nevskii stock, introduction of Putilov stock onto the Paris Exchange, the addition of two positions on the Putilov board for a total of seven directors, and changes in the company charter to allow one director to be a "foreigner of Christian faith." Among the Putilov Company's 336 shareholders, 124 (representing 767 votes and 78 percent of the total shares) participated in the meeting.[22]

Analyzing votes instead of total shares offers another perspective to assess the "takeover." After all, it was possible for the Russo-Asiatic Bank to have more votes, even though it did not have more shares, because of actual voter participation at the meeting and the limitations on the number of votes any individual shareholder could cast. Under the terms of the company charter, anyone with more than 300 shares could cast four votes, but no one could cast more than ten votes as a representative of his own and others' shares combined. If we assume that the Russo-Asiatic Banks' clientele were all entitled to cast the maximum number of votes in the 1912 meeting, then they could account for 160 votes. However, a total of 767 votes were represented at the 1912 meeting. So the Russo-Asiatic Bank's network, as described by A. I. Putilov, could muster approximately one-fifth of the total votes.

At the Extraordinary Meeting of Putilov shareholders on 16 May 1912, the mechanics of the Nevskii acquisition again dominated the agenda, although the meeting was slightly different in details from the general meeting in April. The first order of business was to obtain all the shares of the Nevskii enterprise and issue 60,000 shares of new Putilov stock, at 100 rubles per share, for a total of 6 million rubles. Having acquired Nevskii, the firm would then be able to rebuild and reequip the works for a sum of 1,250,000 rubles. The proposals also called for a total of 1,750,000 rubles for plant expansion at Putilov itself and the issue of 30,000 shares of new stock to cover these expenditures for both Nevskii and Putilov. Henceforth all activities at Nevskii and Putilov were to be coordinated and unified. The proposals called for introducing Putilov stock on the Paris Exchange, expanding the board to seven directors, and allowing one board member to be a foreigner. Participants also voted on whether to supplement the charter to permit the Putilov Company to participate in other similar enterprises by buying and selling stocks or bonds. At this extremely important meeting, 355 stockholders representing 895 votes, agreed to all these proposals.[23] More important, all the issues on the agenda in the 1912 meetings enjoyed the unanimous support of the shareholders. In short, no power struggle or rival factions arose among the shareholders.

A. I. Putilov's depiction of a bitter rivalry between the International Bank and the Russo-Asiatic Bank also does not stand up to scrutiny. Prior to the establishment of the Russo-Asiatic Bank, the Russo-Chinese Bank under A. I. Putilov had become involved in buying Putilov Company stock from the Petersburg International Bank in 1910. Between February and June 1910, the Russo-Chinese Bank cooperated with the PICB in a stock syndicate that sold 7,380 shares of Putilov stock and netted the Russo-Chinese Bank 512,337.5 rubles in the process. The two banks continued to collaborate even after the Russo-Chinese Bank amalgamated with the Northern Bank to become the Russo-Asiatic Bank, and along with the PICB, issued 5 million francs' worth of Putilov Company securities through the Paris section of the Russo-Asiatic Bank in late November 1910. In October 1911 the PICB participated in the Russo-Asiatic Bank's issue of 12 million francs of new Putilov shares. Nor was this kind of cooperative banking exceptional. The Russo-Asiatic Bank also cooperated with the Petersburg Discount Loan and Azov-Don Banks in arranging a loan of 10 million rubles for Bulgaria in 1912.[24]

Around the same time that the Russo-Asiatic Bank was working to form a syndicate to purchase Putilov stock, the Petersburg International Bank was developing similar plans. In February 1911 the PICB notified the Russo-Asiatic Bank that it wanted to put together a syndicate to guarantee 40,000 new shares of Putilov stock for 4 million rubles. The PICB invited the Russo-Asiatic Bank to take part in this syndicate at 25 percent. By 17 March 1911, the Russo-Asiatic Bank had agreed to participate in the International Bank's syndicate for 21.25 percent and had purchased 1948 new shares of Putilov stock.[25]

The cooperative activities of the two banks further weakens the "dueling banks" interpretation. Instead of conceiving of the Putilov Company simply as the object of bank competition, a more compelling explanation for the activity surrounding the company can be found by considering the company as an actor in its own drama. From this perspective, the company could be seen as bringing in the banks in order to secure financial support for its long-term expansion. Before A. I. Putilov appeared on the scene, the company's board already had plans afoot to expand its product line into shipbuilding. In 1903 Putilov's board had begun sounding out British firms as prospective shipbuilding partners. They proposed to approach either Armstrong or Hawthorne and Leslie that fall to make arrangements for constructing merchant vessels for the Russian trade, and they dispatched their head manager to England to that end.

Putilov reentered the naval construction field in 1905 by launching two 570-ton destroyers in May and June 1905, as well as casting the stern frame for a first-class battleship. The company already held a key position in that it provided large castings for the state yards, and these other yards suffered construction delays in 1905 when strikes erupted at Putilov.[26] Since 1904 there had been talk among the firm's administration of establishing a shipbuilding factory on the Gulf of Finland in the Kronstadt region and constructing large warships. On 22 May 1907, the company sent a letter to the Naval Ministry seeking to obtain government agreements for warship construction. For that purpose, the firm declared its willingness to carry out all the required construction for the factory and to create the appropriate equipment.[27]

To be taken seriously by the Naval Ministry, the company initiated steps for naval production. The Putilov board declared to its shareholders in May 1907 that it had actually concluded a preliminary agreement with a large, unidentified English shipbuilding firm for an option of two years. Because the Putilov Company commanded an extensive coastal strip, it had the potential to construct a wharf for building large warships. This prospect attracted the English company enough that it agreed to spend up to 7 million rubles on this project, and the contract with the English company was supposed to last ten years. Still, the naval expansion would probably require a new issue of stocks and bonds. The board told the Putilov shareholders, "Everything depends on the decision about the naval program."[28]

The first Russian naval program, the so-called Small Program, won approval in 1908 and paved the way for the tsarist Navy to build dreadnoughts. The successor building program in 1912 called for still more ships to create a high-seas fleet in the Baltic. Appropriations allowed for comparable programs in 1911 and 1914 for the Black Sea. In 1914 Russia was spending almost as much as Germany for new naval construction, 194 million marks versus 218 million marks.[29]

In February 1908 the Naval Technical Committee (MTK) approached Russian and foreign builders for outlines of 35-ton turbine destroyers to match the new British system laid down the previous year. While determining the technical specifications, the committee invited firms to submit their drawings and in January 1909 evaluated outline drawings received from the various potential suppliers. The Technical Committee declared Putilov the winner of the design competiton and awarded the building contract in July 1909, for 2,190,000 rubles, with a 30 percent advance. The Putilov design received the designation "Novik." The German company Vulkan got the order for boilers and turbines, and Putilov laid the keel in July 1910. Trials began on time in May 1912.[30]

The expanded naval program called for thirty-six destroyers for the Baltic Fleet, and all were to follow Putilov's Novik model. The new fleet plans called for modifications in armament and the goal of interchangeability for turbine parts for all the ships. The final specifications required firms to tender their bids for a 1,322-ton vessel. When the Shipbuilding Commission distributed its orders in October 1912, Putilov garnered eight ships. The remainder went to the St. Petersburg Metal Works, which was to build eight; Russo-Baltic Shipbuilding at Reval, six; Lange and Son at Reval, five; and another nine went to Schichau at its Riga yard.[31]

The Putilov Company succeeded in landing a good portion of the naval expansion up to 1912, and the firm rapidly emerged as a leading naval supplier. The Black Sea destroyer contracts went to four companies in 1911: Naval, Putilov, St. Petersburg Metal Works, and Nevskii. All the St. Petersburg yards were to execute preliminary assembly and then transport the components for final construction at slips on the Black Sea. St. Petersburg Metal Works had no shipbuilding facilities, so Putilov constructed its hulls. To speed up the program, the Naval Ministry also called on Putilov to provide Nevskii and Metal Works with its working drawings. The Baltic program called for four light cruisers, and two for the Pacific, whereas the Black Sea program proposed two light cruisers in 1911. The following year, Putilov competed against the Admiralty yard and the Russo-Baltic works at Reval. The MTK favored Putilov's hull design, but preferred Reval's bow and Admiralty's side protection. In response, Putilov and Reval cooperated in the design, which was accepted in October 1912. After agreeing to reduce their prices from 9,660,000 rubles to 8.3 million, Putilov and Reval split the orders with two apiece in February 1913. Putilov turret design also won approval for the Black Sea dreadnoughts, and the company itself produced the turrets for *Imperator Aleksandr III*. Even when the St. Petersburg Metal Works won the design for battle cruiser turrets, Putilov picked up a piece of the business because of its lower prices. (Obukhov and Nikolaev likewise gained turret orders in this way.)[32]

The timing of the banks' appearance as shareholders in 1907, coinciding as it did with the Putilov Company's dawning financial difficulties with its artillery business, suggests that the company was attempting to line up backing for naval expansion as a way out of its financial squeeze. Because an enormous new port was being built at St. Petersburg, by 1910 Putilov's land on the Gulf of Finland held the prospect of being a good site to locate a new wharf for all types of ships, including 25,000-ton state-of-the-art battleships. In 1910 the company decided to go ahead with construction on the Gulf of Finland. At that time, A. I. Putilov first appeared on the scene as a shareholder in the Putilov Company, with 900 shares.[33] The board had invited him during fiscal year 1911 to fill the fifth director's position on the board.[34]

Rather than seeing A. I. Putilov's entry onto the board as a first step toward taking control of the company on the Russo-Asiatic Bank's behalf, we should consider why the board would want him to serve. First it is necessary to understand the company's position. In 1910 the French firm Schneider assessed Putilov's condition in light of prospects of greater cooperation with the Russian factory. The Schneider representative observed that the company's stock value was comparatively high. Also, at present the state had granted the company substantial submarine orders, and negotiations were under way for torpedo boat contracts worth 20 million rubles. The Schneider representative remarked, "Moreover, according to rumors in this case it will enjoy the financial support of the Russo-Asiatic Bank."[35] The report continued,

> In connection with the expanding activity of the plant, the company needs increasing working capital, since it does not always receive the necessary money punctually from the state. The company sometimes experiences shortfalls in working capital and so it issued new stock for six million rubles.[36]

The Schneider report points to two related reasons why the Putilov board might want to recruit A. I. Putilov. First, the financial participation of the Russo-Asiatic Bank seemed to impress Schneider favorably. Given the Putilov board's desire to collaborate with the French firm, this was extremely important. Also, the French observer noted that the company had cash flow problems. The artillery business caused great financial stress. One way to ease that problem would be to place a banker on the board to facilitate financial support.

In July 1911 the Putilov board approached Schneider-Creusot with a proposition to form a syndicate to guarantee the new stock issue and to consider the question of production of large-caliber artillery. They proposed that Schneider participate for 25 percent of the total. The letter was signed by Vyshnegradskii, of the Petersburg International Bank, and by A. I. Putilov, of the Russo-Asiatic Bank, on behalf of the Putilov Company. Also in July 1911 the Putilov Company and Schneider agreed that Schneider would furnish Putilov with plans for forges and machinery in order to produce large-caliber naval guns with a goal of annual production of twenty-four 12-inch pieces, eighteen 14-inch guns, and twelve 16-inch artillery pieces. Creusot's agent, Mr. Davis, assessed the Putilov Company's position in a letter on 12 October 1911. Davis noted that since 1897 the company had had research and technical agreements with Schneider and that currently the financial situation of the Company was sound. On this point he observed that through the Petersburg International Bank and the Russo-Asiatic Bank the Putilov Company had raised its stock capital from 12 million to 16 million rubles. On 17 October 1911, the bank Société Générale in Paris responded that it would be willing to participate in the artillery syndicate if the Russian banks engaged for more than 50 percent, if Creusot participated for 20 percent and if the French group (Creusot, Banque de Paris, Société Générale) were represented on Putilov's administrative council and had the right to designate a commissioner of accounts.[37]

Now we have sufficient information to appreciate A. I. Putilov's lengthy letter to Dorizon in December 1911. The French wanted a sizable financial commitment from the Russian banks before they would participate. In order to motivate the French, the president of the Russo-Asiatic Bank played the German card. He distorted the nature of the relationship between his bank and the PICB in the Putilov enterprise by portraying the latter as an instrument of German influence, i.e., Krupp. In this way he raised the specter of the Putilov Company falling under the sway of Schneider's archrival. Evidently the ploy worked, because Davis wrote to Putilov on 15 January 1912 that Schneider had a project to increase capital for the fusion of the Putilov Company and the Nevskii Shipbuilding works. In his capacity as head of the Russo-Asiatic Bank, A. I. Putilov responded favorably to Schneider's plan to develop Putilov through the creation of new installations by absorbing Nevskii.[38]

Before we explore the banks' role in the Putilov Company's naval expansion, we need to understand the position of the Nevskii Shipbuilding plant. In the late 1890s, Nevskii Shipbuilding operated as a state enterprise, but the Naval Ministry was not entirely pleased with the factory's performance. As of 1895, Nevskii employed 2,000 workers and was engaged in producing ten torpedo boats, all behind schedule. Even though Nevskii was responsible for executing twenty torpedo boat destroyers, production delays were common because of nondelivery of English machinery. Despite talk of selling off the works to certain English representatives, in 1898 the Naval Ministry decided to postpone the proposed sale of Nevskii indefinitiely.[39] Nevskii did not have to worry about running at a loss, and the chances of the works being closed were slim. The government had invested very little in plant expansion for shipbuilding since 1903, although the locomotive department did increase in size and had full orders. During 1905 Nevskii built three destroyers, had orders for eight more, and was building American-designed Holland submarine boats.[40] The factory seemed to be headed away from shipbuilding and into locomotives, but the navy's heightened interest in submarines after the Russo-Japanese War made Nevskii more attractive. Nevskii's connections with the Holland Submarine Company, along with the American firm's world-class reputation, resulted in an order for three submarines for Nevskii in 1909. By 1910 the War Ministry had also become interested in submarines as part of its defense for Kronstadt. Nevskii developed a smaller class of Holland submarines for this purpose and began production for the War Ministry in October 1912.[41]

The expansion of the Putilov Company's naval business came about through a horizontal acquisition of another ship producer. By the outbreak of war in 1914, the company had purchased the Nevskii Shipbuilding factory and built an entirely new plant, the Putilov Wharves. Nevskii offered an attractive opportunity for Putilov in two important areas of specialization: shipbuilding and locomotive production. In 1912 Nevskii already had started working on orders for two torpedo boats for the Black Sea fleet for 4,000,000 rubles, three submarines for 4,765,000 rubles, and six steamships for 4,427,000 rubles. At the Putilov shareholders' meeting in 1912, the board expressed confidence in Nevskii's potential for gaining significant naval orders from the naval reconstruction program "since it commands the privilege for one of the best submarine systems [Holland] and the patent for internal-combustion turbines for these boats."[42] Additionally, Nevskii had orders for 105 locomotives for 3.5 million rubles and the company expected profits around 1.2 million rubles for the year. Having completed retrofitting its locomotive department in 1910, Nevskii had the capacity to manufacture 200 locomotive units per year. Also, the mechanical workshops of Nevskii's shipbuilding department were technically better than Putilov's.[43]

For its part, Nevskii's board viewed the merger with Putilov favorably. In a report presented to the extraordinary meeting of Nevskii shareholders in November 1912, Nevskii's board identified a number of mutual advantages for the two factories that would accrue from the merger. Both enterprises were essentially similar, were conveniently connected geographically, and therefore under common leadership could fill orders with greater profit than by competing with one another. Also, several branches of production could benefit from transferring operations from Putilov to Nevskii and vice versa. For example, Putilov's boiler production could be allocated to Nevskii, while Nevskii's mechanical pressing business would be transferred to Putilov, and both factories would work together on turbine production. Moreover, the rationalization of production achieved by the reorganization of several workshops at both factories would economize the workshop construction for each. By working together, both factories could also reduce the staff of their technical bureaus.[44]

The Putilov Company expected to begin construction of the new factory in fall 1914. The Council of Ministers had approved the charter for the new Nevskii Company capitalized at 8 million rubles. The largest portion of that capital, 4.4 million rubles, would be provided by Skoda, the defense producer in Austria-Hungary. The Putilov Company had committed to providing 650,000 rubles, and the remaining 2,950,000 rubles would come from the Nevskii factory itself. As of late July 1913, the Putilov Company expected that the new works could be operating by January 1915.[45] Construction of the Putilov Wharf commenced in 1912 as well. The board entered into negotiations with banks for an additional 5 million rubles for wharf construction, but because the company's market position was less favorable than before, the increase in stock capital was

expected to cut into dividends for the first two years of the wharf's operation. The overall sum of orders on hand in May 1913 totaled 90 million
rubles, of which the Putilov factory had 50 million and the wharf was to
fill the remainder.[46] As of 1914, the turbine and small shipbuilding workshops were completed. In fact, the small shipbuilding department had
already started production in May 1914, and the company was engaged in
building two light cruisers (6,800 tons displacement), eight destroyers
(1,260 tons each), three destroyers for the Black Sea (1,110 tons), three
river dredges, and one rescue boat. The general cost of the current construction was 38 million rubles.[47]

A. I. Putilov's role in the Putilov Company is best understood as that
of a financial facilitator for capital investment. In a letter to the board of
the Russo-Asiatic Bank dated 23 December 1911, Putilov wrote, "I inform
you of the results of my negotiations with Kaftal': we are taking on call
4,000 shares of Putilov stock at 120 each at 5 ½ percent; the rate of course
is lower, but he does not want to pay any higher, trusting that his banking
firm will serve only as an intermediary in this matter. I don't know anything about this, but I agree to this rate only on the condition if you will
agree to it."[48] The evidence presented here forces us to revise the standard characterization of A. I. Putilov as the commanding personality
behind the reorganization and expansion of the Putilov Company. In
terms of shareholders, personnel, and policy, strong continuities per-
sisted. For example, the Azov-Don Bank, the banking firms of Junker and
Company and the Dzhamgarov brothers had all worked with the company since the 1890s and were still important investors in 1914. Likewise,
the Russian Trade and Industry Bank and I. P. Manus had also been
actively involved prior to the arrival of A. I. Putilov and continued into his
presidency. Finally, Aleksandr Konstantinovich Von Dreyer, D. S. Khrulev,
N. E. Panafidin, and L. Bischlager carried on in their technical areas on
the board just as they had in the years before the supposed takeover by
the Russo-Asiatic Bank. Indeed, they seemed to be the ones who really
directed the firm after A. I. Putilov became company president in October 1913.[49]

Furthermore, the prominence of these board members was not a
consequence of any previous connections to the Russo-Asiatic Bank.
Instead, they had risen to their positions from within the firm. The
process of specialization in the tasks of board members continued to

develop in the years 1900–1914. The expansion of the naval business required a new division of labor among directors in that period: L. Bischlager primarily handled the artillery projects, Von Dreyer dealt with locomotive affairs, and they both worked on the naval business, including the planning and execution of the Nevskii merger.[50]

If any person can be singled out as the driving force behind the Putilov-Nevskii merger, the most likely candidate is A. K. Von Dreyer. Dreyer had served as a board director at Nevskii since 1899 and was well placed to appreciate the advantages of combining the factories. Alone among Putilov's board members, Dreyer advocated that the productivity of Nevskii's shipbuilding department could be increased, and he outlined to the other directors plans for the following branches of production: (1) constructing swift destroyers of up to 1,300 tons, (2) building submarines of the American and English naval type, and (3) equipping small cruisers with displacement of up to 6,000 tons.[51] Some fragmentary evidence also points to Dreyer as the Putilov Company insider who coordinated arrangements with the Russo-Asiatic Bank. In April 1912, the Russo-Asiatic Bank notified Dreyer that their investment group held 9,455 shares, and therefore his share would increase from 2 to 3 percent. Finally, as part of the Nevskii merger, the Putilov board placed two of its members, Dreyer and Bischlager, on the new Nevskii board.[52]

It is readily apparent from the behavior of the board that the company tended to favor the rise of technical specialists and engineers from within its own ranks. The leading board members all rose to the top of the company because of their technical expertise. More significant, they were all employed by the Putilov Company before the Russo-Asiatic Bank and A. I. Putilov entered the picture. The directors who were officially designated by the French group or the Russo-Asiatic Bank were not the ones responsible for the operations, but actually assumed a purely passive role.

By law, the directors had to be elected from among company shareholders. Therefore, a new perspective on the question of interlocking directorates can be gained by considering the extent to which the shareholders themselves were connected to the various enterprises. If we broaden the conception of the firm to include the active shareholders as well as the boards they elected, then we can properly appreciate the concentration of business activity beyond the narrow confines of supposed banking groups. For example, an examination of the shareholders of the

Russo-Asiatic Bank in 1914 reveals that the Petersburg International Commercial Bank held almost as much stock as president A. I. Putilov. The PICB had 1,750 shares, whereas A. I. Putilov owned 1,869.[53] This fact itself forces the reevaluation of the "dueling banks" interpretation.

Unfortunately, an extensive investigation of the interlocking shareholding patterns in Russian banks is beyond the scope of this study. Nevertheless, even a cursory glance at some of the overlapping spheres of shareholders gives the impression of an extraordinarily complex web. Here I wish to highlight some of the more obvious players in the Putilov Company story. The Dzhamgarov brothers were large shareholders in the Azov-Don Bank, the Petersburg Private Commercial Bank, and the Briansk works. Besides its holdings in the Putilov Company, the Azov-Don Bank possessed 11,800 shares of Briansk in 1912. I. P. Manus controlled a large number of shares in the Azov-Don Bank and the Petersburg Private Commercial Bank. Meanwhile, the Petersburg Trade Bank participated in both the PICB and the Petersburg Private Commercial Bank.[54]

Obviously, banks played a significant role in the tsarist defense sector. An important question is that posed by Peter Gatrell: why did foreign investment take a direct form in defense industries from 1912 to 1914 when indirect investment was the rule in the rest of Russia's industrial sectors? He concludes, "The answer must be, in part, that the complexity of the technological tasks played by contemporary weapons systems encouraged foreign firms to exercise close supervision over capital and labour."[55] Gatrell's answer offers a partial explanation.

A more comprehensive explanation can be found by framing the problem within an analysis of transaction costs. Jean-François Hennart proposes that lenders' choices between loans and equity in foreign direct investment are guided by considerations of efficiency in internalizing capital markets. According to Hennart, lenders will opt for stock ownership rather than loans if the activity to be financed offers little collateral, if it is new and untested and requires rapid, nonstandard decisions, or if there are few personal links between lenders and investors. Loans will also be precluded if the venture requires much research and development because those activities are speculative and produce little collateral. Furthermore, intermediated equity between savers and investors occurs when the information about the activity is complex or rapidly changing, or a great amount of information is needed to make prudent investment decisions. Intermediators centralize the transfer of information between savers and borrowers. Intermediation will also be sought if the investment is too large for a single promoter. An advantage of equity is that the owner has greater control over the use of the funds than a lender. Also, if expected profits for the venture are higher than the return on the loan, lenders are more likely to select stock ownership.[56]

The involvement of the French banking group and Schneider in Putilov's affairs conforms to Hennart's historical model. The Putilov board wanted to expand into naval production, and this decision necessitated large capital expansion. The Russian banks wanted to particpate in the expansion of the Putilov Company but lacked sufficient capital to achieve this goal on their own. The reports from Schneider's representatives in 1910 indicated that they expected Putilov to reap high profits from the upcoming defense orders and that the firm was about to embark into a new area: submarine construction. The French banks and Schneider finally decided to acquire equity in Putilov after A. I. Putilov hinted that if they did not get involved Krupp and the Germans would get the better of them. The motivation and timing of the French indicates that they wanted representation on the Putilov board not simply to look after their investment, but also to preempt the Germans. In this they proved unsuccessful, as the Putilov Company signed a number of agreements with German firms and were directly negotiating with the Austrians and their firm Skoda for another technical agreement for the Nevskii factory in 1914.[57]

Overall, the banks' relationship to the Putilov Company conformed to the general pattern of bank-industry relations in Europe, with some differences. A major factor in inhibiting bank dominance in Britain, France, and Germany was the companies' widespread preference for self-financing through ploughed-back profits. In this way, the companies preserved their financial independence to a significant degree. In contrast, the Putilov Company's board tended to seek outside financing for most of its expansion even before the turn of the century. Putilov may have been less reluctant to seek bank financing than most of its European cohorts because it was not a family firm. Krupp, Schneider, Vickers, and Armstrong sought to preserve family control and worried about the potential influence of outsiders. The Putilov Company had no such qualms. On this score, Putilov more closely resembled Skoda, which became a limited liability company in 1899 thanks to an increase in share capital furnished through the Creditanstalt in Vienna. Creditanstalt later served as the source for one-third of the increase in Skoda's share capital in 1910.

Banks could potentially influence company policy through their shareholding. To avoid this situation, often the large European industrial enterprises worked with several different competing banks at the same time. For example, in Germany the steel company Phoenix maintained accounts with forty-three different banks, including thirty-one foreign ones. Moreover, it was not unusual for the supervisory boards of German companies to include representatives from various Berlin banks. This practice served to mitigate the potential dominance of any one bank by counterbalancing it with a rival or two. We can discern a similar pattern in the Putilov Company's dealings with the Russo-Asiatic Bank, the PICB, and a host of other shareholding banks. Throughout Europe, bankers usually saw their role on company boards as monitoring their investments and maintaining good business relationships with valued customers. By and large they left the business decisions to the industrialists. Again, the Putilov Company fits this trend.[58]

In conclusion, the traditional bases for arguing that banks had a commanding role in organizing the defense sector and manipulating interlocking directorates do not adequately explain the Putilov Company's participation in these activities. The difficulty with such interpretations is that they treat the Putilov Company as merely a prize for contending financial groups or foreign firms rather than as an active participant in its own affairs. On this score, shareholders also receive little attention. Another conceptual problem concerns the association of various board members with other institutions. Should board members best be viewed as representatives of the banks, or primarily as individual shareholders in the Putilov Company? Although a case can be made for considering board members as representatives of competing banks, such an interpretation raises another set of problems. For example, there is as much evidence of cooperation among banks as for competition. The perspective that makes the most sense is to take the company itself as the point of reference.

5

PUTILOV AT WAR

1914–1917

The outbreak of World War I found the Putilov Company in the midst of its planned expansion into naval production, and in that respect the firm could not have been in a more vulnerable position. Because the reorganization of production associated with the Nevskii acquisition had required massive capital outlays, the firm's debt burden began to rise. What was most significant, the first months of the war made it clear that Russia's primary defense needs would be shells and artillery, not warships. For the sake of the country's defense and its own commercial future, the company would have to redirect resources away from shipbuilding and into the production of shrapnel, shell, and artillery pieces. Already financially overextended, Putilov required still more capital to convert fully to wartime production for the empire's land forces. As a result, previous difficulties in civil-military relations regarding payment procedures, along with the increasing role of the banks, combined to weaken the company in the eyes of the Main Artillery Administration (GAU).

The outbreak of war between Russia and the Central Powers in 1914 caught the Putilov Company completely unprepared. It was in the middle of a complicated reorganization and expansion for naval production. The company's position was even more precarious because those plans rested on technical and financial agreements with foreign firms located in the hostile countries. The war not only disrupted those plans, it also made clear that artillery supply would take precedence over naval construction.

Fundamentally, the conflict would be fought on land, and the demands for the army were vast. Hence the board had to scramble to redirect output toward shells and field pieces while the reorganization with Nevskii continued.

Prior to the war, the company had turned to the banks, especially the Russo-Asiatic Bank, for financing in lieu of advances from the War Ministry. During the war, having a banker on the board became a disadvantage as military officers blamed the banks for raising costs and mismanaging production. Even as officials conceded that A. I. Putilov was not really in charge of the Putilov Company, they moved to excise the Russo-Asiatic Bank from defense contracts. In this manner, two important strands in Putilov's development—civil-military relations and the increasing presence of the banks—became intertwined in the imposition of a state sequestration of the Putilov Company in 1916. In addition, the company's lack of strong institutional connections made it vulnerable to both GAU and the lower house of the Russian Parliament, the Duma. At the critical time, the Putilov Company had no real supporters or institutional backers. Therefore, the company stood alone against the Duma and the War and Naval Ministries.

As part of the growing conflict between state and society in the last decade of the tsarist empire, the broader political struggle between the tsarist bureaucracy and the Duma for control over civil-military relations conditioned the company's vulnerability to these outside pressures. Even before the war, Duma members had been advocating greater parliamentary control over the armed forces in the name of society, and they used their authority to vote new budgets for the armed forces as the tool to assert themselves in guiding rearmament and reform in Russia's military and naval establishments. With the outbreak of the war, the struggle intensified as Russia suffered military setbacks against Germany and the army faced severe shell shortages during the long retreat in 1915. Duma opposition placed the blame for the debacle squarely on the incompetence of War Minister Sukhomlinov and his procurement policies, which had given large orders to the Putilov Company. Duma members actively worked to wrest control of military-industrial mobilization from the bureaucracy, and they wanted to reverse the government's policies. For their part, the army officers in GAU resented the potential meddling of civilian amateurs in their area of professional expertise. As the two sides squared off, the Putilov Company became the battleground for the contesting authorities.

On 27 February 1916, the Special Commission for Defense (OSO) voted to sequester the Putilov factory, and thereafter the Main Artillery Administration took over the task of overseeing its operation. Under the terms of sequestration, the company remained private property, but the enterprise was temporarily placed under state administration. The company still operated according to its charter, but the state controlled the board of directors. When the sequestration was lifted, a company would resume normal operations with a board elected from its shareholders. With this move, the largest private armaments factory in tsarist Russia thus came into the hands of the state. More specifically, military officers from the Artillery Department became responsible for running the largest factory in imperial Russia.[1]

Historians and memoirists have offered three main explanations for the sequestration. Foremost is the argument that the decision to take over the Putilov factories was at heart a tsarist attempt to mobilize private industry for wartime expansion of military production. In this respect, the act of sequestration is said to fit into the general process of mobilization that began in January 1915. A second explanation focuses on the more immediate context of labor unrest and the potential threat of social instability in Petrograd caused by the 1916 strike of Putilov workers. In February 1916, the electro-technical workshop presented demands for higher wages, and when the factory administration rejected them, the workers struck. At this time the tsarist government closed the factory, replaced the entire board of directors with a Governing Board composed of predominantly military officers, and reopened the factory as a sequestered enterprise. A third interpretation presents the sequestration as a means of saving the factory owners from huge financial losses. In this view, the Putilov Company faced imminent financial collapse, and so the financial magnates of the Russo-Asiatic Bank and the board of directors of the Putilov Company used the sequestration to get the state to take the debt-ridden factory off their hands.[1]

None of these interpretations, not even the first, directly takes into account the role and interests of the Main Artillery Administration in the decision to sequester the Putilov factories. During the entire war, OSO sequestered only 28 enterprises out of more than 5,200 that worked for defense production in 1916.[2] Therefore it seems misleading to interpret the Putilov sequestration as part of the general process of industrial mobilization because sequestration was not typical, but the exception to the pattern in wartime Russia.

Why would GAU want to sequester the Putilov factories, and what does GAU's role in the sequestration say about civil-military relations in the economic sphere? When the question is placed in the context of civil-military relations, it becomes clear that the sequestration was simply the last act in a three-way conflict among GAU, members of the state Duma, and the board of directors of the Putilov Company. Thus, the case of the Putilov factories frames several broader issues, such as the rivalry between St. Petersburg- and Moscow-based suppliers for war orders, competition between government officials and Duma representatives for authority to direct the war effort, and issues of the mechanics of state sequestration generally. One could explain the motivations of GAU's leaders in terms of their hostility toward the board of directors of the Putilov Company. In this regard GAU was not opposed to private enterprise in itself, only this particular private enterprise and its board of directors. However, we should remember that the impetus to impose sequestration on the Putilov factory originated from the Duma members on the Special Commission for Defense, not from the military. Therefore the sense of professionalism among GAU's officers, and especially GAU's chief, A. A. Manikovskii, was also a consideration because the Duma members were attempting to infringe on GAU's area of technical expertise. In short, GAU could not stand by while the amateurs from the Duma tried to assert themselves as a guiding force in military production.

In May 1915 the Putilov Company first caught the attention of the Special Commission for Defense. The OSO was composed of eighteen Parliament members (eleven Duma members and seven State Council representatives), six military officers, three ministry officials (Finance, Trade and Industry, Transport), two War-Industries members, and two *zemstvo* representatives. So the Duma members by themselves held a plurality and, combined with the State Council representatives, comprised a majority of the votes within the OSO. At that time, the company notified the OSO that it was encountering difficulties in filling all the war orders on time and that it needed an advance payment. The OSO appointed a subcommittee to look into the matter under the direction of A. I.

Guchkov, an important player among Moscow industrialists and a leading proponent of the War-Industries Committees. Guchkov presented his findings to the OSO on 31 July. According to the report, Putilov was heavily in debt and was delaying the completion of old orders in order to complete the newer, more profitable orders issued by the previous war minister, Sukhomlinov. Guchkov also criticized the War Ministry for having given so many orders to Putilov, and the Duma members on the OSO generally echoed Guchkov's criticisms.[3]

To understand why Guchkov was so quick to find fault with the Putilov Company, we must consider his long-standing conflict with War Minister Sukhomlinov. Guchkov had been carrying out attacks against Sukhomlinov since before the war. A self-styled military expert, Guchkov had used his position on the Duma's Defense Committee to establish contacts with officials in the War Ministry and to gain inside information as part of his quest to reform the military. From those contacts, Guchkov had established close connections with Sukhomlinov's deputy, A. A. Polivanov. Sukhomlinov had become alarmed by Guchkov's stinging criticisms of his policies and complained about Polivanov's unscrupulous role in contributing to the influence of outsiders in making policy. In 1912 Polivanov leaked information to Guchkov about Sukhomlinov's plans to create a secret unit to ensure the political loyalty of the military command. Guchkov publicly attacked Sukhomlinov, and Polivanov was dismissed.[4] When given the task of investigating affairs at the Putilov factory, Guchkov seized on the chance to level another attack at Sukhomlinov's policies. As chairman of the Central War Industries Committee in 1915, Guchkov advocated that instead of having GAU place orders directly with factories, defense orders should be distributed through his committee. Such a policy would mean the ascendancy of the Moscow industrialists over their St. Petersburg rivals. Furthermore, since Guchkov's friend and associate Polivanov had replaced Sukhomlinov as chair of the OSO in June 1915, Guchkov's criticisms fell on very receptive ears.[5]

On 27 October 1915, the OSO presented a report highlighting the difficulties at the Putilov factories. The OSO's investigative commission concluded that in order to ensure the punctual fulfillment of state defense orders, the Putilov factories would have to be sequestered soon; moreover, K. K. Spahn, an individual "of German origin," should be removed immediately from the board of directors.[6] In the discussions that

followed on 28 October, OSO members recognized that the Putilov
plants needed an infusion of cash quickly. However, the report continued,

> the issuing of any kind of monetary means to the sitting board of
> directors, who led the factories to so sorry a financial state, seems
> without a doubt inadmissible. At the same time it is necessary to
> call attention to the extremely essential defects in the activity of
> the factory administration. President of the board Mr. Putilov, by
> his own declaration, is not interested in the affairs of the factory
> essentially and is only a representative of the interests of the
> Russo-Asiatic Bank; the chief agent of the factory, Mr. Dreyer, sits
> as a member of so many boards that he cannot possibly devote
> the necessary attention to the Putilov factories, and in particular,
> at so serious a moment for the survival of the factories, Mr. Dreyer
> turned out to be away from Petrograd for three weeks. The
> remaining members of the board are simply extras having no
> active role. Finally, according to the conclusions of the factory
> inspectors, the production is not developed by even half and
> could be increased by 50 percent.[7]

The documents provide no details on how the inspectors arrived at this
figure, and for all practical purposes it seems to have been pulled out of
thin air. In any case, the OSO instructed GAU to assign 5 million rubles
from the war fund to support the activity of the Putilov factories and to
place the following representatives on the Putilov board: Major General
G. G. Krivoshein from the War Ministry, K. N. Ogloblinskii from the Naval
Ministry, and V. Iu. Mebes from Finance.[8]

In a meeting of the Special Commission on 28 October 1915
presided over by War Minister A. A. Polivanov, the consensus of opinion
was that obviously the Putilov Company was on the verge of stopping payments because of lack of free credit. Having a stock capital of 25 million
rubles, the company had received more than 40 million rubles' worth of
advances for state supplies. Yet, "It turned out to be impossible to determine where that money went from the documents presented by the Company." Moreover, "the exclusive significance of the Putilov factories as the
supplier of artillery calls for the necessity to supply financial means
quickly."[9]

Given the sense of urgency among the commission members, two paths lay open. They could either remove the entire board of directors or sequester the enterprise. The commission found the first option unsatisfactory because the new board would still be obligated by the company charter and have to be considered by the stockholders in a general meeting that undoubtedly would lead to friction and nonconfirmation of the desired changes. The choice to sequester, on the other hand, made it possible "to direct the factories with more conformity to its means from the point of view of state defense interests." Thus under sequestration the activity of the factories would continue uninterrupted and the state would be guaranteed completion of the factories' unfulfilled orders amounting to about 180 million rubles. Many members on the Special Commission, predominantly the Duma members, perceived sequestration to be necessary.[10]

Polivanov not only moved on this course of action quickly, but also expanded his role in Putilov company affairs. On 31 October 1915, Polivanov informed the Council of Ministers that he had begun the formation of a state administration for the Putilov factory by replacing the German board member Spahn with N. A. Krylov from the Naval Ministry.[11] Then the war minister extended his sphere of interest to include the Nevskii Shipbuilding factory. In a letter to Nevskii's board of directors on 3 November, Polivanov explained that since the Putilov Company owned the Nevskii stock and Nevskii had significant delays in filling defense orders, he had resolved to appoint a third inspector from the Special Commission to watch over the Putilov factory. Also, all three inspectors were to monitor Nevskii's activity. However, Polivanov did not wish to limit the activities of the inspectors to mere observation. He continued,

I ask the board to present to the mandated inspectors the possibility to attend the sessions of the board with voting rights, to give all necessary information upon their request and to present for examination the company books and all definitive documents which concern the activities of the factory.[12]

The board of directors of the Putilov Company defended their policies and refuted the various charges of negligence hurled at them by the Duma members. The board declared,

Since May of this year, from the time of the formation of the Special Commission, the board of the Putilov Company, for reasons about which it is possible only to guess, has been subjected to systematic attacks and accusations. Up to now denunciations which originated from below have served as the main, if not the only fodder for these accusations from the dregs of the factory and low-ranking official people. They are directed almost exclusively to members of the State Duma who are actually unfamiliar with the state of affairs, and to officials of various departments, mainly to those who for various reasons were dissatisfied with the board of the factory. In the end this has created an atmosphere under which it has become impossible either to live or to work.[13]

The Putilov board complained that the commission had concentrated exclusively on the defects and deficiencies of the factories and that such disorders were unavoidable in any large reorganized and expanded business.[14] The board strove to prove that rather than being detached and uninvolved, it had actually been working diligently to expand the company's capacity for military production for a number of years. The board recounted how after the Russo-Japanese campaigns the necessity for creating a factory for heavy artillery in Russia had become clear; it reiterated that even back in 1909 it had advanced a proposal to expand and increase the Putilov factory without any aid or subsidies from the government, if only the factory were to be guaranteed an order of 100 guns per month. However, GAU had turned down the board's suggestion. In 1912 when the question of building large-caliber guns within the empire arose a second time, the board again proposed to expand artillery production with a promise of sufficient orders. The government rejected this proposal as well. The board then offered to create a filial division of the Putilov company within Russia, since St. Petersburg had nowhere to locate an enormous artillery factory. This too the state refused. Nevertheless, realizing that the army's demand for guns would continue to grow, in 1913 it took the initiative and entered into an agreement with the firm of Creusot and the French banks and began to develop its own Artillery Department and to strengthen its reconstruction. In two years the board expanded production of the Artillery Division from 7 million to 11 million rubles. The outbreak of the war caught the board completely off guard. Still, the board, with full energy, continued the work and from the beginning, with the support of the Russo-Asiatic Bank and then government loans in the form of company bonds, not only completed what it had begun, but also attended to the further expansion of the business, having increased the production of the artillery division in the course of a year of war from 11 to 27 million rubles, that is, two and one-half times.[15]

The Putilov board also initiated a completely new operation to manufacture shrapnel. On this point the board refuted the commission's characterization of its activity as inert:

At the same time, this same "inert" board, understanding that the army would need an enormous amount of shells and that there was no time to lose, since the construction season was coming to a close, quickly upon the declaration of war in August of last year pledged to have a new shrapnel factory at its own peril and risk, not having even one order, which it received then in October.[16]

The shrapnel factory was built in three months.

The Putilov board presented annual production figures to support its position. From 1910 to 1911, Putilov's production had increased by 23 percent. The following year output expanded by an additional 30 percent. By 1914 annual production reached 26 million rubles, and by 1915 this figure had increased by 80 percent to 47 million rubles. Furthermore, if one also included the output from the new shrapnel factory, then the company's production had actually increased by 150 percent to 65 million rubles in 1915.[17]

The Putilov board argued that by using the time of reception of orders as the measure of lateness, the commission created a false impression of delivery problems at the factory. In contracts with both the Naval and War Departments, delivery times were defined as "time of presentation for reception," that is, when orders were completed. Actually, the factory had produced more than the number of guns recognized by the commission. The problem actually resided with GAU because the Artillery Department was behind in its inspection and certification of the assembled guns. In the board's opinion, the proper and accurate measure of factory delivery should be "time of assembly." When viewed in those terms, Putilov production was almost on target or actually ahead of schedule. For example, the commission considered Putilov to have produced only 108 of 132 3-inch mountain guns for its contract from July 1914, or 29 percent unfulfilled. But the factory had already assembled 126 guns and therefore was only 5 percent below the contract level. Similarly, where the commission found Putilov to be 30 percent below the contract delivery of 48-line howitzers (93 of 132), Putilov had overfulfilled the contract by assembling 2.3 percent above the required number (135 of 132).[18] None of this evidence made any impression on Polivanov. When A. I. Putilov presented his opposition to the sequestration before the Special Commission on 7 November 1915, Polivanov took this opportunity to threaten him by stating, "If the measures to increase production were not taken, then he [Polivanov] will in his own turn be forced to resort to the most decisive actions for the inducement of punctuality of the Putilov factory."[19]

The discussion and vote on the sequestration of the Putilov factories in 1915 offers some valuable insights into the variety of opinions within the War Ministry itself. General N. I. Petrovskii, a GAU representative, spoke out against sequestration. The general noted that some of the deficiencies in the Putilov Company's completion of orders were due in part to changes in the conditions of the contracts made by GAU. In the session of the Special Commission on 18 November 1915, he specifically pointed out that because of changes required by GAU, Putilov was supposed to produce only 944 artillery pieces by 17 October 1915, not 1,208. Thus the company was not as far behind in its delivery schedule as at first appeared. Therefore, in Petrovskii's view the charges of the company's guilt were doubtful, and he opposed the sequestration.[20]

Major General G. G. Krivoshein's reluctance to sequester the factories was rooted in his concern that, initially at least, sequestration would probably reduce output at the factories because the staff and workers would have to get used to the new administration, and the new administration would need the assistance of the old board to become acquainted with all aspects of the company, including its contracts. He stated to the observatory commission of the OSO,

It is necessary to assume that the commercial results of the activity of state administration in regard to the cheapening of production will hardly be positive; . . . the administration of so large and complex an enterprise as the Putilov factories does not fall within the usual framework of administration for state factories; the state administration of the Putilov factories should be granted especially broad authority in relation to both the payment of work by the factory's technical staff and the means of buying materials, giving orders, and calculating costs with suppliers.[21]

Krivoshein acknowledged that war production had increased at the Putilov factories. However, he cited the factory administration, and not the board of directors, as the reason for the actual increase in the pace of production at the Putilov works. Therefore, Krivoshein recommended that the state administration should replace only the board of directors while retaining the factory's administration itself.[22]

While Krivoshein criticized the Putilov Company's board of directors for their laxness in mobilizing the factory's war production, other army officers did not share his view. Thus, a representative of the Artillery Department, General Lekhovich, commended the Putilov board for its accomplishments. Lekhovich noted:

If we take into consideration that production of the factory's cannon workshop consisted in peacetime of no more than 30 guns a month, but now has reached 207, then it is impossible not to recognize that the productivity of the factory increased to an extremely significant degree, and one cannot but attribute this to the service of the company's board of directors.[23]

Lekhovich concluded that for its part the current board of the Putilov Company had actively taken all measures for the implementation of increased war production and had achieved significant results, in that the factory's output had expanded two and a half times even under wartime conditions. He pointed to the general difficult conditions of the times as the main cause of the factory's deficiencies.[24]

Meanwhile, A. A. Manikovskii voiced his support for sequestration. General Manikovskii declared at the voting session that in his capacity as head of the Main Artillery Administration he would be willing to take the Putilov factories under his own administration on the same basis as the other factories of the Artillery Department.[25] Of the military officers with voting rights on the commission, four out of six voted against sequestration. The only two military proponents of sequestration were Generals Manikovskii and G. G. Mileant.[26] Thus the majority of officers did not support the Duma members' move for sequestration, whereas Manikovskii went along with their motion as long as he could be in charge of the enterprise. To put it another way, Manikovskii acted to ensure that qualified military specialists, rather than politicians with no technical expertise, would actually hold the upper hand in administering the factory. Manikovskii believed that the OSO had too many heads to function effectively and later commented, "In this enormous staff there were very few people who actually had an understanding of military technology or the causes of the deficiencies of supply for our army and who were capable of taking measures for its improvement. Indeed, there were many who saw in the OSO chiefly a tool for the political struggle and behaved accordingly."[27] Taken together, the officers' voting behavior can be interpreted as a move to block the Duma, and we can understand Manikovskii's position as part of his distrust of the Duma politicians.

In an extremely close decision, the Special Commission members voted 16–15 not to sequester the Putilov factories. Instead of sequestration, the commission decided to place three inspectors on the Putilov board of directors.[28] This result should not be considered a victory for Putilov and the board. True, the company had avoided being immediately sequestered at this time, but the board had also lost control over the direction of company affairs. Indeed, another "victory" such as this would give the War Ministry effective control of the company.

A breakdown of the voters on the commission reveals the fissures in the attitude toward sequestration. As noted, most of the military officers opposed this course of action. However, the vast majority of Duma members, ten of eleven, voted to sequester. Meanwhile, the majority of State Council members voted 5–2 against. The three representatives from the concerned ministries split their votes. The Ministry of Finance and the Ministry of Trade and Manufacturing voted against, but the Ministry of

Transport supported sequestration.[29] By and large, then, the supporters of sequestration consisted of the Duma members, and the opponents turned out to be just about everyone else: the State Council, the ministries, and the officers. Although Polivanov presided over the meeting and clearly favored the state takeover of the Putilov factories, he did not vote.

In spite of the vote not to sequester taken on 18 November 1915, Polivanov pushed for a more active role in running Putilov affairs. He wanted not only to fill the three positions on the board, but also to remove two additional directors of the company (Dreyer and Sokolovskii). In a letter to Minister of Finance P. L. Bark four days after the failed vote, the war minister proposed filling the five places with four of his own members and one named by the finance minister.[30] Given that the Finance Ministry had voted not to sequester and the vote had been so close, it is reasonable to interpret Polivanov's move as an attempt to win Finance over to his position.

The issue of the Putilov sequestration arose again in February 1916 during a major strike at the Putilov Works. According to General A. S. Lukomskii, the strike arose over economic demands.[31] The Duma members of the Special Commission again pushed for sequestration, and this time a majority of members voted for it. As A. N. Krylov later recounted, "In light of the unceasing tardiness in the completion of all orders, upon the insistence of the State Duma and State Council, it was decided to impose the sequester."[32] Polivanov and Manikovskii now got their hands on the enterprise. Why were these two officers so intent on removing the company's board of directors? Part of the answer lies in the fact that both of them had reasons to oppose A. I. Putilov specifically.

Polivanov had reason to be adversarial toward Putilov. He actively supported the main rivals of A. I. Putilov, namely, A. I. Guchkov and the Moscow industrialists involved in the War-Industries Committees. Before Polivanov's appointment as war minister, the Special Commission had been dominated by St. Petersburg–based suppliers, and in that position A. I. Putilov had managed to put together a deal whereby the Putilov Company was to arrange the distribution of orders worth 113 million rubles among nine firms, along with financing from the Russo-Asiatic Bank. Upon becoming war minister and chairman of the OSO, Polivanov changed the composition of the commission so that the Moscow War-

Industries Committee was represented, while the St. Petersburg group lost any position. He then shifted the procurement policy away from the Putilov Works.[33] The new direction was in keeping with the desires of Polivanov's old ally Guchkov.

Manikovskii was not hostile to private suppliers. In fact, he rather favored them over state factories, although he considered both inadequate. In his view, neither the state military factories nor the private Russian factories were prepared to accomplish the necessary tasks in time, and he included the Putilov works in that assessment. The problem with private factories stemmed from the fact that even though they possessed the necessary equipment, they could not maintain their own preparedness for war production without receiving new orders for military goods. As Manikovskii observed,

> Obviously, for private factories it was extremely unprofitable to leave their own machines inactive for long; having fulfilled military orders, these factories adjusted their production for other work which they received. For private factories it was also unprofitable to maintain reserves of the necessary special materials, which were demanded for military orders.[34]

Still, he found the state factories to be incomparably worse than private ones because of bureaucratic formalism and slow production. In assessing the relationship between the Main Artillery Administration and private industry, Manikovskii felt that the state factories should serve as necessary regulators of prices and technical production.[35]

Although General Manikovskii was not hostile to private suppliers, he felt nothing positive about bankers. In his memoirs he complained that almost all the private military suppliers found themselves "in the tenacious clutches of the bankers, who above all cared about extracting maximum profit and to a much lesser degree about bringing up productivity to maximum limits."[36] No doubt, Manikovskii had A. I. Putilov in mind when he wrote those words. Putilov was the head of the Russo-Asiatic Bank, and from that position he had presided over the bank's foray into defense companies. In this context, it was significant that among the twenty-eight enterprises sequestered by the OSO, three relied on the Russo-Asiatic Bank for their financing.[37]

The actual implementation of the sequestration also reveals Manikovskii's special animosity toward A. I. Putilov and the other company board members. The sequestration order prohibited Putilov and the other former board members from leading the business again even after the termination of the sequestration. This last point is an especially blatant example of the animosity toward the former board in that it was the only concrete instruction for administering the factories that Krylov and the other officers received from their superiors. As Krylov recorded,

> There was no general position about the administration of the sequestered enterprise . . . we were only informed that the business should be conducted on a 'commercial basis' and upon termination of sequestration would be returned again to the board of directors, who would be elected by a general meeting of shareholders; the former board itself being barred from leading the business.[38]

Certainly Manikovskii had reasons for wanting to take over the administration of the Putilov factories other than simple hostility toward the board. To appreciate his possible additional motives, we must consider his general attitude toward the whole procurement process. By the directions of GAU, the stockpiles were produced for the most part by means of "orders on time." The law permitted such means of preparation only when the item required a particularly high degree of skill and purity in finishing or was prepared "according to special drawings." The majority of items ordered by GAU had such requirements. Significant tardiness in delivery compared to the time set by the contracts was a common occurrence. However, it was also common for the factories to suffer additional forfeitures, especially for large orders, since in most cases the state found some defects or carelessness in assembly that held up delivery and payment. Yet, in Manikovskii's view, "The delay in delivery of orders actually rarely was the factories' fault, but was due to detailed changes in the initial blueprints and technical conditions given by the Artillery Commission."[39] These delays in filling orders were unprofitable for the factories, since delivery delays in turn hindered receipt of payment. On the other side, GAU could not get the ordered items from the factories in good time and this adversely affected the army's war readiness.

GAU also gave production assignments to its own state factories and those of the Naval and Mining Departments, but this process was not surrounded by such formality as orders to private factories. The Artillery Department concluded no contracts with the state factories of the Naval and Mining Departments, nor did it have a mechanism to guarantee the punctual fulfillment of orders. The official dealings of GAU with the state factories substituted for a contract, and GAU directed the blueprints, technical conditions, and time of manufacture of goods. However, punctual delivery times were usually not observed, and significant tardiness in the fulfillment of orders by state factories was very common for naval and mining factories because GAU had no way to compel these factories to complete their production on time.[40]

Manikovskii was also critical of the competitive bidding process for orders. He observed that the goal of this policy, lowering prices by means of competition, was not achieved because year after year the same firms took part in the bids. They got together beforehand and agreed to divide the orders among themselves, thus dictating to the state their own prices and eliminating any chance of competition.[41] On this point, Manikovskii seems unduly cynical. Recall that in the detailed contract negotiations between GAU and the Putilov board discussed earlier, GAU used the state factories as price regulators and the Putilov Company had always lowered its prices to conform with GAU's expectations.

Besides not holding down prices, in Manikovskii's opinion the competitive bidding process also contributed to production delays. Although the law recognized orders by competitive contract as the accepted normal operating procedure, he claimed, these contracts were filled even more slowly than others: "This means was employed comparatively rarely for large orders given directly by GAU; however, it was unavoidable for preparations of machines and mechanisms, material, fuel, etc."[42]

If Manikovskii's precise reasons for advocating sequestration prior to February 1916 are unclear, his later administrative policies give some clues as to his motivations. In an attempt to direct the Putilov factories just like any other works owned by GAU, Manikovskii started by eliminating the contractual process for procurement. He announced, "All contracts concluded between GAU and the Putilov factories up to the imposition of the sequester—since February 28—are no longer in force. Goods previously under such contracts will be produced on the general basis in the form of assignments."[43] After the sequestration, the factories technically remained private property, but Manikovskii canceled all the old contracts and eliminated the Russo-Asiatic Bank as a factor in the enterprise.[44] Although these moves may have cut costs, they certainly worked to remove any influence A. I. Putilov might still have had over the company through his bank. Along with removal of the bankers, though, Manikovskii's move to change the basis of the relationship with the Putilov enterprise from contracts to assignments was intended to solve the chief problem that he had identified in his assessment of the procurement process. By getting rid of the contractual basis, Manikovskii was trying to streamline procurement.

Manikovskii reflected, "In time of war it was difficult to force a private factory to convert to [single-type] production, although it would be very important for the army."[45] From the army's standpoint, it was easier to make conversions in production at the state works. For example, "The Putilov factory up until the tranfer to state administration made almost no 152mm shells, [but] after the transfer it began to turn out almost half of the total number of these shells manufactured in Russia."[46] This conversion points to another possible reason for Manikovskii's support for sequestration, namely, that it would enable GAU to control directly the factory's responsiveness to the Artillery Department's technical requirements and product demands. As noted, the general liked that aspect of GAU's dealings with state factories.

Perhaps the most significant advantage Manikovskii saw in sequestration was that it restricted company profits and prices. In a letter to the war minister dated 17 August 1916, Manikovskii instructed the Governing Board to calculate the price for these orders without any profit because the laws gave no precise directives. If some new law were to define what was a fair profit, then Manikovskii would make adjustments in previous prices ordered from Putilov. He also commented, "Even without calculating any profit, the prices estimated by the Governing Board for all goods of the Putilov factories are very high compared with similar private and state factories receiving orders from GAU."[47]

The one aspect of the private procurement process of which Manikovskii approved concerned the compulsion of factories to complete orders on time under the threat of fines and forfeitures. Since the Putilov enterprise was still considered private property, the factory could still be accountable for any delays in delivery. Manikovskii made sure that this condition remained in force for the period of state administration.[48]

In summary, then, Manikovskii identified a number of problems with the existing process of procurement. Although both state and private factories as a rule completed their orders behind schedule, the bidding and contract procedures that were imposed on private firms delayed their commencement of the production line. Also, GAU contributed to the tardiness of private orders by changing the specifications in the middle of the contract time. Meanwhile, state factories fell behind because there was no way for GAU to pressure them to stay on schedule. Viewed in this context, Manikovskii's support for sequestering the Putilov factories is more understandable. In effect, the general created a system of factory administration that (in his view) combined the positive features of the previous state and private procurement procedures.

The fact that GAU was not actually hostile to private enterprise can be seen in the way it administered the Putilov factories after taking control. After closing the books on the account year for 1916, the Governing Board reported a profit for the year of 13 million rubles. This figure was based on the definition of pure profit according to article 41 of the company's charter. However, the board considered that level of profit too high and lowered the amount to 8 million rubles. From this lower amount, the board allocated the bulk of the profits, some 5 million rubles, to be spent on the cancellation of property costs in line with article 45 of the charter. The Governing Board then divided the remaining 3 million rubles of profit between taxes (1 million) and distribution to shareholders (2 million). Unlike a typical profit distribution, though, no sums went for awards to the directors of the board or staff.[49]

It would appear, then, that the state administration of the Putilov factories satisfied the state's demands for defense goods and the shareholders' desire for dividends. However, a closer look at the accounts reveals how the avowedly antiprofit state administration managed to achieve such high profits. The simple answer was loans. In 1916 the Main Artillery Administration paid out a total of 35 million rubles in seven separate loan disbursements between 31 March and 23 November 1916.[50] Put another way, in 1916 GAU loaned the Putilov factories the equivalent of almost the entire annual production of the factories in 1914, or about 40 percent of the value of production in 1916.

In light of the evidence, and especially the testimony of the army officers themselves, the explanation that the sequestration was simply part of the general mobilization effort does not appear very satisfying on two counts. First, as Krivoshein observed, sequestration would probably reduce production, at least at first. Second, other officers provided evidence showing that the Putilov factories were not horrendously behind in the delivery of war items and had actually increased production dramatically. General Drozdov, the officer who ultimately served as chief director of the factory after the imposition of the sequester, reported to the Governing Board in October 1916 that production at the Putilov factories averaged around 3.25 million rubles per month in 1914 and that production jumped to an average of 7.52 million rubles per month in 1915. In terms of total annual output, production had increased under the private board from 39.0 million rubles in 1914 to 90.2 million rubles in 1915.[51] It should also be kept in mind that almost every armament producer in Russia, state-owned or private, was behind in filling orders.[52]

Furthermore, the labor issue did not prove to be the deciding issue for GAU either. Although no doubt the strikes in February 1916 were decisive in switching the votes of State Council members in favor of sequestration, Polivanov started to take control of the board of directors even before the sequestration. So, from the point of view of GAU, the implementation of the Governing Board in February 1916 seems more in line with the creeping expansion of control from the War Ministry than a sudden response to strikes. What is clear from the discussions is that War Minister Polivanov and the head of GAU, Manikovskii, actively supported sequestration. In conclusion, one explanation for GAU's involvement in the sequestration of the Putilov factories can be found in its leaders' resentment toward the company's board of directors, and especially A. I. Putilov. This is not to say that hostility was the sole reason for sequestration. Other players were involved who initiated and advocated such action. Whether they were trying to eliminate a powerful rival supplier to the benefit of Moscow firms, or vying with the bureaucracy for more control in directing the war effort, Guchkov and the Duma members had their own reasons for promoting the sequestration of Putilov.

However, the real impetus for sequestration emanated from the Duma members of the OSO. Polivanov supported them for his own reasons having to do with his personal connections to the Moscow War-

Industries Committee and Guchkov. One can speculate that Manikovskii went along with the sequestration because he wanted to make sure that the Duma members did not get their hands on Russia's largest war enterprise. Manikovskii supported sequestration on the grounds that it would remove the influence of the banks and that it would afford an opportunity to combine the favorable methods of procurement for state and private enterprises. In this respect, there were certain advantages in not simply converting the factory into state property.

The Russian War Ministry's concerns about civilian interference, excessive profits, and the sequestration of private factories has much in common with the situation in other countries during the war years. In Austria, the Emergency War Law empowered the War Ministry to take over and run factories, and wartime decrees provided a legal basis for the complete elimination of private industry, including controls over heavy industry and profit ceilings. In Germany, the Law of Siege allowed the military to interfere in the internal affairs of procurement. In a manner very similar to the Russian case, the German War Ministry changed the system of contracts in 1915 so that old contracts were revised downward and new contracts imposed profit limits. In addition, the new regime enabled ministerial oversight through the examination of company accounts and investigation of company operations. As part of a hardening position toward industry, the new war contracts added clauses concerning punishments for miscalculation of costs or late delivery. In France, the law of 3 August 1914 allowed for the expropriation of civilian-owned factories. This power was left in the hands of the military, not civil authority. The French Ministry of War authorized such requisitions, and it was the army that ran the factory once it was seized. Even in the United States the army evinced suspicion and hostility toward civilian institutions and considered civilian mobilization agencies as a threat to professional military prerogatives.[53]

Manikovskii might have thought he was saving the government money, but in fact the state ultimately paid dearly for his policies. The government's Governing Board began to complain of the same difficulties that the private board had expressed about the artillery business. The Putilov Company's financial difficulties prior to being sequestered continued to plague the Governing Board after it assumed control of the factories. In particular, the cash flow deficit posed a serious problem for the continued operation of the works. Krivoshein reported to the commission that Putilov's financial condition turned out to be even weaker than expected because increases in workers' pay added about 5 million rubles to the factories' costs.[54] Moreover, Ogloblinskii and Krivoshein were almost completely overwhelmed by the company's estimates of income and expenditures. In part, the difficulty was due to insufficient experience with the accounts for the Putilov enterprise. Additionally, they complained that "for various reasons it was extremely difficult to estimate precisely in advance the time of reception of payment for the completion of orders."[55] The old complaints about the delays in payment were now coming from the mouths of state officials.

The Governing Board reported in 1917, "The sale price of a significant part of the manufactured goods reckoned according to contracts concluded in 1913 and 1914 turned out to be extremely unprofitable for the enterprise of the Company under conditions of war time."[56] As a result, the sale prices for orders taken for fulfillment in 1915 and 1916 became insufficient to cover production expenditures. Again, the similarity with A. K. Voigt's complaints in 1905–1907 are striking. Also, there were signs of decreasing worker productivity. For the first six months of 1917, the total of goods produced reached almost 58 million rubles, compared to 47 million rubles for the same period in 1916, but workers' pay for the period in 1917 was 37 million rubles against 14 million in 1916. So while total output increased by about 11 million rubles, labor costs increased by 23 million rubles.[57]

Throughout 1917 the Governing Board continued to experience financial difficulties in administering the Putilov factories. In May Manikovskii petitioned the Ministry of Finance for another loan of 28 million rubles to cover expenses, including workers' pay from March through September. For its own part, the board explained that the Putilov workers were not satisfied with the 23 percent increase they had received in March, and in April they had expressed new demands. This new demand for a 33 percent increase amounted to "almost two times the excessive gross profit estimated by the board of the company for the preceding operating year 1916."[58] The Governing Board noted that the demand for a pay increase had implications for all the factories of the country and could possibly raise the production costs of all goods.[59]

In June the board heard a report regarding workers' demands for pay increases. Upon learning that the additional pay would cost the factory about 3 million more rubles per month, the board observed:

> The Putilov Company does not have any available means, and the money assigned by the state for orders cannot cover these new demands of the workers and employees, in light of this the Governing Board is physically denied the possibility to satisfy the declared demands, . . . the worker demands raise general questions which have significance for all of Petrograd.[60]

Putilov's financial condition continued to deteriorate. GAU learned in late September that the factory had only 200,000 rubles on hand, and that the company needed to receive 8.5 million rubles quickly in order to pay the workers. By October 1917, the board would be unable to pay the workers and to purchase materials. In the wake of the Bolshevik revolution, the Putilov shareholders held what was to be their final meeting on 23 November 1917. At that meeting, the shareholders gave their assent for the Governing Board to approach GAU for another loan. In March 1918 the board at Putilov petitioned the Supreme Soviet of the People's Economy for 7 million rubles to pay workers and another 19.25 million to cover expenditures since January.[61]

Although the important role of Putilov workers in the revolutionary events of 1917 is well established, the business context that pushed them into the streets has not been properly appreciated. The strategic decisions taken by Putilov's board of directors turned the factory into the empire's premiere artillery supplier. However, as a consequence of that achievement, the company endured chronic cash flow shortages because of the War Ministry's payment practices, which delayed full payment for defense contracts until the completion of an entire order. In a way, the board's decisions affected the financial condition of the factory, which in turn carried political implications for the state. Research on the workers' role in 1917 highlights their quest for job security and wages.[62] These sore points had been exacerbated as a result of the board's prewar expansion plans that left the company overextended and insufficiently liquid when World War I broke out. Putilov profits were already decreasing in 1914, compared to the volume of output. The company was feeling the shocks as the board tried to pull out of naval production and retool for greater artillery and shell production. All the resources that had been poured into naval production could not save the company.

By assuming control of the company in 1916, the government now had to confront a problem partially of its own making. After all, the Putilov Company had devoted so much to naval expansion because the government had chosen to reconstruct the fleet over a more expansive equipping of the army. Also, once they were put on the receiving end of War Ministry payment policies, the Governing Board felt the squeeze even more than the private board had because of Manikovskii's insistence that Putilov not make a profit on defense orders. Finally, by taking direct control of the factories, the government could not avoid being identified as the adversary of labor. Although some of the officials on the Governing Board were not unsympathetic to workers' demands for higher wages, the plain and simple truth was that the company did not have the money to give.

6

CONCLUSION

BETWEEN STATE AND MARKET

Internationally, the steel and capital goods markets shared some distinctive characteristics that conditioned the formation of common business strategies regardless of country. Therefore, it is best to avoid any attempt to identify defining "national" characteristics of business behavior. There was no single "Russian way" of doing business any more than there was a single American, French, German, or British way. Firms tended to have more in common with businesses in the same sector regardless of nationality. Generally, firms produced steel commodities only according to specified orders that established quality, size, and quantity. Consequently, steel producers did not maintain large stocks in inventory and did not produce large stocks in periods of slack orders. Sellers could not influence the steel market by holding large stocks, and demand was rarely directed toward existing commodities. Instead, it was a firm's ability and preparedness to produce goods for the future that mattered most.[1] Like the steel producers, capital goods builders faced particular kinds of concerns in market demand, customer relations, and product innovation. As John Brown shows for U.S. locomotive producers, the narrow markets for capital equipment builders gave buyers a strong voice in design, and the producers themselves were constantly forced to innovate to keep up with the pace of technical change. Unlike manufacturers who made goods and then sold them, engineering firms such as locomotive builders most often had to compete for contracts and then create the product according to the specifications of the contract. As a result, capital goods builders could not cushion themselves against fluctuating sales by producing for inventory or by trying to foster demand through advertising. Over the course of the boom-and-bust cycle, competition intensified as sales declined and then weakened as they rose. When demand slackened, engineering producers competed in price and credit terms, whereas in times of strong market demand the firm that could deliver the goods more quickly won out. As a survival strategy, builders sought to optimize their assests and expertise through diversification by turning out a range of complementary products.[2]

The sharp fluctuations in market demand and the corresponding volatility in sales were so frequent and so potentially devastating that engineering firms considered profits to be secondary to long-term survival. Locomotive builders could do little to influence the volume of demand through advertising because in times of slow sales their main customers, the railroads, opted to delay new purchases until they were absolutely necessary. In effect, market demand was identical to output; therefore, advertising or salesmanship could not overcome this basic fact. Since the vital issue for the locomotive industry was the cyclical demand for engines, the industry sought to smooth out the sharp peaks and valleys of the market through price fixing and market-sharing agreements.[3] These agreements constituted the formation of a cartel. Generally speaking, cartels consisted of multiple firms that functioned independently, as opposed to one single economic unit that in itself comprised a marketing unit. The cartel's purposes were to restrict or minimize possible competition among its member firms and to establish collective marketing controls based on mutual agreement.[4]

Soviet historians devoted much effort to characterizing the stages of development of a monopoly. Basing their definitions on Lenin's, they usually defined cartels as characterized by pricing agreements. Cartels then became syndicates, which were distinguished from cartels by the addition of a coordinating sales office that unified the members' activities. The process of monopolization then evolved into finance capitalism whereby the banks coordinated whole enterprises instead of particular divisions.[5] The Putilov Company's participation in cartels and its cooperation with other firms generally do not conform to this framework. The problem with applying the Soviet historians' interpretation is that it denies any agency to the individual firm itself.

Putilov's directors exhibited an ongoing preference for interfirm cooperation over competition. In this regard the company participated in cartel agreements that affected almost all of its various product lines. Beginning with agreements covering rail production, the company expanded its cartel activities to encompass railroad cars, bridge construction, locomotives, artillery shells, and even warship turrets. An examination of Putilov's cartel practices recasts other Gerschenkronian assumptions about the tsarist economy. In Gerschenkron's words, "Like the banks in Germany, the Russian bureaucracy was primarily interested in large-scale enterprises and in amalgamations and coordinated policies among the industrial enterprises which it favored and helped create."[6] Contrary to this view, the Putilov case shows that the impetus for joining cartels originated with the firms themselves; neither the bureaucracy nor the banks played a commanding role.

Rail and Locomotive Cartels

In the United States, beginning in 1877 steel rail producers effectively controlled pricing through the Bessemer Association. By limiting access to technology, the Bessemer Association replaced the competitive market with administrative coordination. Through the association and its successor organizations, American rail producers managed to determine the price for steel rails among themselves until 1915. In the American case, therefore, classic free-market conditions were inoperative. Railroads and steel mills were coordinated because "the users and producers could be owned and controlled by the same (railroad) corporation."[7]

In Western Europe, one of the first international steel cartels grew up around the steel rail market. By 1883 British, Belgian, and German producers of heavy rails had created an International Association of Rail Makers in an attempt to blunt the sharp competition among them for exports. Although this intial association disintegrated in 1890, it was reestablished in 1904 and expanded to include Luxembourg. American firms soon joined as well, and special agreements with Russian, Austrian, and Italian steel works limited the potential destabilizing force of smaller competitors in the export market.[8] In France the Comptoir des Rails was officially formed in November 1887 when six firms agreed to pursue in common all the orders for steel rails and also to set up a market-sharing quota system. The precipitous fall in demand and prices for rails in France prompted the founding of this cartel.

With the completion of the French domestic railroad network, investment dwindled. Furthermore, since railroads ordered rails and rolling stock only during the expansion phase, the downward cycle of the market led to a virtual collapse in production by 1885. French producers therefore looked to the Comptoir des Rails as a defensive measure to prevent any further decline in their market position. To that end, the Comptoir was organized on the basis of market sharing (quotas) and price fixing. The Comptoir des Rails was the first steel cartel, and it continued until 1914, growing to include ten firms. However, it did not have a central sales office to establish common pricing in advance. Instead, Comptoir participants met monthly to decide the distribution of orders based on the inquiries each had received from potential customers. The cartel set quotas based on tonnage. In Germany a similar steel rail syndicate had been organized in 1876 as a result of the same market pressures.[9]

The very first cartel in Russia concerned rail producers. On 1 June 1882, five factories (Putilov, Briansk, Warsaw Steel, Huta-Bankova, and Alexandrov) signed an agreement to form a union *(soiuz)* for pooling all orders for steel rails and dividing them among the union members. The firms agreed in principle to all charge the same price, and they created an administrative representative to negotiate for and to distribute the orders. The agreement lasted five years.[10] At the time of the signing, the Putilov Company actually belonged to the State Bank, but in 1883 the Warsaw and Briansk group bought Putilov and held it until 1885. After 1885 Putilov resumed operation as an independent firm under its own board of directors but continued to honor the cartel agreement.[11]

Almost simultaneously, Putilov engaged in a trilateral agreement with Briansk and Lilpop, Rau, and Löwenstein affecting bridge construction. Like the rail producers' cartel, the purpose of the bridge producers' convention concerned the distribution of orders and setting prices among the three factories. Putilov occupied the most junior position in this arrangement and was allocated only 18 percent market share, compared to 44 percent for Briansk and 38 percent for Lilpop. Specifically, the contracting parties sought "to struggle successfully against competing factories."[12] Although the original agreement had a three-year term, the basic contours remained in effect until 1892.[13]

After the rail producers' cartel had lapsed, Putilov entered into a similar arrangement for cars. In 1889 Putilov, Briansk, and Kolomna established the Union of Railroad Car-building Factories.[14] The number later expanded to include Dneprovsk, Lilpop, and the Baltic Wagon Factory in 1893.[15] From these beginnings emerged the more formal structure of the railroad car builders' syndicate, Prodvagon, which ultimately embraced fourteen producers and received formal sanction by the government in 1904.[16]

Price fixing and collusive behavior among locomotive producers proved to be common phenomena in industrializing countries in the nineteenth and early twentieth centuries. The frequent recourse to these practices in different national settings derived from the shared general characteristics of locomotive markets. In each country a limited number of heavily capitalized producers regularly faced periods of declining sales and too much productive capacity. Some form of cooperative arrangement among producers could help spread the risks and ensure survival. In the United States, locomotive firms often tried to fix prices, although these agreements never proved to be long-lived. In 1857 twelve American locomotive producers met for the first time to establish fixed pricing among themselves, and they repeated such efforts in 1862 and 1872. In 1891 ten firms created the American Locomotive Manufacturers Association. Beginning in 1892, the firms considered forming a horizontal combination, and these plans came to fruition in 1901 when the majority of American locomotive producers established the American Locomotive Company (ALCO) as a holding company. The ten firms in ALCO in combination achieved a rough parity with the Baldwin Locomotive Works, which was the largest U.S. locomotive builder and not a member of ALCO. By 1901 the American locomotive industry consisted of ALCO and Baldwin.[17]

In France, too, locomotive builders responded to the problems of the boom-and-bust pattern by coming together formally as a cartel. French engineering firms lacked the productive capacity to handle all the orders during the boom of the 1890s, with the result that Belgian and German firms gained orders at French expense. This prompted the French locomotive builders to found the Railroad Matériel Manufacturers' Association in 1899. The Association aimed to pressure the railroad companies to pursue more regular purchasing policies. As in the American case,

French railroads placed equipment orders during peak years so that they could pay for them from current receipts, and this amplified the intensity of the boom-and-bust cycle. The French association envisioned a sales policy along the lines of the German model whereby the state railroad administration cooperated with the producers' groups to distribute annual orders with greater regularity.[18]

The Russian locomotive cartel commenced operation on 3 December 1901. Originally, members agreed to a five-year term, and they renewed the arrangement through 1914. In 1907 the organization's council applied to the government for legal recognition as the Company for Trade in Goods of Russian Locomotive-Building Factories. The organization included all of Russia's locomotive producers except three enterprises. The state, however, refused to grant permission.[19] According to the protocol from the founding session, the union's activities included distributing orders, establishing prices, and setting assembly times for locomotives and tenders. Under the initial division, four of the founding companies received 14.75 percent each (Putilov, Kolomna, Briansk, Sormovo), while two were apportioned 14 percent (Hartman and Khar'kov). The remaining 13 percent was designated for the Nevskii Shipbuilding factory, which did not formally sign at this time but agreed to adhere to the provisions.[20]

The union's council coordinated the distribution and exercised oversight for affairs. The council consisted of one representative from each member company, from whom a president and his assistant were elected. The factories receiving orders were not to transfer them in full or in part, and equally could not cancel orders among themselves without the permission of the union.[21] Under article 16 of the protocol, "The council discusses all enquiries put forth by state and private persons and institutions, makes considerations about probable time of filling orders, about proposals for the transfer to foreign factories or for output for the foreign market, and about competing prices with foreign factories."[22] Finally, all matters and decisions of the union required the agreement of no fewer than four votes of those representatives present at the council's sessions, and the council could levy fines against members for infractions of the terms.[23]

For the most part, the management of the union's affairs flowed smoothly. If companies appeared to stray from the agreement, the council did intervene. However, such interventions were rare, and the council tended to rebuke errant participants verbally rather than disciplining them financially through fines. In September 1902 the council learned that Putilov had petitioned the State Railroad Administration for an order of twenty-six locomotives instead of securing them through the council. Basing its decision on article 1 of the union protocol, the council forced Putilov to entrust its order to the council. As a result, Putilov only received an order for eight locomotives, while the remaining eighteen were reapportioned among other union members.[24]

In another case in September 1903, Putilov and Kolomna were competing for a private locomotive order simultaneously. To resolve this problem, the council announced that in the future factories had to inform the council no more than a week from the day they received official notification of a proposal from a customer.[25] Two weeks later, Putilov and Kolomna again confronted each other over orders. This time the council assigned the order to Kolomna.[26] As yet another example of the types of minor friction between Putilov and the union, in the session of 16 February 1905 the board of the Putilov Company informed the council of an inquiry from the Khar'kov factory asking how many locomotives Putilov could prepare that year. The council noted that all factories had to process inquiries through the council rather than dealing directly with one another.[27] Despite these instances, apparently the benefits of cooperation outweighed those of more independent behavior for the Putilov Company; in the session of 3 November 1906, the Putilov representative, S. V. Zhdanov, declared a proposal to extend the existing charter of Prodparavoz, since the cartel was scheduled to expire the following month.[28] Obviously, the Putilov board found the arrangement advantageous enough to warrant its continuation.

In the years ahead, Putilov seemed to chafe less under the restrictions of the union. This was evident from the decreasing complaints about Putilov's behavior from the other members. The only notable exception occurred in January 1908 when the Nevskii representative called the council's attention to the improper activity of the Putilov factory. Specifically, "The board of the Nevskii Company considers it necessary to express its protest of the appearance of competition among participants of the Council."[29] Nevskii's complaint centered on Putilov's attempts to steal orders away by offering the Southeastern Railroad an earlier delivery date than Nevskii could accomplish. Nevskii explained to the council that in late December 1907 it had been negotiating with the president of the Southeastern Railroad for the assembly of eleven locomotives by August 1908. The railroad's board of directors did not want to wait until August, since the Putilov factory had said that if the order were transferred to it, these eleven locomotives could be delivered in February and March, and on the basis of this statement the Southeastern Railroad considered the order given to the Nevskii factory to be void.[30] In this case, the council resolved the dispute by prohibiting Putilov from fulfilling this order.[31]

Judging by the sales results, it seems that the council achieved an equitable division of locomotive orders among union members. The council recorded the following distribution of locomotive orders for the years 1902–1911: Briansk, 1,127 locomotives; Hartman, 1,197; Nevskii, 1,064; Putilov, 1,004; Sormovo, 1,137; and Khar'kov, 1,001. In terms of value, Hartman, Putilov, and Sormovo each received 43 million rubles' worth of locomotive orders; Nevskii had 40 million; Khar'kov 38 million; while Briansk received the most, with almost 50 million rubles.[32]

The locomotive cartel functioned as an empirewide distribution system for the firms that were geographically dispersed. The firms themselves were situated in the Moscow region, in Nizhnii-Novgorod, in Lugansk, and in Khar'kov, and two were in St. Petersburg: Putilov and Nevskii. Part of the reason for the dispute between Putilov and Nevskii in 1908 could have been their location.[33] They were the only two participants in the same place. Ultimately, Putilov eliminated any further con-

Table 6.1

Number of Locomotives Produced by the Putilov Company, 1894–1914

	Russian Total	*Putilov Company*	*(%)*
1894–1898	2,391	534	(22)
1899–1903	5,187	786	(15)
1904–1908	5,102	564	(11)
1909–1914	3,129	378	(12)

Source: Il'inskii and Ivanitskii, *Ocherk istorii russkoi,* 79, 90, 98, 103.

flicts by purchasing Nevskii and unifying the operations of the two firms. This also effectively doubled the share of the enterprise within the cartel. A similar merger occurred between Sormovo and Kolomna.

Putilov's prominence in Russian locomotive production is evident in the figures shown in table 6.1.

The locomotive cartel provides important clues to the condition of the private market in Russia. In keeping track of all the orders for union members, the council amassed fairly complete output statistics. More important, as a matter of course the council divided the orders between state and private customers. Although it would be premature to draw any definitive conclusions for the entire Russian locomotive market without a truly comprehensive study of all railroad companies, state purchases, and suppliers, it is possible to assess the role of the state as a customer both for Putilov and the cartel as a whole. By far the most dramatic evidence for the preeminence of private over state orders in Putilov's production comes from the figures reported to the locomotive cartel after the turn of the century. A glance at Putilov's distribution reveals the overwhelming predominance of the private market over state customers. For the period 1901–1912, the Putilov Company's annual output for private customers averaged approximately 81 percent. However, the trend clearly favored a decreasing state share from 28 percent in 1901 to 10 percent by 1912.[34] Putilov's ever increasing business in the private market before 1914 calls into question the notion that armaments became the driving engine for growth in the Russian economy.[35]

Even though Putilov relied much more on private customers than the state for its total sales, the company's state orders were hardly insignificant. A breakdown of its locomotive sales, for example, reveals heavy reliance on the State Railroad Administration. Between 1902 and 1911, Putilov sold 733 locomotives to the state, as opposed to 271 to private customers. The difference was also reflected in the total value of the sales. State orders generated 32.1 million rubles, compared to only 11.2 million rubles from private sales.[36]

The preponderance of locomotive orders by the state was characteristic of the cartel as a whole. While the private share generally increased, it did so as part of a shrinking total after 1906. For example, in 1903 cartel producers made 220 locomotives for private customers, as opposed to

762 for the state. By 1911 private locomotive orders amounted to 109, while state orders had dropped to 193.[37] Moreover, in none of those years did private orders exceed state orders in either quantity or ruble value.

The output figures for the companies together paint a more complicated picture. The total business of the cartel companies including all goods, not just locomotives, averaged about 50 percent private over the 1901–1912 period. However, the trend toward a larger percentage of private customers than state orders became clear from 1910 onward. The value of state sales peaked in 1905 at 55.7 million rubles and dropped to 23.9 million rubles in 1912. Meanwhile, the value of private orders increased from 24.1 million rubles in 1905 to 62.0 million in 1912.[38] Thus, Putilov turned out to be less dependent on state orders than the cartel as a whole.

Another way of gauging the company's perception of the available consumer market is to consider its approach toward commercial advertising. The Putilov Company pursued only limited advertising. The few examples of public advertising appeared in the trade journal *Promyshlennost' i Torgovlia*, which was published by the Association of Industry and Trade. The journal itself had a circulation around 3,000 copies, both domestically and abroad, and its readership consisted of business groups and government officials. Although Putilov's advertisements were not particularly imaginative, they did reflect a changing profile of primary products offered by the company away from varieties of steel and locomotive goods toward factory and construction equipment. For example, in 1911 Putilov's full-page advertisement consisted of a simple list of product categories. Various kinds of steel stood at the top of the list, followed by instrument steel, locomotives, railroad cars, bridges, railroad switches, cranes, coal unloaders, oil presses, and rolling presses. Artillery and shipbuilding were at the bottom of the list.[39]

By 1913 Putilov's advertisements rearranged the order of the products and gave priority to oil presses, factory equipment for cotton factories, presses for flour mills, paper shops, and resin factories as the first category. Internal combustion motors, steam machinery, and turbines moved up to second place, followed by iron structures in third. Other new products near the top included presses for stearin, plywood, pasta, and gramophone records in fourth place. Locomotives, railroad cars, and artillery all disappeared from the advertisements.[40] In short, Putilov's product line as advertised was now oriented toward supplying other factories with equipment for manufacturing consumer goods.

Conclusions

Before turning specifically to the question of the state's role in Putilov's development, we must first consider the problem of state and market, and Putilov's position between the two. As an ideal "pure" form, a market is usually conceived as composed of a number of buyers and sellers who have command of all the appropriate information for making transactions, and competition among the sellers (and perhaps the buyers) that leads to a uniform price that the market can bear. However, in actual practice a number of "impurities" exist in the real market. Perfect information is unlikely, and many prices are not actually set by competition, but "administered."[41] Furthermore, the relationship between state and market is not necessarily a zero-sum game, that is, a conflict between the two.[42] If an enterprise manufactures goods to sell to a customer, and that customer happens to be a government agency, it does not automatically follow that the transaction was excluded from the market. Yet often a stigma is attached to an enterprise that serves a state customer. Such an enterprise is considered in some way artificial or dependent because it seems unable to sustain itself legitimately in the "real" consumer market. This brings up an important point: neither the state nor the market is a monolithic entity, and one must recognize the differentiated nature of any given market.[43]

Nevertheless, the attempt to distinguish between production for the state from production for the market is not inappropriate. Putilov's directors themselves made the distinction, as did their contemporaries. In the early period of the company, the term *market* identified the chaotic realm where large quantities of low-cost goods were sold. For example, in the Putilov Company's annual accounts for 1883–1892, a regular section was designated "goods for market sale."[44] In this instance, the market was not contrasted to the state. The term was used to identify goods that were not produced according to a specific contract, but instead were sold according to unsolicited and unpredictable demand. Such items for the market included railroad ties, nails, and other small metal objects. Beginning in 1893, such products were recorded under the relevant departmental production figures, and the heading "goods for market sale" fell into disuse. Even around the turn of the century, though, the official history of the Putilov Company observed that the crucible workshop was the first in Russia to produce steel instruments "for the market" (na rynok).[45] At one of the shareholders' meetings in 1910, the board of directors announced that prospects looked encouraging because not only had the company received a large artillery order, but "besides this, the work of the Putilov plant for the market was growing stronger."[46]

Yet there were also indications that Putilov's directors did not perceive production for the state as inherently artificial. When discussing the prospects for naval construction, the board expressed the view that since the creation of a modern shipbuilding works with state-of-the-art equipment and large special technical capabilities would be possible only if there were some guarantee of continued work, the naval rearmament program offered an excellent opportunity for sustained growth. In this instance, Putilov's shipbuilding could grow because it would have a multiyear time frame and "a program sufficiently broad that the work of private works would not be artificial but actually a necessity for the aid to existing state works."[47] Here, *artificial* implied a one-time production prospect as opposed to long-term orders. So state orders for warships were not necessarily considered artificial if they provided multiyear contracts.

In combination, the advertisements and the cartel figures would seem to confirm Gerschenkron's argument for a decreasing role of the state and the growth of an autonomous market prior to the outbreak of the First World War. Yet we are confronted with a paradox. How can we reconcile the apparently low share of Putilov's total output for the state with the much higher percentages for artillery output presented in the annual account books and the firm's behavior as the classic defense producer? Since artillery must be considered a product for state consumption rather than private, how can we explain the contradictory impressions given by the data? How could artillery comprise 30–40 percent of the factory's annual output when the state share of Putilov's total production did not exceed 20 percent in any of those years?

The answer lies in the difference between the time of production and the time of realization of the sale. In effect, artillery production did not really count as a part of factory income until the company could sell the pieces and receive payment. However, under the payment policies of the Artillery Department and the War Ministry, the company could be paid only after the completion of the entire contract. As Putilov committed more and more to the artillery business, the proportion of its backlog of inventory increased. Thus, during the years 1911–1914 the annual unsold inventory amounted to the equivalent of about 40 percent of annual output, most of it consisting of artillery and naval products.[48] So in terms of the overall company performance, the state share did not predominate, but it did occupy a pivotal position in the company's financial well-being, and that share was increasing up to 1914. To consider it in another way, Putilov could survive financially in any given year without artillery sales because it maintained a sufficient private market share to sustain itself. The proof lies in the fact that the company endured the long intervals between payments for artillery orders and still achieved sizable profits. Essentially, the state served as Putilov's single biggest customer, but the private customers provided the backbone of the company's profits in any given year.

For artillery and naval orders, obviously the company looked to the state as its customer, but any defense producer relies on some state somewhere as its market. The state called the tune on pricing, length of terms, and fines. Also, the government's choice to favor naval construction over field artillery after 1905 created a demand to which Putilov responded. This proved to have negative consequences both for the state and Putilov during World War I.

In terms of financial support, the state role in Putilov's development was indirect. The State Bank did bail out the company under N. I. Putilov, but after 1883 the company most definitely turned to private sources for investment. Initially, Moscow banking firms provided the financial backing, and in its second incarnation the company drew on the resources of the joint-stock banks, including some German ones. Primarily, the Putilov Company arranged its own financing and capital from domestic banks. Only in 1912 did French capital become directly involved, and then as a minority.

In the process of advanced technology transfers from the West to Russia, again the firm was not dependent on the state, but in fact demonstrated independence. Putilov developed its own technical agreements with foreign firms or designed its own product line, as in the case of the 3-inch field gun. Also, Putilov served as the transmitter of new technology and processes to state arsenals and shipyards. In effect, Putilov pulled the state up to its level.

How dependent was Putilov on the state? It can rightly be said that the state created the demand for many of the company's product lines. This was especially true in the case of artillery and naval orders. However, the company itself created the means to supply that demand and in addition developed its own private markets, which enabled it to persevere in the long intervals without payment from the government. As a strategy to secure that vital private market share, the directors of the Putilov Company participated in multiple cartel arrangements that covered almost all its diverse product lines. Judging from the evidence, it would seem that the Putilov Company survived in spite of artillery orders, rather than because of them. As a conclusion, regarding the question of Putilov's degree of state dependence, it is more accurate to say that Putilov's board was responsive to the state rather than dependent on it. For its market the company was already relying much more on the private sector by 1900.

How dependent was the state on Putilov? Except for artillery supplies, the answer seems to be that its dependence was negligible. The company rarely got what it wanted from the state. Putilov could not renegotiate the terms of payment, and the government avoided complete dependence on any single supplier. Nor were there signs of any real military-industrial complex, although retired low-level bureaucrats and low-ranking retired officers did work for the company. There was hardly a cozy relationship on either side. The absence of strong support from state institutions helps to explain why Putilov was sequestered in 1916: the company had few supporters or sympathizers in the ministries and only enemies in the Duma after 1907. The elaborate financial and technical arrangements with Skoda and licensing deals with Blohm und Voss, which were arranged in the years immediately preceding the outbreak of World War I, clearly reveal how unexpected the war was for these arms producers. They also show how far out of official circles war industrialists were in Russia.

Unfortunately, owing to the lack of sufficient material from Putilov's board members, one can only speculate about their political views. The directors left no memoirs, nor were they active participants in the political and professional organizations of the time. Antsyforov, Voigt, and Von Dreyer, the key actors in the company's leadership, remain virtually invisible to us. Nor did they figure as players in the industrial associations. A. I. Putilov did appear as a leading character, but, as this study has argued, his role in the Putilov Company itself has been greatly overstated. The absence of such behavior suggests that the company's directors concerned themselves primarily with business and did not see themselves as any kind of bourgeoisie.

The Putilov Company's market behavior was consistent with that of other European and American industrial enterprises. Through its participation in a wide array of cartel agreements, Putilov managed to exploit a national distribution network. Also, the firm's activities within the locomotive cartel seemed relatively harmonious and can fairly be interpreted as showing a preference for market sharing along the lines practiced in Germany or France.[49] The commonality of this business behavior should mitigate any notions that it represented a particular cultural attribute. Cartels were not peculiar to the United States, Germany, France, or Russia. Moreover, such preferences were not manifestations of a culturally conditioned rejection of competition. There was a regional component to competition in Russia that erupted in full force during World War I. It is enough to conclude that Putilov's behavior in the Russian market would have been intelligible to directors in the West.

That is not to say that Russia was not unique in other ways. Certainly the autocratic tradition and conceptions of political power and authority in tsarist Russia did not find analogues in the West. Based on the peculiarities of Russian autocracy, Owen argues that tsarist autocracy and the modern corporation were fundamentally incompatible. He writes, "The corporation is only one of many cultural artifacts that emerged in Europe, came to Russia, and, because of its essential incompatibility with the nature of autocracy, lost much of its dynamism and became subordinate to bureaucratic control after transplantation to Russian soil."[50]

The Putilov case demonstrates from the vantage point of a private joint-stock corporation in the tsarist economy that a contemporary corporation could indeed coexist and prosper under the autocratic state. More important, Putilov's business practices such as market strategies, long-term investment choices, and cartel behavior so closely paralleled those of its Western cohorts because all companies at that time faced similar market challenges. Despite differences between tsarist legal and political structures and Western systems, those market realities acted more powerfully to shape the Putilov Company's behavior along lines similar to those of Western firms than Russian autocracy worked to condition uniquely different behavior.

7

EPILOGUE

PUTILOV'S SUCCESSORS
1991–1998

Certainly the immediate legacy of the Soviet system weighs heavily on Russian defense enterprises today. However, there are also important parallels with the business experience of the late tsarist era that can help us navigate the waters between state and market in today's Russia. This usable past offers grounds for optimism. The largest factory in St. Petersburg is the Putilov Company's successor, Kirovsky Zavod, a firm that has undergone privatization before. Similarly, both firms searched for foreign partners to provide financial and technical support and developed diversified market strategies for long-term growth. In coming to terms with defense conversion following the fall of the Soviet Union, Kirovsky is moving away from a reliance on defense orders. However, the motivation for taking its current direction recalls the older goals of seeking to diversify production to satisfy a variety of commercial markets.

The Soviet legacy is not entirely negative, either. An unexpected positive effect of Soviet policy is that, unlike the experience of its tsarist-era predecessor, for the first time in its history as a private firm Kirovsky's board looks to export goods to foreign markets. Another Soviet legacy is that defense enterprises in the USSR had a long history of making nondefense goods. In the 1980s, roughly 40 percent of the defense sector's output was designed for civilian use, and even in 1990 defense enterprises produced more than 25 percent of all nonfood consumer goods in the USSR (such as radios, televisions, VCRs, sewing machines, and washing machines).[1]

During the Soviet era, the Putilov Works was renamed the Kirov Plant (Kirovsky Zavod) and was part of the huge Kirovsky Zavod Production Association. The association played a leading role in the design and enhancement of Soviet tractors. After the 1917 revolution, the plant started making farm tractors (under license from a Western producer), steam turbines, and tanks. After World War II, Kirovsky's manufacturing lines were further diversified to include nuclear power equipment, marine turbines, and tunneling equipment. Since 1962 the best-known Kirovsky plant product, both in the USSR and abroad, was the large agricultural tractor, the Kirovets. In 1979 Kirovsky participated in designing experimental 250hp caterpillar tractors. This tractor was the first Soviet tractor with a hauling capacity of 5 tons. Kirovsky was also involved in developing a 500hp tractor that was 50 percent more powerful than the K-701 model. As a defense enterprise, Kirovsky's output included T-80 tanks, self-propelled artillery guns, turbines for naval surface vessels and submarines, and silent reduction gears for submarines.

Additional product lines ranged from turbines for electric power generation, circulating pumps for nuclear power stations, and construction machinery (including bulldozers, cranes, front-end loaders, and canal digging machinery) to automated packaging machinery for agriculture, mining equipment, road construction, and equipment for the repair of oil wells and oil pipelines. Along with these heavy industrial goods, Kirovsky also manufactured some consumer items such as kitchen appliances (juice pressers and meat grinders), window locks, and children's swings.[2]

Kirovsky figured prominently at the beginning of Gorbachev's efforts to spur productivity. In May 1985 Gorbachev visited Kirovsky, and the enterprise's managers, engineers, and technical workers informed him of their implementation of the new resolutions from the Communist Party's April plenum. In particular, the Kirovsky staff stressed giving greater attention to applying scientific and technical progress in production. In one machine shop, the general secretary expressed special interest in a new automatic production system for the manufacture of parts. The system had been developed by Kirovsky, and all the components were linked by local computing equipment. Such techniques raised the hope for increased labor productivity. Gorbachev spoke with the foremen, who told him that the managers understood the connection between

Kirovsky's future and advanced technology. Kirovsky had manufactured more than 300,000 Kirovets tractors, and the plant had filled its production quota for dozens of K-701s with the necessary spare parts ahead of schedule. As reported by the BBC, "The entire increase in gross production is to be achieved in the current Five-Year Plan period through progress in technology, maximum use of equipment and saving of resources."[3] As part of Gorbachev's perestroika, the Kirovsky enterprise took up the issue of creating new economic management conditions. Issues up for discussion included increasing tractor output and raising the standards of the Kirovets product line, as well as speeding up reconstruction of the country's leading machine-building plant. Workers focused special concern on improving the food supply for the plant's workers and expanding the production of consumer goods.[4]

Kirovsky already had an eye to exports in Soviet times, and Kirovets tractors were well known abroad. In 1989 the first consignments of the new, large K-701M tractors were delivered to Soviet and foreign customers. In addition to the expected customers in the East Bloc, such as Czechoslovakia and Hungary, other purchasers included China, Australia, Italy, and Canada. The opinions of Canadian farmers were especially taken into account in modifying the Kirovets. The Canadian influence resulted in better working conditions for the tractor driver, including air conditioning, a refrigerator, and a radio-tape player on board. More than 11,000 Kirovets tractors were exported to twenty countries. In 1990 the tractor was modified for use in construction, mining, and other industries.[5]

Kirovsky also was developing new mini-tractors just before the collapse of the Soviet Union. Experimental prototypes were in the works for a four-wheeled mini-tractor with a 30hp diesel engine and all-wheel drive. However, organizational delays slowed down implementation. Kirovsky experts thought that the only way to initiate production quickly would be to find some way to bypass the usual bureaucratic routine that required obtaining permission from a host of offices and seeking subsidies from central planning in Moscow. Kirovsky plant administrators hoped to accelerate the process by negotiating directly with the auto works in Togliatti and Naberezhnye Chelny on the Volga River to arrange for output of the new tractor prototypes.[6]

With the collapse of the Soviet Union, Kirovsky, like many enterprises, faced rough times in 1992. At the peak of the arrears crisis in mid-1992, estimates placed the value of enterprise nonpayments to one another at about 78 percent of GDP, and four-fifths of Russia's industrial enterprises had either overdue accounts receivable or accounts payable.[7] Kirovsky had thousands of unsold tractors in inventory, and factory debt amounted to almost 1 billion rubles. Farmers were reluctant to buy a tractor priced at 800,000 rubles and rising. Kirovsky was on the verge of halting its tractor line, and the factory's director expressed the belief that large low-interest government credits should be extended to all suppliers of Kirovets components. Otherwise, the operation would fold.[8]

Meanwhile, Kirovsky's financial condition continued to deteriorate. In May 1992, the plant was on the verge of total shutdown because its water supplies were cut off. The Water and Canals Board of St. Petersburg cut off Kirovsky, along with about twenty other enterprises, because of nonpayment of bills. Water authorities needed money to buy reagents for water-processing works, and without them city inhabitants would be without water for their homes. The deputy chairman at the Water Board blamed the managers, saying, "Better for incompetent managers to suffer. Now they might put their houses in order, so that we don't have to resort to extreme measures."[9]

Under these pressing circumstances, Kirovsky's management began contemplating privatization in 1992. In general, Russian enterprise directors had two goals in privatizing their operations: assuring the survival of their large enterprises intact and gaining control over them.[10] Kirovsky's management was no exception. The enterprise's economic service drafted a strategy for privatizing the plant's assets. According to these plans, the factory would gradually be transformed into a joint-stock company, and its units would become subsidiaries. The plant managers hoped to complete privatization by the end of 1993. The enterprise's charter capital at the start of privatization comprised 8,149,005 shares of common stock and 2,176,335 shares of preferred stock each, with a par value of 100 rubles. Employees were to acquire up to 75 percent of the stock, and 10 percent of the stock was to be made available to foreign investors.

In April 1993 the newly privatized joint-stock company AO Kirovsky Zavod emerged. The firm's key facilities consisted of the Kirovsky machine-building and metalworking factory, the former All-Union Scientific Research Institute of Transport machinery in Gorelovo, and the

Transmash plant in Tikhvin (Leningrad Oblast). The Kirovsky Company was a vertically integrated association that also produced its own steel, its own sheet metal, and its own forgings and stampings. The Kirovsky plant ceased producing tanks in November 1991. It continued to make turbines, tractors, construction machinery, and rolled steel. Gorelovo formerly designed and field-tested tanks and now produces Kirovets tractors. Tikhvin produces castings, as well as machinery, spare parts, and consumer goods.[11]

Although the form was new, the general director of the newly privatized Kirovsky Company, Petr Georgievich Semenenko, was a Kirovsky insider. A graduate of the Leningrad Shipbuilding Institute, Semenenko (b. 1946) had worked his way up from within Kirovsky's management after starting in the turbine assembly department in 1970. He subsequently advanced as head of tank production at Kirovsky and then became the general engineering director for production. In 1987 he was named general director for the unified Kirovsky plant. Since November 1992, Semenenko has held the position of general director of the Kirovsky joint-stock company, and in 1994 the shareholders elected him general director and president of the council of directors.[12]

Kirovsky's place as a defense enterprise was also jeopardized by the state's collapse. With the prospect of state abandonment looming, Kirovsky began initiating defense conversion. To that end, the enterprise looked to the manufacture of civilian trucks and acquired the production lines for light trucks in the former East Germany. Volkswagen served as intermediary, and Kirovsky took hold of the Barkas light truck range in Karl-Marx-Stadt. The submanufacture of components was distributed among twenty enterprises in St. Petersburg, and regular production was expected to start by the end of 1992, although actual production has not been confirmed.[13]

During the Soviet era, the Kirovsky Works was an important producer of tanks. Since the breakup of the USSR, however, the company has opted to diversify and abandon military production. Defense industry conversion and the severe Russian economic recession of 1992–1995 seriously affected Kirovsky Zavod's activities. During 1992–1994 the T-80 tank line was phased out as a result of a Russian government defense conversion program. Kirovsky's conversion activity included large-scale production of household appliances and other consumer goods. An effort commenced to produce mini-tractors and attachments (K-20, using 35hp engines from Germany) for small farms. The firm also began production of municipal service vehicles. It produced annually about 21,000 225hp and 300hp tractors, 600,000 meat grinders, and 400,000 juice pressers. Late in 1994, Kirovsky worked on the task of converting 3,000 decommissioned Soviet tanks into agricultural implements.[14] By 1995, Robin Pertenava, vice-director at Kirovsky, commented, "The plant, which was producing tanks, does not work for war any more."[15]

The directors of the recently privatized Kirovsky factory, like their prerevolutionary predecessors, have looked to technical agreements with leading Western firms. Kirovsky and the German firm Landtechnik AG Schonebeck set up a joint venture to produce self-propelled fodder harvesters in May 1993. Kirovsky planned to put out 400 machines the first year, and eventually reach a volume of 5,000 per year after three years. The first Landtechnik machine was to be assembled with German components in June. Ultimately, Kirovsky would assemble the harvesters and make the components. Kirovsky's company president, Semenenko, expected the joint venture to create 1,000 jobs, thereby mitigating the effects of work force downsizing.[16]

In spite of these efforts, Kirovsky's tractor production ran into serious difficulties. The company was forced to halt the line in December 1993, and workers were sent on forced leave. Even workers at the metallurgical plant were furloughed. Although the turbine production continued in operation, workers there experienced a reduced workweek. In the plant's yard several hundred Kirovets tractors, worth 10 billion rubles, stood ready to go, but they had been ordered by Russian agricultural enterprises that could not pay for them. Other problems plagued the mini-tractors. Some 150 K-20 mini-tractors had been manufactured in 1993 as part of a test batch, but production delays for lack of cheap diesel fuel, coupled with defects in cabin construction, meant that the model had to be overhauled before it could possibly compete for foreign sales. Work on Kirovsky's main tractor production line suffered another two-month shutdown due to lack of product demand and did not resume until 5 September 1994, by which time 350 tractors worth 21 billion rubles had finally been sold.[17]

Tractor production continued to drop off sharply. In the period 1992–1995, agricultural consumers were no longer able to pay for large tractors, and the disintegration of large collective farms required smaller tractors. This resulted in dramatically reduced demand for the Kirov plant's main product, the Kirovets tractor. In the late Soviet years, the factory was turning out around 20,000 wheeled tractors annually, but now the company consciously decreased production. The Kirovsky plant administration was forced to stop tractor production lines and to furlough workers temporarily several times during 1993–1995. In June 1995 the plant lacked enough orders to keep assembly lines operating through the summer. After this enforced stoppage due to shortage of components and lack of solvent demand, workers on the tractor line were called back to work in September to put out about 100 tractors by the end of the month.

Kirovsky's tractor line sputtered to a halt again in December 1995. This time, failing floating assets caused the shutdown. All told, in 1995 Kirovsky turned out about 900 tractors, and plans for the following year reduced output to 600 for the Russian market, with a possible addition of 100 for export to Germany.[18] As Deputy Director-General Alexander Krikunov explained, "Knowing the market situation, the company is not interested in producing tractors that will not be sold."[19] However, the company has demonstrated some creative flexibility in maintaining ties to the cash-strapped agricultural sector. In 1996 the Kirovsky tractor plant created one of St. Petersburg's largest wholesale foodstuffs depots. The firm signed contracts with farmers from Stavropol, Krasnodar, Voronezh, Kransoyarsk, and Orenburg regions, as well as with farmers from Ukraine and Belarus, to arrange a large-scale barter exchange. The principles of the deal call for Kirovsky to supply tractors and spare parts to the farmers in exchange for grain, meat, and vegetables. Kirovsky then sells the agricultural produce in St. Petersburg. Krikunov believes it is the only efficient method to organize a trade when there is no money.[20]

By 1994, St. Petersburg's machine-building factories were looking to escape their critical state, and foreign joint ventures assumed even greater importance for salvaging the cash-strapped works. Kirovsky approached Ford, Volkswagen, and General Motors in an aggressive effort to obtain a Western partner for joint automobile production. An automotive joint venture with Mitsubishi was also contemplated for existing facilities at Gorelovo. Production of small multipurpose tractors through a joint venture has also been considered, as well as jeep production. Kirovsky was also studying the possibility of wheelchair production.[21]

Although these initial attempts did not land any foreign partners, the firm's persistence yielded positive results, and among St. Petersburg machine-builders Kirovsky was the first to accomplish a major foreign deal. In February 1994 Kirovsky entered into a joint venture with the U.S. firm Caterpillar. Under the terms of the agreement, Caterpillar and Kirovsky formed NevaMash, which serves as a Caterpillar supplier. The Petersburg plant produces base frames for Caterpillar's plant in Belgium, and production began in 1994. Caterpillar is a 65 percent owner in the venture. According to a Caterpillar representative, "Kirovsky Zavod has made enormous progress in adjusting to the challenges of a market-based economy, and we are confident that this new partnership will enable both our companies to take full advantage of expanding opportunities in Europe and the Commonwealth of Independent States."[22]

NevaMash itself is a $5.5 million joint venture (10 billion rubles), and is expected to create only seventy-five new jobs.[23] The new joint venture would also produce hydraulic power shovels and machines for road construction, and the first products came out in 1995. According to the contract, NevaMash was established on Kirovsky's facilities in the Gorelovo district near St. Petersburg. These facilities had originally been planned for tank production in the late Soviet era but were never used. Semenenko looked to the joint venture as a way to save jobs and guarantee sales for Kirovsky, even though he did not expect it to yield profits in the first two years. On the American side, Caterpillar had been trying to establish a venture in Russia for three years and finally picked Kirovsky because of the firm's high skills, good location, and a well-considered marketing program developed at the works for the joint venture.[24] The NevaMash deal marked the thirteenth venture for Caterpillar in Russia and contributed to a boost of $2.75 for Caterpillar stock on the New York Stock Exchange.[25] In the partnership, Kirovsky's 35 percent stake took the form of production facilities over an area of 11.6 acres (4.7 hectares) and also equipment, while Caterpillar's 65 percent share included deposit components and know-how, including assistance in promoting the venture's output for external markets. [26]By summer 1995, the Defense Enterprise Fund, an American nonprofit organization founded to help fund conversion, was ready to commit to the Caterpillar-Kirovsky deal for production of platforms for excavators. The fund kicked in $1.8 million of the $5 million needed.[27]

Besides Caterpillar, the Kirovsky factory has also established a foreign partnership with General Electric. After completing a feasibility study in 1994, G.E. and Kirovsky teamed up in 1995 to create a joint venture for the assembly and production of gas turbines for distribution within the Russian market. Kirovsky owns 30 percent of the venture, and production commenced in 1996. According to Semenenko, "Combining our understanding of the Russian market and our manufacturing experience with G.E.'s world-class technology will provide Russian customers with locally produced gas turbine products from a strong Russian company."[28] From Kirovsky's perspective, the purpose of the deal with G.E. Power Systems was to expand gas turbine production in Russia over the next ten to fifteen years with the goal of attracting $350 million in foreign investment. The gas turbines were to be primarily for Russian power stations, but production for export was a consideration as well. The joint venture's less expensive gas turbines were expected to be competitive against comparable foreign-made ones, and the first products were manufactured in 1996.[29]

G.E.'s interest was to secure a place in Russia's modernizing turbine market. Russia's domestic heavy turbine engineering has been practically stagnant for the previous two decades, and as much as 80 percent of the country's electric power has been generated by inefficient and ecologically substandard steam turbines. The potential for Russia's turbine industrial growth is immense, but the lack of funding has inhibited development. The G.E. subsidiary Nuovo Pignone SPA, which has played an active role in the Russian turbine market for twenty years, provided the modernized compressor and turbine production technology for the new partnership.[30] In this instance, G.E.'s strategy has already paid off. Based on Nuovo Pignone's participation in 1994, the firm won a contract worth $1.6 billion with Gazprom to replace and modify Russia's antiquated pipelines and gas turbines in 1996.[31]

As part of its diversification strategy, Kirovsky's management also pursued an important domestic joint venture. In April 1994 the company allied itself with the huge truck producer KamAz in Tatarstan, the largest heavy truck manufacturer in the Russian federation, to establish a bus production line. The new joint-stock venture, Peterburg-Avto-Kam, is to produce buses in St. Petersburg at an estimated unit cost of 60 million rubles. The new enterprise's price effectively undercut the Hungarian-made Ikarus buses, which cost between 80 and 120 million rubles each.

The potential demand for city buses in Russia is estimated at 20,000 units annually. This demand can be only partially met by domestic manufacturers. The Hungarian firm Ikarus, the traditional supplier to Russia within the old Council for Mutual Economic Assistance, had become too expensive for Russian customers. The new bus made by the joint venture is to cost about half of comparable imported brands. The Kirovsky program calls for a total investment of 30 billion rubles, and the St. Petersburg Mayor's office invested the first billion after preparing a feasibility study. The new line at the Kirovsky works was expected to create 2,500 new jobs. KamAz had already made the first ten engines for a trial batch of buses, and serial production launched in the second quarter of 1994.[32]

As of 1 August 1994, St. Petersburg was home to 480 industrial enterprises employing 479,000 workers. Massive nonpayment problems were endemic and had interrupted wage payments at local companies. The 459 enterprises in the city employing 500 or more workers were operating 385.8 billion rubles in the red, with outstanding credits of 617.5 billion rubles. The mayor's economic and financial committee prepared to audit prospective enterprises that needed government assistance. Kirovsky Zavod made it onto the list. Under the terms of the bailout program, Kirovsky and KamAz would assist government auditors in advising troubled enterprises. Opening a bus assembly plant at Kirovsky formed part of the municipal government's economic policy, a program for which the government promised $5 million worth of rubles. Overall, federal authorities promised 877 billion rubles in assistance to thirty-two St. Petersburg enterprises.[33] The St. Petersburg government also planned to grant certain loan privileges, city guarantees on foreign investment, and local budget payment delays to Kirovsky, Izhorskye, Baltiisky, and seventeen other industrial enterprises in the city in 1997.[34]

In 1995 the St. Petersburg authorities approved a municipal bus production program to be filled by Peterburg-Avto-Kam. The city government allocated 7.5 billion rubles to implement the program. KamAz became the major supplier of assembly units, and Kirovsky started making accessories in addition to serving as the assembly plant. Avto-Kam planned to produce 2,000 buses annually by 1997. As prospects for the bus venture improved, the stocks of both Kirovsky and KamAz rose.[35]

Increasingly, Kirovsky has been moving toward the fuel and energy sector and away from tractors. Already in 1991 Kirovsky was poised to enter the natural gas and pipeline industries. An American consortium signed a contract with a St. Petersburg enterprise to repair defective natural gas pipelines running from Siberia to the European parts of the Soviet Union. The consortium planned to set up a factory to build 25-megawatt turbines designed by General Electric. The Kirovsky Zavod landed the job of building the turbines.[36] Semenenko has noted that because the Kirovets tractors are no longer in high demand on the Russian market, Kirovsky had to slash production to 60 percent of the 1993 level in 1997, even though these tractors were once the major product of the plant. Assessing company prospects in May 1995, Semenenko considered the joint venture with KamAz promising but risky, whereas gas turbine production had proved to be the most lucrative line. On this score, the beginnings of the plant's business relationship with Gazprom back in 1991 were paying off. Russian oilmen also have paid attention to Kirovsky's potential products. Lukoil specialists are interested in the new design of Kirovsky's branch, the PKB Automatica pumping device ANA-105. The 350hp machine is designed to pump working liquid into drills under pressure of 140 atmospheres. The device costs $700,000, which is cheaper than its U.S. analogue, and two Kirovsky sample machines are at present undergoing testing.[37]

The new diversification strategies seem to be working. Among the new product lines are mini-tractors, armored security cars, gas pumping turbines for pipelines, and carrot-gathering machines. Kirovsky is competitive in world markets because its production prices are about 40 percent cheaper than Western costs. In 1994 the company posted its first net profit of approximately 352 million rubles, and for 1995 Kirovsky profits totaled 163 billion rubles ($32 million), yielding dividends to shareholders amounting to 4.27 billion rubles ($854,000). Company profits have been positive in recent years, although return on equity is still fairly low, at 6 percent in 1995.[38]

At the beginning of 1995, the company was completely privatized. Kirovsky shares began to be listed on the St. Peterburg stock exchange, and the stock price grew by a factor of four during 1995. At a recent shareholders' meeting it was decided that the company would buy the land occupied by the factory from the municipal government of St. Petersburg. The new Western-style management structure treats the several former divisions of the company now operating in the market as independent legal entities. Kirovsky has twenty-six such subsidiaries wholly owned by the parent firm. The largest are the rolling mills, the castings and forgings production division, the agricultural machinery division, the construction machinery division, the power generation equipment division, and the consumer hardware division. Service divisions include engineering, automation, international operations, logistics, and training. This structure has encouraged the subsidiaries to be more active in the market since their profits depend entirely on their own activities.[39]

In 1995 the recession bottomed out for Kirovsky Zavod, and the company began to show signs of recovery. The rapid pace of production declines slowed considerably, mass staff reductions leveled off, and the factory's leadership announced management reorganization. The company's new direction has not come without pain, however. By 1994 employment had fallen from about 50,000 to 22,000, and in 1995 the company employed only 18,000 workers. By 1999, the company employed only 8,000 workers. Still, Kirovsky was the largest plant in St. Petersburg. The company's situation and its market position had stabilized. Kirovsky saw its sales increase by around one-third in 1996 to reach 1.12 trillion rubles ($218.15 million) up from 740 billion rubles ($161.9 million) in 1995. The 1996 figures point to a continued stabilization at the plant after it reached a low point in 1994, with sales of just 200 billion rubles ($83.4 million).[40]

Company management expects the positive trend to continue. In 1997 Kirovsky planned to increase output by almost 17 percent and boost ruble sales proceeds by 22 percent to 1.37 trillion rubles—a projected increase of some 5–7 percent in real terms. The company has undergone downsizing and restructuring. The factory has increased its output of steel and rolled products through the subsidiary Pertostal, which produced 294,000 metric tons of crude steel in 1996 (10 percent above 1992 output), one-third of which was exported. Steel production now accounts for around 50 percent of Kirovsky's revenues, but the company is also seeking niches in lucrative areas of small tractors and sweepers, buses, and armored vehicles, as well as oil and gas equipment. The factory hopes to export an increasing share of small tractors to European markets.[41]

New tractor models designed in 1996 are expected serve as the means for increased output. At present, twenty-two models of machines for road construction, as well as branches for oil, gas, building, forestry, and agriculture have been created using the new Kirovets as a base model. In 1996 the AO Kirovsky Zavod (the privatized joint-stock company formed in 1993) sold products, works, and services in the amount of 1,124 billion rubles in comparable prices. Over 20 billion rubles were invested in the enterprise's development. According to the 1997 plan, the volume of products and sales was to reach 1,373 billion rubles.[42] In 1997 the Russian stock markets were booming. The *Moscow Times* index of leading Russian shares rose 140 percent in the first half of 1997, while St. Petersburg equities grew only slightly less, rising by 105 percent. In St. Petersburg the local blue chips Baltika Brewery and Kirovsky saw their shares skyrocket up over 500 percent, and price to earnings ratio (ratio of share's price to per-share earnings) are similar to top Western shares.[43]

Kirovsky's good fortune has continued even with the fiscal crisis and ruble devaluation of 1998. For the firm, 1998 yielded the biggest profits to date. At the shareholders' meeting in May 1998, the company reported post-tax profits of 69.3 million rubles ($11.55 million), up from $80,000 the previous year. The dramatic jump in profits is mostly due to cost-cutting, as the company was able to eliminate its tax debt and transfer its social services costs (such as workers' housing) to city government. Kirovsky also signed a $120 million deal with Gazprom in May.[44] Only time will tell whether Kirovsky can sustain its long-term viability.

The role of the banks in Kirovsky's management offers still another parallel with the Putilov Company's experience, including having a board director named Putilov. Kirovsky's stock is currently controlled by several institutional investors. In 1995 the shareholders of Rosneft, a large state-owned Russian oil company, voted to place their president, Alexander Putilov, on Kirovsky's board of directors. The new board of directors for Kirovsky now includes three officials from Kirovsky Zavod, two from Promstroibank, and one each from Rosneft and the Generalny investment fund. Rosneft holds a 4 percent stake in the Kirovsky plant, and Kirovsky also enjoys close relations with the oil company Yukos. The single largest shareholder in late 1996 was the St. Petersburg Promstroibank, with a 13.8 percent stake.[45] As with the Putilov Company board and its banks prior to 1914, despite the presence of these large institutional shareholders, the effective management of the firm remains in the hands of Kirovsky's general director, Semenenko.

Good bank relations have enabled Kirovsky to arrange the necessary infusion of capital to proceed with final privatization. In 1997 Kirovsky crossed an important legal threshold of privatization when it gained full ownership of the 184 hectares of land it occupies, Russia's largest-ever land privatization to date. The deal was approved by St. Petersburg's Governor Vladimir Yakovlev and funded by the politically connected Balt-Uneximbank, a local branch of the Moscow-based Uneximbank. The result is a complicated agreement to liquidate a chain of mutual debts between the factory, the City Property Fund, and various city enterprises. Kirovsky received the land in return for debts of about 13 billion rubles ($2.2 million) owed it by both federal and municipal budgets. In July Kirovsky formally signed a three-way contract with the City Property Fund and the bank and received the deed to the land. Balt-Uneximbank in essence put up the money to buy the land for the factory in return for an unspecified number of shares in Kirovsky and other securities.

The land-debt swap is part of a complex debt chain. Balt-Uneximbank will provide the cash to the City Property Fund, which will in turn pay off various municipal debts to other enterprises. For providing the 12.9 billion rubles over the next three years, the bank acquired equity in Kirovsky, and Kirovsky has already received its land in payment for various debts. Those enterprises in debt to Kirovsky will be obliged to pay off their Kirovsky debts directly to the bank. The bank's initial installment of 4 billion rubles will be paid within the month. The City Property Fund initiated the debt payment plan as part of the desire to push forward the land market in St. Petersburg. Kirovsky hopes to attract foreign investment, now that it owns the land. With clear title to its land, Kirovsky has become fully privatized, and some of its property is adjacent to the city port along the old Putilov Canal. This strategic location, once the key to Nikolai Putilov's grand plans, again figures prominently in the current company's hopes to attract large investors for long-term projects.[46]

Kirovsky's successful transformation into a private, market-oriented producer is not unique or exceptional. To appreciate Kirovsky's experience, it is helpful once again to compare it with its old cohort Skoda, now in the Czech Republic. Skoda serves as an especially useful comparative case because of the firm's parallel developments with Putilov prior to World War I and its post-Soviet privatization experience in the 1990s. As we have seen, Skoda Plzen had become the main defense firm in the Hapsburg Empire while also offering a vast array of heavy engineering goods. By the end of World War II, the bulk of the works had been destroyed, but they were rebuilt along the lines of a Soviet state enterprise after the communist takeover in 1948. As a socialist state enterprise in the Soviet bloc, Skoda employed 40,000 workers and produced an array of heavy industrial goods, ranging from locomotives and turbines to machine tools and metallurgy. Thus Skoda was similar to Kirovsky in both the scale and scope of its operations.

Like Kirovsky, Skoda too felt the effects of the collapse of its previous customer base in the Soviet Union. Skoda Plzen became a state-owned joint-stock company on 1 January 1991. At that time, the company consisted of twenty-one factories and 38,000 employees. The company had posted a profit of about $26 million in 1990, mostly from exports to the Soviet market. However, the enterprise saw its existing markets evaporate as the Soviet-led trading bloc Comecon disintegrated.[47] Skoda then endured the financial squeeze of mounting debts and suspended production. In September 1992, 7 billion kroners' worth of debt forced line closings, and 1,200 people lost their jobs, with an additonal 2,000 workers placed on half pay. Skoda was stuck with several billion kroners' worth of unpaid orders, and banks refused to postpone payments. As the owner of the enterprise, the Czech government faced the prospect that Skoda's bankruptcy could trigger an economic avalanche within the country because the enterprise owed money to some 4,000 other companies.[48]

In these circumstances, the government launched a privatization program as a means to solve the financial crisis. The privatization process culminated in June 1993 when Lubomir Soudek, manager of Skoda in 1990–1991, took control of the enterprise with a 20 percent stake. Soudek had put together a financial partnership with two banks, Investicni and Komercni, to bail out the enterprise in return for managerial control. Soudek reorganized the enterpise and converted some of the divisions into joint ventures with foreign firms, including Dorries-Scharmann (a German company), Brown and Root (Anglo-American), Siemens (German), and Russian rail factories. Skoda also established a new division for military equipment. By this time, Skoda employed 25,000 workers and produced locomotives, trolley buses, electric power turbines, machine tools, and raw steel.[49]

Under Soudek, a former "rank-and-file communist," Skoda Plzen has been transformed into a privatized joint-stock company with an extensive foreign business. Exports have been a vital component of Soudek's plan. In 1994 export sales more than doubled to 5.9 billion kroner, and Skoda is looking to southeast Asia and China for expanding market opportunities. Skoda is also returning to its traditional market in Russia, and the firm signed a contract with the Russian engineering group VMZ to make trolley buses for the Russian market in April 1995.[50]

The Skoda product lines correspond closely with Kirovsky's. Both enterprises manufacture buses, steam turbines, foundries, forges, agricultural equipment, and machinery for power generation, reactors, and nuclear power production. In addition to making diversification decisions similar to those of Kirovsky, Skoda has also paired up with G.E. Power Systems Europe. In April 1994 Skoda and G.E. announced a ten-year agreement for "cooperation and strategic association" between them in power systems. G.E. supplies gas turbines for Skoda-designed power plants in eastern Europe, and Skoda provides the components. The American company would invest $5–10 million over two years.[51]

In another parallel development with Kirovsky, Skoda branched out into the truck industry. In 1996 Skoda acquired a 43.5 percent share in the truck maker Tatra. This acquisition, in combination with the 1995 takeover of the haulage vehicle firm Liaz, gave Skoda control of the entire heavy truck sector in the Czech Republic. Customers for Tatra vehicles include the oil exploration, construction, and forestry industries. The Czech truck industry had been devastated by the collapse of its main markets in the former Soviet Union, but Tatra had managed to climb back into the black by 1994.[52] Nevertheless, by 1997 it appeared that the truck business might be pulling Skoda down as the company's fortunes declined in 1998.

This study has aimed to bring the Russian firm squarely into mainstream discussions of business history and to explore the unmapped terrain of private enterprise in late imperial Russia. It is a testimony to the unexamined state of the field of Russian business history that to advocate the existence of a market economy in tsarist Russia in the second half of the nineteenth century seems a bold statement.[53] My experience in grappling with the topic has brought an acute awareness that we need to learn more about Russian economic history and business performance and that the views of the old intelligentsia have continued to shape the understanding of the tsarist economy for far too long. This is especially true when one attempts to assess the role played by the state and to reexamine notions of the St. Petersburg industrialists' dependence on the state. It is time to rethink interpretations that stress state dependency and artificiality as the chief attributes of Petersburg's heavy industry firms. The old characterization of the Putilov Company and of St. Petersburg industrialists in the late tsarist era emphasized their "artificiality" and slow adjustment to new market conditions. These complaints are made against Russian firms today. However, the picture needs to be redrawn because Russian business leaders in the tsarist era successfully made those adjustments.

A dominant theme running through this study has been the similarities between Putilov and its Western counterparts. If we consider the Putilov board's strategies for growth and compare them with those of analogous industrial enterprises elsewhere in Europe, then the evidence supports the proposition that Russian entrepreneurs not only adopted the techniques of industrial capitalism but, more important, the strategic outlook as well. Thus the image of Russia as fundamentally exceptional in its economic development should be discarded.

In its relationship with state control, the Putilov factory has come full circle. Having left state hands when N. I. Putilov purchased the factory in 1868, the company returned briefly to state receivership in 1880–1883 and found itself again under state administration during the First World War, beginning in 1916. The Soviet government took over control of the works in 1918 and never relinquished it. However, now that the Soviet Union has departed, the old Putilov factory has taken on the guise of the Kirovsky Zavod. Given the enterprise's track record, it would be premature to rule out the possibility that a new team of managers and financial specialists might once again grasp the essentials of contemporary capitalism and develop them in Russia.

NOTES

Introduction

Unless otherwise indicated, all translations [from the Russian] are by the author.

1. Amberger, *Deutsche in Staat;* Amberger, "Das Haus Wogau & Co.," in *Fremde und Einheimishce,* 62–83; Anan'ich, *Bankirskie doma v Rossii;* Ruud, *Russian Entrepreneur;* Tolf, *The Russian Rockefellers;* Friedgut, *Iuzoka and Revolution;* Bovykin and Petrov, *Kommercheskie banki rossiiskoi imperii.*

2. Ruckman, *The Moscow Business Elite,* 12.

3. Ermanskii, "Krupnaia burzhuaziia do 1905 goda," 313–48; Miliukov, *Russia and Its Crisis,* 552–64.

4. Owen, *Russian Corporate Capitalism;* McCaffray, *The Politics of Industrialization.*

5. Rieber, *Merchants and Entrepreneurs;* King, "The Emergence of the St. Petersburg Industrialist Community," 36–44; Goldstein, "Military Aspects," 71.

6. Goldthorpe et al., *The Affluent Worker,* 30–32.

7. Walicki, *A History of Russian Thought,* chaps, 5, 12, 18; Rubenshtein, *Russkaia istoriografia.*

8. I am indebted to David McDonald for calling to my attention Chaadaev's concept of the advantages of backwardness. See McNally, *The Major Works of Peter Chaadaev,* 199–220; Gerschenkron, *Economic Backwardness.*

9. Black et al., *The Modernization of Japan and Russia,* 342–54.

10. Moore, *World Modernization,* 26–27.

11. Gerschenkron, *Economic Backwardness,* 19–22; 135–36.

12. Crisp, *Studies in the Russian Economy;* Gatrell, *The Tsarist Economy;* Gregory, *Before Command.*

13. McKay, *Pioneers for Profit.*

14. A notable work that argues in favor of Russian exceptionalism is Owen, *The Corporation.* The notion of economic exceptionalism is not confined to Russian historiography. Examples can be found in the German *Sonderweg,* American exceptionalism, the "special case" of Britain, and the problem of French industrialization (Dunlavy, *Politics and Industrialization,* 12–13); Skocpol, *States and Social Revolutions,* 19–22; Blackbourn and Eley, *The Peculiarities of German History.*

15. Scott, "Latin America and Modernization,"; Ghosh, *Developing Africa,* 12–13.

16. Anderson, *Internal Migration;* Gregory, *Russian National Income;* McDaniel, *Autocracy.*

17. Carstensen and Guroff, "Economic Innovation," 353.

18. Bradley, *Guns for the Tsar,* 3–11. See also Brown, "The Problematics of Armory Modernization."

19. Apter, *Rethinking Development;* Moore, *World Modernization;* Scott, "Latin America and Modernization," 2, 9.

20. Chandler, *Strategy and Structure;* Chandler, *Scale and Scope.*

21. Chandler, *Scale and Scope,* 8.

22. Carstensen and Guroff, "Economic Innovation," 352.

23. Cassis, *Big Business,* 6–10, 80.

24. See Beskrovnyi, *Russkaia armiia i flot;* Beskrovny, *Armiia i flot Rossii v nachala XX v.* See also Grechaniuk, *Baltiiskii flot,* 98–150; Kovalenko, *Oboronnaia promyshlennost' sovetskoi Rossii.*

25. Bovykin, "Banki i voennaia promyshlennost'"; Shatsillo, "Inostrannyi kapital i voenno-morskie programmy Rossii"; Shatsillo, *Gosudarstvo.*

26. Bokhanov, *Delovaia elita Rossii 1914 g.*

27. For studies on the workers' movement at the Putilov Works, see Mitel'man et al., *Istoriia Putilovskogo zavoda;* and Taits, *Korabelshchiki Narvskoi zastavy.* Regarding the workers and the naval factories, see S. Zav'ialov, *Istoriia Izhorskogo zavoda* (Moskva: Ogiz Gos. Izdat., 1934).

28. For studies of the Moscow merchants, see Owen, *Capitalism and Politics in Russia;* Ruckman, *The Moscow Business Elite;* Rieber, *Merchants and Entrepreneurs.* A good example of the memoir literature for the Moscow group is Buryshkin, *Moskva kupecheskaia.*

29. Owen, *Russian Corporate Capitalism,* 126–38.

30. Roosa, *Russian Industrialists;* Hogan, *Forging Revolution;* on relations between industrialists and the government regarding labor policy, see McKean, *St. Petersburg Between the Revolutions,* 269–96. Rieber gives some attention to St. Petersburg (*Merchants and Entrepreneurs,* 243–55, 345–72).

31. McKay, *Pioneers for Profit;* Carstensen, *American Enterprise;* Beaud, "De l'expansion internationale."

32. Goldstein, "Vickers Limited and the Tsarist Regime"; Bradley, *Guns for the Tsar.* Both of these works draw heavily from the business records of the foreign firms. In addition, Dietrich Geyer summarizes the standard Soviet secondary works in his chapter on the arms trade in Russia. See Geyer, *Russian Imperialism,* 255–72.

33. Kipp, "The Russian Navy and Private Enterprise"; Gatrell, "After Tsushima."

34. Gatrell, *Government,* 215–23.

35. Ibid., 216.

36. *K stoletiiu Putilovskogo zavoda, 1801–1901 gg.* (Sankt-Peterburg: Izdanie Putilovskogo zavoda, 1902).

37. Gatrell, *The Tsarist Economy,* 188–91, 207–30.

38. Gindin, "Balansy aktsionernykh predpriiatii kak istoricheskii istochnik," 108–09.

39. Mitel'man et al., *Istoriia Putilovskogo zavoda,* 415–16.

40. For proof that Breitigam was actually the accountant in 1913, see RGIA f. 120, op. 1, d. 80, ll. 70–71. For Ioganson's appearance as the new accountant in 1917, see RGVIA f. 505, op. 3, d. 22, l. 237.

41. Cassis (*Big Business,* 77) writes, "Published accounts, however, should not be readily dismissed. They provide for all countries at best a fairly accurate picture, at worst a rough idea of a company's state of affairs, and there is no reason a priori to believe that discrepancies between published and real profits were more pronounced in one country than in another. In addition, even if 'untrue' published profits do reflect the image a company wishes to project."

42. Orlovsky, *The Limits of Reform,* 197–205; Fuller, *Civil-Military Conflict,* 219–63; Anan'ich et al., *Krizis samoderzhaviia;* Chernukha and Anan'ich, "Russia Falls Back."

Chapter 1. The Rise and Fall of a Rail Giant

1. King, "The Emergence of the St. Petersburg Industrialist Community," 20–21, 36–44; Rieber, *Merchants and Entrepreneurs,* 251; Goldstein, "Military Aspects," 71. PRO FO 65/1141, Report Arthur Herbert, St. Petersburg, 22 November 1882. Enclosed in Thornton to Granville, 22 November 1882.

2. Falkus, *The Industrialisation of Russia,* 53–54.

3. PRO FO 65/1141, Report Arthur Herbert, St. Petersburg, 22 November 1882. Enclosed in Thornton to Granville, 22 November 1882.

4. *K stoletiiu Putilovskogo zavoda,* 9–16.

5. *Obscchii morskoi spisok,* Chast' XI (Sanktperterburg: Tip. Morskogo Ministerstva, 1900), 294–96; Zelnik, *Labor and Society in Tsarist Russia,* 213, 336–40; "Putilov, N. I.," *Russkii biograficheskii slovar',* 151–53.

6. King, "The Emergence of the St. Petersburg Industrialist Community," 27; Zelnik, *Labor and Society in Tsarist Russia,* 287.

7. Gorodkov, *Admiralteiskie izhorskie zavody,* 121–23.

8. Bradley, *Guns for the Tsar,* 144–49.

9. *K stoletiiu Putilovskogo zavoda,* 17–18; *Golos,* 6 [18] June 1870, 2; ibid., 16 [28] June 1870, 1–2; *Zavody N. Putilova,* 53.

10. Del'vig, *Moi vospominaniia,* 4:352.

11. PRO FO 65/1163, Thornton to Granville, 16 July 1883.

12. Del'vig, *Moi vospominaniia,* 4:354.

13. *Pravitel'stvennyi Vestnik,* 4 [16] December 1875, 1; Del'vig, *Moi vospominaniia,* 4:175; Zelnik, *Labor and Society in Tsarist Russia,* 220.

14. Keppen, *Materialy dlia istorii,* 118–21; *Golos,* 16 [28] June 1870, 1–2; ibid., 6 [18] June 1870, 2.

15. Keppen, *Materialy dlia istorii,* 118–21; Zelnick, *Labor and Society in Tsarist Russia,* 309.

16. Del'vig, *Moi vospominaniia*, 4:355.

17. Ibid., 356–58. See also the diary of Fedor Chizhov in the Russian State Library (RGB), fond 332, Karton 2.11, l. 25 (ob). I am indebted to Thomas Owen for generously providing me with this citation and with excerpts from his unpublished manuscript of Chizhov's diary.

18. Rieber, *Merchants and Entrepreneurs*, 173–74, 188, 194.

19. Owen, *The Corporation*, 18.

20. Ibid., 20–21.

21. Golikov and Naumova, "Istochniki po istorii aktsionirovaniia promyshlennosti," 92.

22. This information comes from articles 2 and 25–30 of the 1872 Ustav published in *Pravitel'stvennyi Vestnik*, No. 15, January 18 [30], 1873, 1–2.

23. Ibid., articles 31–35.

24. Ibid., articles 48–56. In the company's charter of 1904 the maximum number of votes was raised to 10. RGVIA f. 369, op. 16, d. 32, ll. 391–408. Article 56 of Charter, 19 December 1904.

25. *Pravitel'stvennyi Vestnik*, No. 15, January 18 [30], 1873, 1–2, articles 59–66.

26. Keppen, *Materialy dlia istorii*, 118–21; Del'vig, *Moi vospominaniia*, 4:359.

27. Ibid., 361; *Otchet, 1873–1875*, 21.

28. Hayward, "Official Russian Policies Concerning Industrialization," 309; PRO FO 65/1141, Report Arthur Herbert, St. Petersburg, 22 November 1882. Enclosed in Thornton to Granville, 22 November 1882.

29. Del'vig, *Moi vospominaniia*, 4:360; *K stoletiiu Putilovskogo zavoda*, 19; *Otchet, 1876*, 27.

30. *Otchet, 1876*, 31–32.

31. Del'vig, *Moi vospominaniia*, 4:364–67, 370–73; *Pravitel'stvennyi Vestnik*, 4 [16] December 1875, 1; RGIA f. 626, op. 1, d. 816, l. 2; PRO FO 65/1163, Thornton to Granville, 16 July 1883. RGB f. 332, karton 3.4, l. 82 (ob) (courtesy of Thomas Owen).

32. Del'vig, *Moi vospominaniia*, 4:362–63; *K stoletiiu Putilovskogo zavoda*, 17–20; 69. See also Owen, *The Corporation* 101–02; Rieber, *Merchants and Entrepreneurs*, 194–95; RGB f. 332, karton 3.5, l. 10 (courtesy of Thomas Owen); Bovykin and Petrov, *Kommercheskie banki rossiiskoi imperii*, 215–16.

33. *Pravitel'stvennyi Vestnik*, 1 [13] July 1881, 4; *Birzhevye Vedomosti*, 7 April 1881, 842; *Torgovo-Promyshlennaia Gazeta*, 27 January [8 February], 1893, 3; ibid., 29 January [10 February], 1893, 3.

34. Hogan, *Forging Revolution*, 5–6.

35. *Birzhevye Vedomosti*, 11 October 1885, 3; ibid., 3 June 1881, 958; *Otchet, 1877*, 21; *Otchet, 1878*, 53; Hayward, "Official Russian Policies Concerning Industrialization," 272–73.

36. RGB f. 332, karton 3.3, l. 124; karton 3.4, l. 2 (ob); ibid., l. 64 (ob). Again, I am indebted to Thomas Owen for providing me with these materials from Chizhov's diary.

37. Misa, *A Nation of Steel*, 20–21, 42, 97.

38. Chandler, *Scale and Scope*, 26.

39. RGIA f. 1263, op. 1, d. 4180, art. 564.

40. Gaza, *Putilovets v trekh revoliutsiiakh*, 7–9; RGIA f. 268, op. 1, chast' 2, d. 1618, ll. 1–2; *K stoletiiu Putilovskogo zavoda*, 21.

41. Chernukha and Anan'ich, "Russia Falls Back", 82–83.

Chapter 2. Engineering Growth

1. "Ustav Obshchestva Putilovskikh zavodov," 9 November 1884, articles 23–26; "Dopolnenie k ustavu Obshchestva Putilovskikh zavodov," 20 September 1912, article 23, in RGVIA f. 369, op. 16, d. 32, ll. 388–90.

2. This information is gleaned from the following sources: RGIA f. 626, op. 1, d. 415, l. 62; ibid., d. 816, l. 44, 55; *K. stol.*, 20–22; *Pravitl'stvennyi Vestnik*, 6 [18] November 1873, 3; ibid., 11 [23] October 1876, 2; ibid., 27 March [8 April] 1880, 5; *Birzhevye Vedomosti*, 7 April 1881, 842; ibid., 31 March 1887, 4; ibid., 1 December 1885, 3.

3. RGIA f. 626, op. 1, d. 459, ll. 18–19; ibid., d. 415, ll. 4, 6, 47, 51, 62, 84, 212. For Voigt, see ibid., ll. 150, 174, 217.

4. *K stoletiiu Putilovskogo zavoda*, 1, 33; Levitskii, *Putilovskii staliteinyi*, 11.

5. Shepelev, *Tsarizm i burzhuaziia*, 100: RGIA f. 20, op. 3, d. 2206, l. 10; *K stoletiiu Putilovskogo zavoda*, 22, 93; McCaffray, *The Politics of Industrialization*, 89–90.

6. Gorodkov, *Admiralteiskie izhorskie zavody*, 124.

7. For discussion of the professionalization of engineers since 1890, see Hogan, *Forging Revolution*, 65–71; McCaffray, *The Politics of Industrialization*, 73–94; Fenin, *Coal and Politics in Late Imperial Russia*. On the relationship between state and professions, see Balzer, "The Problem of Professions in Imperial Russia." See also Orlovsky, "The Lower Middle Strata in Revolutionary Russia."

8. Levitskii, *Putilovskii staliteinyi*, 11; Owen, *The Corporation*, xi, 92.

9. Karpin'skii, "Kommercheskoe obrazovanie v Rossii."

10. *K stoletiiu Putilovskogo zavoda*, 21.

11. *Doklad pravleniia obshchestva Putilovskikh zavodov obshchemu sobraniiu aktsionerov. 7 Noiabria 1887*, 1–2.

12. Ibid., 1–2.

13. Ibid., 2.

14. Ibid., 3–4.

15. Ibid., 5.

16. Ibid., 4–5.

17. Ibid., 5.

18. *K stoletiiu Putilovskogo zavoda*, 22.

19. RGIA f. 626, op. 1, d. 415, ll. 3–10.

20. PRO ADM 231/16 Rept. 216 Russian Fleet, Guns, etc. 1889. by Capt. Sir Cecil Domville, 12; PRO ADM 231/18 Rept. 249 Russia. Guns, Torpedoes, Torpedo Boats, etc. 1890. by Capt. Sir Cecil Domville, 6; ADM 231/19 Rept. 258 Russian Fleet,

Dockyards etc. (Baltic Sea) 1890. By Capt. Sir Cecil Domville, 11.

21. PRO ADM 231/20, Rept. 294. Russia. Fleet, Dockyards, etc. (Baltic Sea), 1891, 11–23; ibid., 231/23 Rept. 376 Russia. Fleet, Dockyards (Baltic Sea). 1893, by Capt. G. Le C. Egerton, 17.

22. *Torgovo-Promyshlennaia Gazeta,* 12 [24] January 1893, 3; ibid., 6 [18] April 1893, 3; *K stoletiiu Putilovskogo zavoda,* 22–23, 93–94.

23. *K stoletiiu Putilovskogo zavoda,* 77.

24. Ibid., 78; PRO ADM 231/20, Rept. 294. Russia. Fleet, Dockyards, etc. (Baltic Sea), 1891, 23.

25. *K stoletiiu Putilovskogo zavoda,* 80.

26. RGVIA f. 504, op. 9, d. 717, ll. 28, 174.

27. *K stoletiiu Putilovskogo zavoda,* 80–86; Levitskii, *Putilovskii staliteinyi,* 39, 56, 71–74.

28. *K stoletiiu Putilovskogo zavoda,* 87; *Torgovo-Promyshlennaia Gazeta,* 6 [18] April 1893, 3. *Otchet, 1895–1896,* 8–9; *Otchet, 1896–1897,* 8; *Otchet, 1897–1898,* 8; *Otchet, 1898–1899,* 8–9; *Otchet, 1899–1900,* 8–9.

29. PRO ADM 231/26 Rept. 453. Russia. Fleet, Dockyards (Baltic Sea) 1895. By Capt. Wintz, 27–28.

30. ADM 231/29 Rept. 540. Russia. Baltic and Black Sea Fleets, Dockyards etc. 1898. Capt. Henry Jackson, 42.

31. RGVIA f. 504, op. 2, d. 112, ll. 20–21.

32. *Torgovo-Promyshlennaia Gazeta,* 17 [29] November 1898, 5.

33. RGVIA f. 514, op. 1, d. 52, ll. 25–26.

34. *Torgovo-Promyshlennaia Gazeta,* 8 [20] April 1899, 5.

35. *Torgovo-Promyshlennaia Gazeta,* 12 [24] November 1899, 5.

36. Bradley, *Guns for the Tsar,* 7–11.

37. Misa, *A Nation of Steel,* 97–101.

38. Ibid., 95.

39. Ibid, 102–05; 129–31.

40. PRO ADM 231/19. Rept. 259 Austria. Guns, Torpedoes, Torpedo Boats, etc. 1890. By Capt. Domville, 6–8.

41. PRO ADM 231/22 Rept. 337 Austria. Guns, Torpedoes, etc. 1892. By Capt. William May, 11.

42. PRO ADM 231/27 Rept. 473. Austria. Guns, Torpedoes, etc. 1896. By Capt. Lewis E. Wintz, 6–8.

43. Collier, *Arms and the Men,* 47–48, 61; Boelcke, *Krupp unde Die Hohenzollern, aus der Korrespondenz,* 9–13, 35–38, 63–68.

44. Ropp, *The Development of a Modern Navy,* 64–65.

45. Collier, *Arms and the Men,* 54.

46. Trebilcock, *The Vickers Brothers,* 26, 29, 31, 36–37.

47. Ibid., 27.

48. PRO ADM 231/23 Rept. 364, Russia Coast Defence Ordnance and Torpedoes. 1894, 8, 12, 20–21.

49. *Torgovo-Promyshlennaia Gazeta,* 17 [29] November 1898, 5.

50. *K stoletiiu Putilovskogo zavoda,* 26.

51. Gatrell, *The Tsarist Economy,* 154; Il'inskii and Ivanitskii, *Ocherk istorii russkoi,* 79, 90, 98, 103.

52. Gatrell, *Government,* 51; *K stoletiiu Putilovskogo zavoda,* 33–34; 1.

53. Solov'eva, "Pribyli krupnoi promyshlennoi burzhuazii, 44. Putilov's figures are calculated from the annual account books for 1893–1900.

54. Trebilcock, *The Vickers Brothers,* 156.

55. *Torgovo-Promyshlennaia Gazeta,* 5 [18] May 1903, 2.

56. *K stoletiiu Putilovskogo zavoda,* 3; *Torgovo-Promyshlennaia Gazeta,* 6 [19] May 1904, 4.

57. RGIA f. 120, op. 1, d. 58, ll. 1.

58. *K stoletiiu Putilovskogo zavoda,* 1. See Boelcke, *Krupp unde die Hohenzollern in Dokumenten,* 98.

59. *K stoletiiu Putilovskogo zavoda,* 126.

60. Ibid., 125.

61. Ibid., 125–26.

62. Ibid., 126.

63. Ibid., 127.

Chapter 3. The Russian Krupp

1. Gatrell, *Government,* 215. A similar view is expressed by Shatsillo, *Gosudarstvo,* 140.

2. Jindra, *Der Rüstungs-Konzern Fried,* 52; Trebilcock, *The Vickers Brothers,* 20, 25.

3. For 1908–1911, see RGIA f. 630, op. 2, d. 477, l. 10; for 1912, see *Otchet, 1912,* 16; *Otchet, 1902,* 17; *Torgovo-Promyshlennaia Gazeta,* 2 [15] May 1904, 4. According to Gatrell, the shift to armaments began in 1908 when armaments accounted for 30 percent of production. He sees the increasing arms share as a result of A. I. Putilov's control of the company, which he mistakenly dates in 1908. Putilov did not appear on the scene until 1910 (Gatrell, *Government,* 217, 223).

4. PRO ADM 231/37 Rept. 689. Reports on Foreign Naval Affairs 1903 (vol. 2), 90–91.

5. ADM 231/41 Rept. 738. Foreign Naval Progress and Estimates. 1904, 137.

6. Krause, *Arms and the State,* 58–59; Jindra, *Der Rüstungs-Konzern Fried,* 106, 115.

7. Ropp, *The Development of a Modern Navy,* 63, 68; Krause, *Arms and the State,* 60.

8. PRO ADM 231/37 Rept. 689. Reports on Foreign Naval Affairs 1903 (vol. II), 129.

9. Ibid., 130.

10. Stevenson, *Armaments and the Coming of War,* 29–30. As of 1912, Schneider's plant at Creusot was worth about one-tenth of Krupp's plant.

11. PRO ADM 231/46 rept. 804. Reports on Foreign Naval Affairs. 1906. (Vol. I), 172, 186–87.

12. Ibid., 187.

13. PRO ADM 231/23 Rept. 364. Russia Coast Defence Ordnance and Torpedoes. 1894, 7. For a schematic of the War Ministry, see Beskrovnyi, *Russkaia armiia i flot*, 200.

14. Manikovskii, *Boevoe snabzhenie russkoi armii*, 41–42.

15. Kovalenko, *Oboronnaia promyshlennost' sovetskoi Rossii*, 17.

16. Gudmundsson, *On Artillery*, 21; Herrmann, *The Arming of Europe*, 17; Stevenson, *Armaments and the Coming of War*, 17.

17. Gudmundsson, *On Artillery*, 17–18; Herrmann, *The Arming of Europe*, 18.

18. RGVIA f. 514, op. 1, d. 52, ll. 2–6.

19. Ibid., l. 7.

20. Ibid., ll. 9, 17; RGVIA f. 514, op. 1, d. 67, l. 210; ibid., d. 80, l. 40, 167.

21. Gatrell, *Government*, 260–61.

22. RGVIA f. 514, op. 1, d. 52, l. 7.

23. RGVIA f. 514, op. 1, d. 84, ll. 2, 3 (quoted).

24. Ibid., l. 3.

25. Ibid., ll. 3-4.

26. Ibid., ll. 4, 26.

27. Ibid., l. 5.

28. RGVIA f. 514, op. 1, d. 93, ll. 3, 6, 12–13, 27; ibid., d. 95, l. 8.

29. RGVIA f. 514, op. 1, d. 95, ll. 77, 153, 4.

30. RGVIA f. 514, op. 1, d. 105, l. 3 (quoted), 4–5.

31. RGVIA f. 514, op. 1, d. 108, l. 3.

32. ADM 231/41 Rept. 738. Foreign Naval Progress and Estimates. 1904, 137.

33. RGVIA f. 514, op. 1, d. 108, l. 4.

34. *Otchet, 1901*, 1–4; ibid., 1902, 1–4; *Torgovo-Promyshlennaia Gazeta*, 2 [15] May 1904, 4; ibid., 6 [19] May 1904, 4.

35. Surh, *1905 in St. Petersburg*, 51, 66, 96, 147–56, 179; Ascher, *The Revolution of 1905*, 80–92.

36. Surh, *1905 in St. Petersburg*, 194, 210, 263, 271, 292, 359–60; *Torgovo-Promyshlennaia Gazeta*, 19 May [1 June] 1905, 4; ibid., 17 [30] May 1906, 5.

37. RGVIA f. 514, op. 1, d. 108, l. 71.

38. RGVIA f. 514, op. 1, d. 131, ll. 117–18, 225–26.

39. Ibid., ll 226, 426.

40. Ibid., ll. 226–27.

41. Ibid., ll. 117, 227.

42. Ibid., l. 228.

43. Ibid., l. 229.

44. Ibid., l. 490.

45. Ibid., l. 490.

46. Ibid., l. 490.

47. Ibid., l. 491.

48. Ibid., l. 491.

49. Ibid., l. 491.

50. Ibid., l. 561.

51. Ibid., l. 492.

52. Ibid., ll. 493–97.

53. Ibid., ll. 615–16.

54. Ibid., l. 616.

55. McDonald, *United Government and Foreign Policy in Russia,* 5–7.

56. RGVIA f. 514, op. 1, d. 131, l. 617.

57. Ibid., l. 612.

58. Ibid., l. 612.

59. The Putilov figures are calculated from *Otchet, 1904–1907;* the figures for Sormovo and Kolomna can be found in Golikov and Naumova, "Istochniki po istorii aktsionirovaniia promyshlennosti," 118–19.

60. Stevenson, *Armaments and the Coming of War,* 23.

61. RGVIA f. 514, op. 1, d. 131, l. 491.

62. Trebilcock, *The Vickers Brothers,* 24.

63. Ibid., xi.

64. PRO WO 106/6187. Rept. on Changes in Foreign Armies During 1910, 91.

65. *Otchet, 1911,* 3, 16.

66. Goldstein, "Military Aspect," 195.

Chapter 4. Banks, Boards, and Naval Expansion

1. The number of these works is vast, but examples which deal with the Putilov Company and banks in detail include K. F. Shatsillo, *Gosudarstvo,* 140–61; Mitel'man et al., *Istoriia Putilovskogo zavoda,* 361–71, 415–22; Bovykin, "Banki i voennaia promyshlennost'"; Livshin, "K voprosu o voenno-promyshlennykh monopoliiakh;" Bovykin and Tarnovskii, "Kontsentratsiia proizvodstva."

2. Rieber, *Merchants and Entrepreneurs,* 364–71; Hogan, *Forging Revolution,* 157–161; Gatrell, *Government,* 215–18.

3. Cassis, *Big Business,* 177.

4. The older positions based on Hilferding and the new revisionist views are outlined in Tilly, "An Overview on the Role of the Large German Banks up to 1914"; Bonin, "The Political Influence of Bankers and Financiers"; James, "Banks and Bankers"; Lee, "The Paradigm of German Industrialisation"; Feldenkirchen, "Banking and Economic Growth."

5. Bovykin, "Banki i voennaia promyshlenost,'" 83–101; Mitel'man et al., *Istoriia Putilovskogo zavoda,* 353–67. More recently Bovykin has presented a more nuanced view that combines competition between the banks with cooperation. See Bovykin and Petrov, *Kommercheskie banki rossiiskoi imperii,* 170–76.

6. Shatsillo, *Gosudarstvo,* 147–51. Gatrell's study acknowledges the banking groups but does not take a clear position on cooperation or competition between the groups. See Gatrell, *Government,* 218–25.

7. Rieber, *Merchants and Entrepreneurs,* 366; Anan'ich, *Bankirskie doma v Rossii,* 179.

8. RGIA f. 630, op. 2, d. 474, ll. 28–29.

9. Ibid., l. 33.

10. Ibid., l. 33.

11. *Otchet, 1887–1888*, 19. The original debt amounted to 3.5 million rubles. See *Otchet, 1884–1885*, 20.

12. RGIA f. 626, op. 1, d. 423, ll. 5–6.

13. *Torgovo-Promyshlennaia Gazeta*, 17 [29] November 1895, 6.

14. RGIA f. 626, op. 1, d. 459, ll. 5; 8–9; 30.

15. *Torgovo-Promyshlennaia Gazeta*, 20 November [3 December] 1903, 3.

16. *Torgovo-Promyshlennaia Gazeta*, 15 [28] May 1907, 3.

17. This information comes from *Torgovo-Promyshlennaia Gazeta*, 15 [28] May 1907, 3; ibid., 18 [31] May 1908, 5; 1 [14] May 1909, 4; 6 [19] May 1910, 3; 29 April [12 May] 1911, 2; 1 [14] May 1912, 3; 17 [30] May 1913, 2–3; 21 May [3 June] 1914, 3.

18. RGIA f. 630, op. 2, d. 470, l. 16.

19. Ibid., l. 17; *Torgovo-Promyshlennaia Gazeta*, 6 [19] May 1910, 3; ibid., 1 [14] May 1912, 3; ibid., April 29 [12 May], 1911, 2.

20. RGIA f. 630, op. 2, d. 474, ll. 77, 79.

21. RGIA f. 630, op. 2, d. 472, l. 72.

22. *Torgovo-Promyshlennaia Gazeta*, April 8 [21], 1912, 8; ibid., 1 [14] May 1912, 3.

23. *Torgovo-Promyshlennaia Gazeta*, 17 [30] May 1912, 3.

24. RGIA f. 630, op. 2, d. 469, ll. 2–11; 16; 23–24; ibid., f. 626, op. 1, d. 273, ll. 2., 13; PRO FO 371/1521 Buchanan to Grey, 5 December 1912.

25. RGIA f. 630, op. 2, d. 473, ll. 1–2, 9–10.

26. PRO ADM 231/37 Rept. 689. Reports on Foreign Naval Affairs 1903 (vol. II), 90; ADM 231/43 Rept. 757. Reports on Foreign Naval Affairs. 1905 (Vol. I), 34; ADM 231/44 Rept. 777. Report on Foreign Naval Affairs. 1905. (vol. II), 127.

27. Taits, *Korabelshchiki Narvskoi zastavy*, 14–15.

28. *Torgovo-Promyshlennaia Gazeta*, 15 [28] May 1907, 3.

29. Westwood, *Russian Naval Construction*, 2.

30. Ibid., 78–83.

31. Ibid., 85–86.

32. Ibid., 77, 90–97.

33. *Torgovo-Promyshlennaia Gazeta*, 6 [19] May 1910, 3.

34. *Torgovo-Promyshlennaia Gazeta*, April 23 [6 May] 1911, 2.

35. RGIA f. 630, op. 2, d. 470, l. 14.

36. Ibid., l. 15.

37. RGIA f. 630, op. 2, d. 474, ll. 5, 8–9, 47–50.

38. Ibid., ll. 51, 67.

39. ADM 231/26 Capt. Wintz, Rept. 453, Russia. Fleet, Dockyards (Baltic Sea) 1895, 26; ADM 231/29 Capt. Henry Jackson, Rept. 540, Russia. Baltic and Black Sea Fleets, Dockyards etc. 1898, 13, 30, 41.

40. ADM 231/43 Rept. 757. Reports on Foreign Naval Affairs. 1905 (Vol. I), 33, 36; ADM 231/44 Rept. 777. Report on Foreign Naval Affairs. 1905. (vol. II), 135.

41. Westwood, *Russian Naval Construction*, 112–15.

42. *Torgovo-Promyshlennaia Gazeta,* 16 [29] May 1912, 5.

43. RGIA f. 597, op. 2, d. 310, ll. 18–19, 23–24.

44. Ibid., l. 7.

45. RGIA f. 630, op. 2, d. 430, ll. 10, 17.

46. *Torgovo-Promyshlennaia Gazeta,* 15 [28] May 1913, 3.

47. RGAV-MF, f. 418, op. 1, d. 2352, l. 283.

48. RGIA f. 630, op. 2, d. 474, l. 41.

49. This conclusion is drawn from a reading of the pattern of their signatures on a variety of contracts in 1910–1914. See RGIA f. 120, op. 1, d. 80 *passim;* f. 630, op. 2, d. 484, l. 89, 114; ibid., d. 470, l. 1; ibid., d. 430, l. 17; ibid., d. 482, ll. 1–4, 5; ibid., d. 425, ll. 102, 371.

50. RGIA f. 630, op. 2, d. 425, ll. 199–207; ibid., f. 120, op. 1, d. 80, ll. 37, 40, 43, 49, 61, 92–93; RGVIA f. 504, op. 9, d. 366, ll. 1–6; ibid., d. 370, ll. 1–6; ibid., d. 390, ll. 2, 28.

51. *Nevskii sudostroitel'nyi i mekhanicheskii zavod,* 21; *Torgovo-Promyshlennaia Gazeta,* 17 [30] May 1912, 3.

52. RGIA f. 630, op. 2, d. 472, ll. 78, 11.

53. *Torgovo-Promyshlennaia Gazeta,* 8 [21] May 1914, 3.

54. Ibid., 7 [20] April 1913, 3; ibid., 25 April [8 May], 1912, 3; ibid., 13 [26] May 1912, 3; ibid., 18 April [1 May], 1912, 3.

55. Gatrell, *Government,* 242–43.

56. Hennart, "International Financial Capital Transfers."

57. RGIA f. 597, op. 2, d. 310, ll. 9–10; f. 630, op. 2, d. 430, l. 10; RGVIA f. 369, op. 16, d. 32, l. 187.

58. Cassis, *Big Business,* 181–85; Stevenson, *Armaments and the Coming of War,* 31.

Chapter 5. Putilov at War

1. Examples of the first category of interpretation can be found in Mitel'man et al., *Istoriia Putilovskogo zavoda,* 554; Krylov, *Vospominaniia i ocherki,* 208. For interpretations that emphasize the labor issue, see Siegelbaum, *The Politics of Industrial Mobilization in Russia,* 117; Lemeshev, "Na Putilovskom zavode v gody voiny," 196; McKean, *St. Petersburg Between the Revolutions,* 449. The case for the sequestration as a means to save the owners from financial loss is made by Shatsillo, "Iz istorii."

2. Shatsillo, "Iz istorii," 217; Kovalenko, *Oboronnaia promyshlennost' sovetskoi Rossii,* 27.

3. Siegelbaum, *The Politics of Industrial Mobilization in Russia,* 70; RGVIA f. 369, op. 1, d. 54, l. 46; ibid., op. 4, d. 32, ll. 18–20; ibid., op. 16, d. 32, l. 104.

4. Pinchuk, *The Octobrists in the Third Duma,* 189–90; Hosking, *The Russian Constitutional Experiment,* 76; Polivanov, *Iz dnevnikov,* 40–43; Suchomlinow, *Errinerungen,* 199, 279; Senin, *Aleksandr Guchkov,* 28–29, 39, 42, 61, 75, 92; Gleason, *Alexander Guchkov,* vol. 73, pt. 3, 33–34, 58–59.

5. Rieber, *Merchants and Entrepreneurs,* 378; Siegelbaum, *The Politics of Industrial Mobilization in Russia,* 38.

6. RGVIA f. 369, op. 16, d. 32, l. 58.

7. RGVIA f. 369, op. 1, d. 54, l. 60.

8. RGVIA f. 369, op. 16, d. 32, l. 59.

9. RGVIA f. 369, op. 1, d. 54, l. 60.

10. RGVIA f. 369, op. 1, d. 54, l. 61.

11. Polikarpov, "Putilovskii zavod nakanune fevralia 1917 goda."

12. RGVIA f. 369, op. 16, d. 32, l. 66.

13. Ibid., l. 18.

14. Ibid., l. 19.

15. Ibid., l. 20.

16. Ibid., l. 20.

17. Ibid., l. 27.

18. Ibid., l. 27.

19. RGVIA f. 369, op. 1, d. 54, l. 75.

20. Ibid., l. 82.

21. RGVIA f. 369, op. 16, d. 32, ll. 146–47.

22. Ibid., l. 147.

23. Ibid., l. 153.

24. Ibid., l. 154.

25. Ibid., l. 85.

26. Ibid., ll. 85–86.

27. Manikovskii, *Boevoe snabzhenie russkoi armii,* 72.

28. RGVIA f. 369, op. 16, d. 31, l. 87.

29. RGVIA f. 369, op. 1, d. 54, ll. 85–86.

30. RGVIA f. 369, op. 16, d. 31, l. 88.

31. RGVIA f. 369, op. 1, d. 54, l. 225.

32. Krylov, *Vospominaniia i ocherki,* 208.

33. Siegelbaum, *The Politics of Industrial Mobilization in Russia,* 31–33, 38, 70–71, 77–79.

34. Manikovskii, *Boevoe snabzhenie russkoi armii,* 122–23.

35. Ibid., 124–25, 141.

36. Ibid., 384–85.

37. Shatsillo, "Iz istorii," 217.

38. Krylov, *Vospominaniia i ocherki,* 208.

39. Manikovskii, *Boevoe snabzhenie russkoi armii,* 42.

40. Ibid., 43.

41. Ibid., 46–47.

42. Ibid., 43.

43. RGVIA f. 505, op. 3, d. 21, l. 31.

44. RGVIA f. 505, op. 3, d. 21, l. 8; ibid., d. 22, ll. 71–72; Polikarpov, "Putilovskii zavod nakanune fevralia 1917 goda," 105.

45. Manikovskii, *Boevoe snabzhenie russkoi armii,* 143.

46. Ibid., 143.

47. RGVIA f. 505, op. 3, d. 21, l. 49.

48. Ibid., l. 52.

49. RGVIA f. 505, op. 3, d. 22, l. 162.

50. Ibid., l. 165.

51. The exact figures reported by General Drozdov were in 1914: 39,008,587 rubles (av. 3,250,715 rubles per month); 1915: 90,181,421 rubles (av. 7,515,118 rubles per month), and for 1916 including the first seven months of state administration of the factories 87,078,312 rubles (or an average of 9,675,368 rubles per month). RGVIA f. 505, op. 3, d. 22, l. 129.

52. Siegelbaum, *The Politics of Industrial Mobilization in Russia,* 105–07.

53. Wegs, "Austrian Economic Mobilization," 11–16, 158–59; Feldman, *Army, Industry and Labor,* 31–33, 60–61, 228–29; Godfrey, *Capitalism at War,* 144–49; Koistinen, *Mobilizing for Modern War,* 106, 186, 296.

54. RGVIA f. 505, op. 3, d. 22, l. 77.

55. Ibid., l. 84.

56. Ibid., l. 235.

57. Ibid., l. 235.

58. Ibid., ll. 207–08.

59. Ibid., l. 208.

60. Ibid., ll. 200–01.

61. Ibid., ll. 319, 352, 408.

62. Mandel, *The Petrograd Workers and the Fall of the Old Regime;* Mandel, *The Petrograd Workers and the Soviet Seizure of Power;* Smith, *Red Petrograd.*

Chapter 6. Between State and Market

1. Hexner, *The International Steel Cartel,* 24.

2. Brown, *The Baldwin Locomotive Works,* xxvi–xxix.

3. Ibid., 28–34.

4. Hexner, *The International Steel Cartel,* 44–46.

5. There are numerous examples of this interpretation; see Bovykin, *Formirovanie;* Bovykin, *Zarozhedenie;* Liashchenko, "Iz istorii monopolii v Rossii"; Sidorov, "Nekotorye problemy."

6. Gerschenkron, *Economic Backwardness,* 20.

7. Misa, *A Nation of Steel,* 20–21.

8. Hexner, *The International Steel Cartel,* 18–19.

9. Rust, "Business and Politics in the Third Republic," 40–44, 142–45.

10. RGIA f. 626, op. 1, d. 406, ll. 2–7.

11. The best summary of the rail producers' cartel can be found in Bovykin, *Zarozhdenie,* 99–115. Some of the archival documents have also been published in A. L. Sidorov ed., *Materialy po istorii SSSR,* tom VI (Moskva: Izdatel'stvo Akademii Nauk SSSR, 1959), 18–24.

12. *Materialy,* 28–30.

13. Bovykin, *Zarozhdenie,* 118–21.

14. RGIA f. 626, op. 1, d. 414, ll. 1, 10.

15. Ibid., ll. 22–23.

16. Bovykin, *Formirovanie*, 218–19.

17. Brown, *The Baldwin Locomotive Works*, 49–54.

18. Rust, "Business and Politics in the Third Republic," 81–83, 186–89.

19. Bovykin, *Formirovanie*, 217–18; RGIA f. 120, op. 1, "Predislovie," ii–iii.

20. RGIA f. 120, op. 1, d. 1, l. 1, 7.

21. Ibid., ll. 2–3.

22. Ibid., l. 3.

23. Ibid., l. 3.

24. RGIA f. 120, op. 1, d. 2, l. 88.

25. RGIA f. 120, op. 1, d. 4, l. 21.

26. Ibid., l. 23.

27. RGIA f. 120, op. 1, d. 1, l. 17.

28. Ibid., l. 30.

29. Ibid., l. 40.

30. RGIA f. 120, op. 1, d. 14, l. 2.

31. Ibid., l. 5.

32. RGIA f. 120, op. 1, d. 58, l. 67.

33. I am indebted to Andrew Verner for pointing out the geographic dimension to the cartel's activity.

34. RGIA f. 120, op. 1, d. 58, ll. 1–24.

35. Gatrell, *Government*, 256.

36. RGIA f. 120, op. 1, d. 58, ll. 70–71.

37. Ibid., l. 51.

38. Ibid., ll. 1–24.

39. *Promyshlennost' i Torgovlia*, 1 January 1911 (no. 1); on the trade journal, see Roosa, *Russian Industrialists* 34, 36–37, 178, 189–90.

40. *P i T*, 15 June 1913 (No. 12), 28.

41. Moore, *World Modernization*, 38.

42. Evans et al., *States versus Markets*, 11–12.

43. Ibid., 25.

44. *Otchet, 1883–1892*. This category appeared under the section for output by departments.

45. *K stoletiiu Putilovskogo zavoda*, 22.

46. *Torgovo-Promyshlennaia Gazeta*, 15 [28] June 1910, 3.

47. RGAV-MF, f. 418, op. 1, d. 2352, l. 291.

48. This information is based on the *Otchety* for 1911–1914 under the heading "obrotnoe imushchestvo."

49. Chandler, *Scale and Scope*, 423–27, 501, 587–89. For the French case, see Freedeman, *The Triumph of Corporate Capitalism*, 112–28.

50. Owen, *The Corporation*, 215. A similar sentiment is expressed in Von Laue, *Sergei Witte*, 305.

Epilogue

1. O'Prey, *A Farewell to Arms?*, 19–23.

2. Akansky, "Industrial Company Profile—Kirovsky Zavod"; "Tractors and Agricultural Machinery," *BBC Summary of World Broadcasts*, 16 February 1979.

3. "Gorbachev's Visit to Leningrad," *BBC Summary of World Broadcasts*, 17 May 1985.

4. "End of Zaykov's Visit to Leningrad," *BBC Summary of World Broadcasts*, 7 September 1988.

5. "Kirovets Tractor—New Modification," *TASS*, 13 April 1989; Akansky, "Industrial Company Profile—Kirovsky Zavod."

6. "New Tractor Prototypes," *SovData Dialine–BizEkon News*, 22 February 1991.

7. Gaddy, *The Price of the Past*, 95–99.

8. "On the Verge of Stoppage," *SovData Dialine–BizEkon News*, 2 March 1992.

9. "Company News," *BBC Summary of World Broadcasts*, 29 May 1992.

10. Gaddy, *The Price of the Past*, 78–80.

11. "We Will Divide Everything," *SovData Dialine–BizEkon News*, 22 April 1992; Rye, Man and Gor Securities, "Analytical Note," 17 April 1997.

12. Hofheinz, "Who to Call in the Soviet Union Now," *Fortune*, 2 December 1991, 163; "Semenenko, Petr Georgievich," in Vasil'ev et al., *Kto est' kto v Sankt-Peterburge 1996;* "Semenenko, Petr Georgievich," in *Kto est' kto v Rossii*, 306.

13. *Izvestia*, 31 March 1992.

14. Akansky, "Industrial Company Profile—Kirovsky Zavod"; *St. Petersburg Press*, no. 85, 20–26 December 1994, business section.

15. Yevgenia Borisova, "Local Plants Find Private Success," *St. Petersburg Press*, no. 118, 8–14 August 1995, business section.

16. "Russia's Demand for Fodder Harvesters Will Be Met," *SovData Dialine–BizEkon News*, 14 May 1993.

17. "Petersburg Tractor Plant Announces 'Pre-strike Status,'" *BBC Summary of World Broadcasts*, 14 December 1993; ibid., 6 May 1994; ibid., 23 September 1994.

18. Ibid., 8 September 1995; Akansky, "Industrial Company Profile—Kirovsky Zavod"; "Kirovsky Zavod is Putting Its Tractors Out Again," *SovData Dialine–BizEkon News*, 16 January 1996.

19. Lev Frolov, "Tractor assembly conveyer line stopped at Kirovsky Zavod," *TASS*, 5 June 1995.

20. *A&G Information Services*, 20 September 1996.

21. *Directory of Russian Enterprises (Part 2)*, Defense Conversion Directories for the Newly Independent States (Internet Version).

22. Bob Bouyea, "Cat Signs New Joint Venture, Puts Down More Roots in CIS," *Peoria Journal Star*, 8 February 1994, business page.

23. Katya Yuspova, "New Deal," *St. Petersburg Press*, no. 80, 15–21 November 1994, business section.

24. "NevaMash to be One-Third Russian," *SovData Dialine–BizEkon News*, 9 February 1994.

25. "Caterpillar Takes Another Step in Russia," *Central European Business Guide*, no. 4, vol. 1, April 1994.

26. "Kirovsky Zavod Forms Venture with Caterpillar," *CIS Economics and Foreign Trade*, 29 August, 1994.

27. O'Prey, *A Farewell to Arms?*, 88.

28. Rachel Katz, "Arms Giants Team Up in New Deal," *St. Petersburg Press*, no. 95, 28 February–6 March 1995, business section. See also ibid., no. 64, 26 July–1 August, 1994.

29. "General Electric Subsidiary in Russian Gas Turbine Deal," *Russia Express–Perestroika: Executive Briefing*, 27 February 1995; "Russian Turbine Engineering Still Attractive to Foreign Capital," *SovData Dialine–BizEkon News*, 10 February 1995.

30. "So Far Only Foreign Investors Are Interested in Supporting Russia's Turbine Engineering," *SovData Dialine–BizEkon News* 7 March 1995.

31. Peter Koenig, "If Europe's Dead, Why is GE Investing Billions There?," *Fortune*, 9 September 1996.

32. "Kirovsky Zavod to Produce Buses," *CIS Economics and Foreign Trade*, 1 April 1994; Akansky, "Industrial Company Profile—Kirovsky Zavod."

33. Vladimir Kovalov, "Mayor's Office Takes Action As Industrial Crisis Looms," *St. Petersburg Press*, no. 70, 6–12 September 1994.

34. *A&G Information Services*, 21 January 1997.

35. "Kirovsky Zavod to Make Buses," *CIS Economics and Foreign Trade*, 15 March 1995; "The Weekly Indicators of Stock Trading Activity," *Moscow News*, 30 June 1995.

36. "U.S. Firm to Help Build Gas Turbines for Soviet Pipeline," *Agence France Presse*, 3 September 1991.

37. *A&G Information Services*, 29 August 1997.

38. Kirovsky Zavod web page http://www.spb.su/bw/49.html; Yevgenia Borisova, "Major Factories Celebrate Birthdays," *St. Petersburg Times*, nos. 165–66, 3–9 June 1996, business section; Borisova, "Local Plants;" Rye, Man and Gor Securities, "Analytical Note."

39. Akansky, "Industrial Company Profile—Kirovsky Zavod";.

40. Borisova, "Local Plants;" Akansky, "Industrial Company Profile-Kirovsky Zavod"; Rye, Man and Gor Securities, "Analytical Note."

41. Rye, Man and Gor Securities, "Analytical Note."

42. *A&G Information Services*, 27 February 1997.

43. Lena Berezanskaya and Jeff Grocott, "Raging Bull: 1997 Financial Year in Review Shows Stock Market the Best Place to Invest," *St. Petersburg Times*, nos. 282–83, 28 July–3 August 1997.

44. John Varoli, "Kirovsky Bounces Back with Bigger Profits," *St. Petersburg Times*, no. 371, 9 June 1998.

45. "Former 'Tank Director' Stakes on Partnership," *CIS Economics and Foreign Trade*, 1 May 1995; Rye, Man and Gor Securities, "Analytical Note."

46. Yevgenia Borisova, "Kirovsky Factory Uses Debt Deal to Privatize Its Land" *St. Petersburg Times,* nos. 286–87, 11–17 August 1997.

47. "Czech Firm Skoda Plzen Seeks Foreign Partners," *Eastern European Report,* 4 March 1991.

48. "Skoda Plzen Freezes Production," *East European Markets,* 2 October 1992.

49. "Plans Unveiled for Skoda-Plzen Privatisation," *European Information Service,* 17 November 1992; "Czech Skoda Director Takes Control of Major Stake," *Reuters European Business Report,* 17 June 1993.

50. "Survey of Czech Finance, Industry and Investment," *Financial Times* (London), 2 June 1995.

51. Andrew Baxter, "GE and Skoda in Power Co-operation," ibid., 27 April 1994.

52. Vincent Boland, "Skoda Plzen to Take Tatra Stake," ibid., 28 February 1996.

53. Gregory, *Before Command,* 82–83.

SELECTED BIBLIOGRAPHY

Archival Sources

Rossiiskii Gosudartsvennyi Arkhiv Voenno-Morskogo Flota (RGAV-MF)

Fond 418 (Materials pertaining to the Shipbuilding Commission)

Opis' 1 : Dela 2352, 1616

Rossiisskii Gosudartsvennyi Istoricheskii Arkhiv (RGIA)

Fond 120 (Materials of the Locomotive Producers Cartel)

Opis' 1: Dela 1–2, 4, 7, 9, 14–16, 52, 58, 60, 64, 72, 80–81, 84

Fond 268 (Department of Railroad Affairs)

Opis' 1, part 2: Delo 1618

Fond 597 (St. Petersburg Private Commercial Bank)

Opis' 2: Dela 309–10

Fond 626 (St. Petersburg International Commercial Bank)

Opis' 1: Dela 406, 410, 413–15, 423, 459, 816

Fond 630 (Russo-Asiatic Bank)

Opis' 2: Dela 425–26, 428–31, 469–70, 472–74, 476–82, 484, 840

Fond 1263 (Journal of the Committee of Ministers)

Opis' 1: Delo 3601, art. 561; 4106, art. 466; 4180, art. 564; 4399, art. 770; 5129, art. 571

Opis' 2: Delo 5744, art. 1050; 5112, art. 53

Fond 1276 (Council of Ministers)

Opis' 7: Delo 104

Opis' 10: Delo 134

Fond 1333 (Senatorial Revision of D. B. Neidgart)

Opis' 2: Dela 52–54

Rossiisskii Gosudarstvennyi Voenno-Istoricheskii Arkhiv (RGVIA)

Fond 369 (Special Commission for Defense)

Opis' 1: Delo 54

Opis' 4: Delo 32

Opis' 16: Dela 31, 32, 33

Fond 504 (Main Artillery Administration)

Opis' 2: Dela 112, 116, 127

Opis' 7: Dela 1520, 438

Opis' 9: Dela 342, 356, 366, 370, 390, 717, 1165

Opis' 52: Delo 26

Fond 505 (Technical Artillery Establishment)

Opis' 3: Dela 21, 22

Fond 514 (Journals of the Commission for Rearmament of Field Artillery)

Opis' 1: Dela 52, 67, 80, 84, 93, 95, 108, 131, 149, 199, 208, 256

Russian State Library (RGB)

Fond 332

British Public Record Office, Kew (PRO)

ADM 231: 16, 18–20, 22–23, 26–27, 29, 37, 41, 43–44, 46

   WO 106: 6187

   FO 65: 1141, 1163

Published Primary Sources and Contemporary Works

A&G Information Services

Agence France Presse

Birzhevyia Vedomosti

BBC Summary of World Broadcasts

Central European Business Guide

CIS Economics & Foreign Trade

Del'vig, A. I. *Moi vospominaniia*, tom. IV. Moskva: Izdatel'stvo Imperaterskogo Moskovskogo i Rumiantsovskogo Muzeia, 1913.

Doklad pravleniia obshchestva Putilovskikh zavodov obshchemu sobraniiu aktsionerov. 7 noibria 1887.

East European Markets

Eastern European Report

European Information Service

Financial Times (London)

Fortune

Gaza, I. I., ed. *Putilovets v trekh revoliutsiiakh: sbornik materialov po istorii Putilovskogo zavoda.* Leningrad: OGIZ, 1933.

Golos, 1870

Izvestia

Karpin'skii, S. "Kommercheskoe obrazovanie v Rossii." *Promyshlennost' i Torgovlia* 13 (1 July 1908): 7–12.

Keppen, A. *Materialy dlia istorii rel'sovogo proizvodstva v Rossii.* Sanktpeterburg, 1899.

Krylov, A. N. *Vospominaniia i ocherki.* Moskva: Voennoe Izdatel'stvo Ministerstva Vooruzhennykh Sil SSSR, 1949.

K stoletiiu Putilovskogo zavoda, 1801–1901 gg. SanktPeterburg: Izdanie Putilovskogo zavoda, 1902.

Levitskii, M. *Putilovskii staleliteinyi, zhelezodelatel'nyi i mekhanicheskii zavod.* Kronshtadt: Tip. D. M. Komarova, 1898.

Manikovskii, A. A. *Boevoe snabzhenie russkoi armii v mirovuiu voinu.* Moskva: Gos. Voennoe Izdatel'stvo, 1937.

Moscow News

Nevskii sudostroitel'nyi i mekhanicheskii zavod 1910. K vypusku 3000 parovoza s osnovaniia zavoda. Sankt-Peterburg, 1910.

Obshchii morskoi spisok, chast' XI. Sanktpeterburg: Tip. Morskogo Ministerstva, 1900.

Otchet pravleniia obshchestva Putilovskikh zavodov. Sanktpeterburg: Izdanie Putilovskogo zavoda, 1873–1902; 1911–1914.

Peoria Journal Star

Polivanov, A. A. *Iz dnevnikov i vospominanii po dolzhnosti voennogo ministra i ego pomoshchika, 1907–1916 g.* Moskva: Vysshii Voennyi Redaktsionnyi Sovet, 1924.

Pravitel'stvennyi Vestnik, 1870–1880.

Reuter European Business Report

Russia Express-Perestroika: Executive Briefing

St. Petersburg Press

St. Petersburg Times

Sidorov A. L., ed. *Materialy po istorii SSSR,* tom VI. Moskva: Izdatel'stvo Akademii Nauk SSSR, 1959.

SovData DiaLine-BizEkon News

Suchomlinow, W. A. *Errinerungen: deutsche Aufgabe.* Berlin: Verlag von Reimar Hobbing, 1924.

TASS

Torgovo-Promyshlennaia Gazeta, 1893–1914.

Zavody N. Putilova, 1857–1870 g. Sanktpeterburg, 1870.

Secondary Works

Akansky. "Industrial Company Profile—Kirovsky Zavod," *IMI series,* 13 March 1996.

Amberger, Erik. *Deutsche in Staat, Wirtschaft unde Gesellschaft Russlands. Die Familie Amburger in St. Petersburg, 1770–1920.* Wiesbaden: Otto Harrassowitz, 1986.

———. *Fremde und Einheimishce im Wirtschafts- und Kulturleben des Neuzeitlichen Russland.* Wiesbaden: Franz Steiner Verlag, 1982.

Anan'ich, Boris V. *Bankirskie doma v Rossii, 1860–1914 gg.* Leningrad: Nauka, 1991.

Anan'ich, Boris V., et al. *Krizis samoderzhaviia v Rossii, 1895–1917.* Leningrad: Akademiia Nauk SSSR, 1984.

Anderson, Barbara A. *Internal Migration During Modernization in Late Nineteenth-Century Russia.* Princeton: Princeton University Press, 1980.

Apter, David E. *Rethinking Development: Modernization, Dependency, and Postmodern Politics.* Newbury Park: Sage Publications, 1987.

Ascher, Abraham. *The Revolution of 1905: Russia in Disarray.* Stanford: Stanford University Press, 1988.

Balzer, Harley. "The Problem of Professions in Imperial Russia." In *Between Tsar and People: Educated Society and the Quest for Public Identity in Late Imperial Russia*, ed. Edith W. Clowes, Samuel D. Kassow, and James L. West, 183–98. Princeton: Princeton University Press, 1991.

Beaud, Claude. "De l'expansion internationale à la multinationale Schneider en Russie (1896–1914)." *Histoire Économie et Société* 4 (1985), 575–602.

Beskrovnyi, L. G. *Armiia i flot Rossii v nachale XX v.* Moskva: Nauka, 1986.

———. *Russkaia armiia i flot v XIX veke.* Moskva: Nauka, 1973.

Black, Cyril, et al. *The Modernization of Japan and Russia, A Comparative Study.* London: Free Press, 1975.

Blackbourn, David, and Geoff Eley. *The Peculiarities of German History: Bourgeois Society and Politics in Nineteenth-Century Germany.* Oxford: Oxford University Press, 1989.

Boelcke, Willi. *Krupp und Die Hohenzollern, aus der Korrespondenz der Familie Krupp 1850–1916.* Berlin: Rütten & Loening, 1956.

Boelcke, *Krupp unde die Hohenzollern in Dokumenten.* Frankfurt: Akademische Verlagsgesellschaft Athenaion, 1970.

Bokhanov, A. N. *Delovaia elita Rossii 1914 g.* Moskva: Rossiiskaia Akademiia Nauk Institut Rossiskoi Istorii, 1994.

Bonin, Hubert. "The Political Influence of Bankers and Financiers in France in the Years 1850–1960." In *Finance and Financiers in European History, 1880–1960*, ed. Youssef Cassis, 219–42. Cambridge: Cambridge University Press, 1992.

Bovykin, V. I. "Banki i voennaia promyshlennost' Rossii nakanune pervoi mirovoi voiny." *Istoricheskie Zapiski* 64 (1959): 82–135.

———. *Formirovanie finansovogo kapitala v Rossii.* Moskva: Izdatel'stvo Nauk, 1984.

———. *Zarozhdenie finanansovogo kapitala v Rossii.* Moskva: Izdatel'stvo Moskovskogo Universiteta, 1967.

Bovykin, Valerii Ivanovich, and Iu. A. Petrov. *Kommercheskie banki rossiiskoi imperii.* Moskva: Perspektiva, 1994.

Bovykin, V. I., and K. N. Tarnovskii. "Kontsentratsiia proizvodstva i razvitie monopolii v metalloobrabatyvaiushchei promyshlennosti Rossii." *Voprosy Istorii* 2 (1957): 19–31.

Bradley, Joseph. *Guns for the Tsar: American Technology and the Small Arms Industry in Nineteenth-Century Russia.* De Kalb: Northern Illinois University Press, 1990.

Brown, John K. *The Baldwin Locomotive Works 1831–1915: A Study in American Industrial Practice.* Baltimore: Johns Hopkins University Press, 1995.

Brown, Peter B. "The Problematics of Armory Modernization in Late Imperial Russia." *Russian History* 21 (Spring 1994): 65–81.

Buryshkin, Pavel A. *Moskva kupecheskaia.* New York: Izdatel'stvo imeni Chekhova, 1954.

Carstensen, Fred V. *American Enterprise in Foreign Markets: Studies of Singer and International Harvester in Imperial Russia.* Chapel Hill: University of North Carolina Press, 1984.

Carstensen, Fred V., and Gregory Guroff. "Economic Innovation in Imperial Russia and the Soviet Union: Observations." In *Entrepreneurship in Imperial Russia and the*

Soviet Union, ed. Fred V. Carstensen and Gregory Guroff, 347–60. Princeton: Princeton University Press, 1983.

Cassis, Youssef. *Big Business: The European Experience in the Twentieth Century.* Oxford: Oxford University Press, 1997.

Chandler, Alfred D. *Scale and Scope: The Dynamics of Industrial Capitalism.* Cambridge: Belknap Press of Harvard University Press, 1990.

———. *Strategy and Structure: Chapters in the History of the Industrial Enterprise.* Cambridge: MIT Press, 1962.

Chernukha, Valentina G., and Boris V. Anan'ich. "Russia Falls Back, Russia Catches Up: Three Generations of Russian Reformers," in Theodore Tarnanovski (ed.), *Reform in Modern Russian History, Progress or Cycle?* New York: Woodrow Wilson Center Press, 1995, 55–96.

Collier, Basil. *Arms and the Men: The Arms Trade and Governments.* London: Hamish Hamilton, 1980.

Crisp, Olga. *Studies in the Russian Economy Before 1914.* London: Macmillan, 1976.

Directory of Russian Enterprises (Part 2), Defense Conversion Directories for the Newly Independent States (internet version).

Dunlavy, Colleen A. *Politics and Industrialization: Early Railroads in the United States and Prussia.* Princeton: Princeton University Press, 1994.

Ermanskii, A. "Krupnaia burzhuaziia do 1905 goda." In *Obshchestvennoe dvizhenie v Rossii v nachale XX-go veka,* ed. L. Martov et al., 313–48. The Hague: Mouton Russian Reprint Series, 1968.

Evans, Peter, Dietrich Rueschemeyer, and Evelyne Huber Stevens, eds. *States versus Markets in the World-System.* Beverly Hills: Sage Publications, 1985.

Falkus, M. E. *The Industrialisation of Russia 1700–1914.* London: Macmillan Press, 1983.

Feldenkirchen, Wilfried. "Banking and Economic Growth: Banks and Industry in Germany in the Nineteenth Century and Their Changing Relationship During Industrialisation." In *German Industry and German Industrialisation,* ed. W. R. Lee, 116–47. London: Routledge Press, 1991.

Feldman, Gerald D. *Army, Industry and Labor in Germany, 1914–1918.* Princeton: Princeton University Press, 1966.

Fenin, A. I. *Coal and Politics in Late Imperial Russia: Memoirs of a Russian Mining Engineer.* Trans. A. Fediaevsky. Ed. Susan McCaffray. De Kalb: Northern Illinois University Press, 1990.

Freedeman, Charles E. *The Triumph of Corporate Capitalism in France, 1867–1914.* Rochester, N.Y.: Rochester University Press, 1993.

Friedgut, Theodore H. *Iuzoka and Revolution.* Vol. 1. Princeton: Princeton University Press, 1989.

Fuller, William C. *Civil-Military Conflict in Imperial Russia, 1881–1914.* Princeton: Princeton University Press, 1985.

Gaddy, Clifford G. *The Price of the Past: Russia's Struggle with the Legacy of a Militarized Economy.* Washington, D.C.: Brookings Institute Press, 1996.

Gatrell, Peter. "After Tsushima: economic and administrative aspects of Russian naval rearmament, 1905–1913." *Economic History Review*, 2nd ser., 43, no. 2 (1990): 255–70.

———. *Government, Industry and Rearmament in Russia, 1900–1914.* Cambridge: Cambridge University Press, 1994.

———. *The Tsarist Economy 1850–1917.* New York: St. Martin's Press, 1986.

Gerschenkron, Alexander. *Economic Backwardness in Historical Perspective.* Cambridge: Belknap Press, A Division of Harvard University Press, 1962.

Geyer, Dietrich. *Russian Imperialism: The Interaction of Domestic and Foreign Policy, 1860–1914.* New Haven: Yale University Press, 1977.

Ghosh, Pradid K., ed., *Developing Africa: A Modernization Perspective.* Westport, Conn.: Greenwood Press, 1984.

Gindin, I. F. "Balansy aktsionernykh predpriiatii kak istoricheskii istochnik." In *Maloissledovannye istochniki po istorii SSSR XIX–XX vv.*, ed. N. A. Ivnitskii, 74–147. Moskva: Nauka, 1964.

———. *Banki i promyshlennost' v Rossii do 1917 g.* Moskva: Promizdat, 1927.

Gleason, William. *Alexander Guchkov and the End of the Russian Empire*, vol. 73, pt. 3. Philadelphia: American Philosophical Society, 1983.

Godfrey, John F. *Capitalism at War: Industrial Policy and Bureaucracy in France, 1914–1918.* Leamington Spa: Berg Publishers, 1987.

Goldstein, Edward Ralph. "Military Aspects of Russian Industrialization: The Defense Industries, 1890–1917." Ph.D. diss., Case Western Reserve University, 1971.

———. "Vickers Limited and the Tsarist Regime." *Slavonic and East European Review* 58 (October 1980): 561–71.

Goldthorpe, John H., David Lockwood, Frank Bechhofre, and Jennifer Platt. *The Affluent Worker in the Class Strucrure.* Cambridge: Cambridge University Press, 1969.

Golikov, A. G., and G. P. Naumova. "Istochniki po istorii aktsionirovaniia promyshlennosti." In *Massovye istochniki po sotsial'no-ekonomicheskoi istorii Rossii perioda kapitalizma*, ed. I. D. Koval'chenko, 87–120. Moskva: Izd. Nauka, 1979.

Gorodkov, Grigorii Ivanovich. *Admiralteiskie izhorskie zavody: kratkii istoricheskii ocherk.* Sanktpeterburg: Tip. Morskogo Ministerstva, 1903.

Grechaniuk, N. *Baltiiskii flot.* Moskva: Voennoe Izdatelstvo Ministerstva Oborony Soiuza SSR, 1960.

Gregory, Paul. *Before Command: An Economic History of Russia from Emancipation to the First Five-Year Plan.* Princeton: Princeton University Press, 1994.

———. *Russian National Income, 1885–1913.* Cambridge: Cambridge University Press, 1982.

Gudmundsson, Bruce I. *On Artillery.* Westport, Conn.: Praeger, 1993.

Hayward, Oliver Stoddard. "Official Russian Policies Concerning Industrialization During the Finance Ministry of M. Kh. Reutern, 1862–1878." Ph.D. diss., University of Wisconsin, 1973.

Hennart, Jean-François. "International Financial Capital Transfers: A Transaction Cost Framework." *Business History* 36 (January 1994): 51–70.

Herrmann, David G. *The Arming of Europe and the Making of the First World War.* Princeton: Princeton University Press, 1996.

Hexner, Ervin. *The International Steel Cartel.* Chapel Hill: University of North Carolina Press, 1943.

Hilferding, Rudolf. *Das Finanzcápital.* Viennas Verlag der wiener Volksbuchhandlung, 1923.

Hofheinz, Paul. "Who to Call in the Soviet Union Now," *Fortune,* 12-02-1991.

Hogan, Heather. *Forging Revolution: Metalworkers, Managers, and the State in St. Petersburg, 1890–1914.* Bloomington: Indiana University Press, 1993.

Hosking, Geoffrey. *The Russian Constitutional Experiment: Government and Duma, 1907–1914.* Cambridge: Cambridge University Press, 1973.

Il'inskii, D. P., and V. P. Ivanitskii. *Ocherk istorii russkoi parovozistroitel'noi i vagonstroitel'noi promyshlennosti.* Moskva: Transpechat' NKPS, 1929.

James, Harold. "Banks and Bankers in the German Interwar Depression." In *Finance and Financiers in European History, 1880–1960,* ed. Youssef Cassis, 263–81. Cambridge: Cambridge University Press, 1992.

Jindra, Zdenek. *Der Rüstungs-Konzern Fried. Krupp AG., 1914–1918.* Prague: Univerzita Karlova, 1986.

Karpin'skii, S. "Kommercheskoe obrazovanie v Rossii," *Promyshlennost' i Torgovlia,* no. 13 (1 July 1908).

King, Victoria Anne Palmer. "The Emergence of the St. Petersburg Industrialist Community, 1870 to 1905: The Origins and Early Years of the Petersburg Society of Manufacturers." Ph.D. diss., University of California, Berkeley, 1982.

Kipp, Jacob W. "The Russian Navy and Private Enterprise, A Peculiar MIC." In *War, Business and World Military-Industrial Complexes,* ed. Benjamin Franklin Cooling, 84–105. Port Washington, N.Y.: Kennikat Press, 1981.

Koistinen, Paul A. C. *Mobilizing for Modern War: The Political Economy of American Warfare, 1865–1919.* Lawrence: University of Kansas Press, 1997.

Kovalenko, D. A. *Oboronnaia promyshlennost' sovetskoi Rossii v 1918–1920 gg.* Moskva: Nauka, 1970.

Krause, Keith. *Arms and the State: Patterns of Military Production and Trade.* Cambridge: Cambridge University Press, 1992.

Kubitskaia, O. A. "Evoliutsiia monopolisticheskoi organizatsii na primere Soveta predstavitelei parovozostroitel'nykh zavodov)." In *Monopolisticheskii kapital v Rossii,* ed. V. I. Bovykin, 86–103. Moskva: Akademiia Nauk, 1989.

Lee, W. R. "The Paradigm of German Industrialisation: Some Recent Issues and Debates in the Modern Historiography of German Industrial Development." In *German Industry and German Industrialisation,* ed. W. R. Lee, 1–46. London: Routledge Press, 1991.

Lemeshev, F. A. "Na Putilovskom zavode v gody voiny" In *Krushenie tsarizma i vospominaniia uchastnikov revoliutsionnogo dvizheniia v petrograde (1907 g.-Fevral' 1917 g.,* ed. R. Sh. Ganelin and V. A. Ulianov, 189–214. Leningrad: Lenizdat, 1986.

Liashchenko, P. I. "Iz istorii monopolii v Rossii." *Istoricheskie Zapiski* 20 (1946): 150–88.

Liu, Guoli. *States and Markets: Comparing Japan and Russia.* Boulder: Westview Press, 1994.

Livshin, Ia. I. "K voprosu o voenno-promyshlennykh monopoliiakh v Rossii v nachale XX veka (po materialam senatskikh revizii)." *Voprosy Istorii* 7 (1957): 55–70.

Mandel, David. *The Petrograd Workers and the Fall of the Old Regime.* New York: St. Martin's Press, 1983.

———. *The Petrograd Workers and the Soviet Seizure of Power.* London: Macmillan, 1984.

McCaffray, Susan P. *The Politics of Industrialization in Tsarist Russia, The Association of Southern Coal and Steel Producers 1874–1914.* De Kalb: Northern Illinois University Press, 1996.

McDaniel, Tim. *Autocracy, Modernization, and Revolution in Russia and Iran.* Princeton: Princeton University Press, 1991.

McDonald, David MacLaren. *United Government and Foreign Policy in Russia, 1900–1914.* Cambridge: Harvard University Press, 1992.

McKay, John P. *Pioneers for Profit: Foreign Entrepreneurs and Russian Industrialization, 1885–1913.* Chicago: University of Chicago Press, 1970.

McKean, Robert B. *St. Petersburg Between the Revolutions: Workers and Revolutionaries, June 1907–February 1917.* New Haven: Yale University Press, 1990.

McNally, Raymond T. *The Major Works of Peter Chaadaev: A Translation and Commentary.* Notre Dame: University of Notre Dame Press, 1969.

Miliukov, Paul. *Russia and Its Crisis.* Chicago: University of Chicago Press, 1905.

Misa, Thomas J. *A Nation of Steel: The Making of Modern America 1865–1925.* Baltimore: Johns Hopkins University Press, 1995.

M. Mitel'man, M., B. Glebov, i A. Ul'ianskii. *Istoriia Putilovskogo zavoda, 1789–1917.* Moskva: Leningradskii Institut Istorii, 1939, 1941.

Moore, Wilbert E. *World Modernization: The Limits of Convergence.* New York: Elsevier North Holland, 1979.

O'Prey, Kevin P. *A Farewell to Arms? Russia's Struggle with Defense Conversion.* New York: The Twentieth Century Fund Report, 1995.

Orlovsky, Daniel. *The Limits of Reform: The Ministry of Internal Affairs in Imperial Russia, 1802–1881.* Cambridge: Harvard University Press, 1981.

———. "The Lower Middle Strata in Revolutionary Russia." In *Between Tsar and People: Educated Society and the Quest for Public Identity in Late Imperial Russia,* ed. Edith W. Clowes, Samuel D. Kassow, and James L. West, 248–55. Princeton: Princeton University Press, 1991.

Owen, Thomas. *Capitalism and Politics in Russia: Moscow Merchants, 1855–1905.* Cambridge: Cambridge University Press, 1981.

———. *The Corporation under Russian Law, 1800–1917.* Cambridge: Cambridge University Press, 1991.

———. *Russian Corporate Capitalism from Peter the Great to Perestroika.* New York: Oxford University Press, 1995.

Pinchuk, Ben-Cion. *The Octobrists in the Third Duma, 1907–1912.* Seattle: University of Washington Press, 1974.

Polikarpov, V. V. "Putilovskii zavod nakanune fevralia 1917 goda." *Voprosy Istorii* 10 (1983): 99–101.

Pollard, Sidney. *Peaceful Conquest, The Industrialization of Europe 1760–1970*. Oxford: Oxford University Press, 1986.

"Putilov, N. I.," *Russkii biograficheskii slovar'*, tom 15, 151–53. Moskva: Aspekt Press, 1998.　＼

Rieber, Al. *Merchants and Entrepreneurs in Imperial Russia*. Chapel Hill: University of North Carolina Press, 1982.

Roosa, Ruth AmEnde. *Russian Industrialists in an Era of Revolution, The Association of Industry and Trade, 1906–1917*. Armonk, N.Y.: M.E. Sharpe, 1997.

Ropp, Theodore. *The Development of a Modern Navy: French Naval Policy, 1871–1904*. Annapolis: Naval Institute Press, 1987.

Rubenshtein, N. L. *Russkaia istoriografia*. Moskva: Ogiz, 1941.

Ruckman, Jo Ann. *The Moscow Business Elite: A Social and Cultural Portrait of Two Generations, 1840–1905*. De Kalb: Northern Illinois University Press, 1984.

Rust, Michael Jared. "Business and Politics in the Third Republic: Comité De Forges and the French Steel Industry, 1896–1914." Ph.D. diss., Princeton University, 1973.

Ruud, Charles A. *Russian Entrepreneur, Publisher Ivan Sytin of Moscow, 1851–1934*. Montreal: McGill-Queen's University Press, 1990.

Rye, Man & Gor Securities. "Analytical Note," 17 April 1997.

Schmitz, Christopher J. *The Growth of Big Business in the United States and Western Europe, 1850–1939*. London: Macmillam Press Ltd, 1993.

Schwartz, Herman M. *States versus Markets: History, Geography, and Development of the International Political Economy*. New York: St. Martin's Press, 1994.

Scott, John, and Catherine Griff. *Directors of Industry: The British Intercorporate Network, 1904–1976*. London: Polity Press, 1984.

Scott, Robert E. "Latin America and Modernization." In *Latin America Modernization Problems: Case Studies in the Crises of Change*, ed. Robert E. Scott, 1–22. Urbana: University of Illinois Press, 1973.

"Semenenko, Petr Georgievich," in *Kto est' kto v Rossii*. Moskva: Russkaia Kadrovaia Assotsiatsiia, 1996, 306.

"Semenenko, Petr Georgievich." In V. K. Vasil'ev, O. S. Kuzin, and V. B. Ugriumov, *Kto est' kto v Sankt-Peterburge 1996*, 165–66. Sankt-Peterburg: Leninzdat, 1996.

Senin, A. S. *Aleksandr Guchkov*. Moskva: Skriptorii, 1996.

Shatsillo, K. F. *Gosudarstvo i monopolii v voennoi promyshlennosti Rossii konets XIX v.–1914*. Moskva: Nauka, 1992.

———. "Inostrannyi kapital i voenno-morskie programmy Rossii." *Istoricheskia Zapiski* 69 (1961): 73–100.

———. "Iz istorii ekonomicheskoi politiki tsarskogo pravitel'stva v gody pervoi mirovoi voiny." In *Ob osobennostiakh imperializma v Rossii*, ed. A. L. Sidorov, 215–33. Moskva: Izdatel'stvo Akademii Nauk SSSR, 1963.

Shepelev, L. E. *Tsarizm i burzhuaziia v 1904–1914 gg*. Leningrad: Akademiia Nauk SSSR, 1987.

Sidorov, A. L. "Nekotorye problemy razvitiia rossiiskogo kapitalizma v Sovetskoi istoricheskoi nauke." *Voprosy Istorii* 12 (1961): 26–62.

Siegelbaum, Lewis H. *The Politics of Industrial Mobilization in Russia, 1914–1917: A Study of the War-Industries Committees.* New York: St. Martin's Press, 1983.

Skocpol, Theda. *States and Social Revolutions: A Comparative Analysis of France, Russia, and China.* Cambridge: Cambridge University Press, 1979.

Smith, S. A. *Red Petrograd, Revolutions in the Factories 1917–1918.* Cambridge: Cambridge University Press, 1983.

Solov'eva, A. M. "Pribyli krupnoi promyshlennoi burzhuazii v aktsionernykh obshchestvakh Rossii v kontse XIX-nachale XX veka." *Istoriia SSSR* 3 (1984): 34–49.

Stevenson, David. *Armaments and the Coming of War: Europe, 1904–1914.* Oxford: Clarendon Press, 1996.

Strange, Susan. *States and Markets.* London: Pinter Publishers, 1988.

Surh, Gerald D. *1905 in St. Petersburg: Labor, Society, and Revolution.* Stanford: Stanford University Press, 1989.

Taits, R. M. *Korabelshchiki Narvskoi zastavy.* Leningrad: Lenizdat, 1967.

Tilly, Richard. "An Overview on the Role of the Large German Banks up to 1914." In *Finance and Financiers in European History, 1880–1960,* ed. Youssef Cassis, 93–112. Cambridge: Cambridge University Press, 1992.

Tolf, Robert W. *The Russian Rockefellers: The Saga of the Nobel Family and the Russian Oil Industry.* Stanford: Hoover Institution Press, 1976.

Trebilcock, Clive. *The Vickers Brothers, Armaments and Enterprise 1854–1914.* London: Europa Publications Ltd., 1977.

Von Laue, Theodore H. *Sergei Witte and the Industrialization of Russia.* New York: Columbia University Press, 1963.

Walicki, Andrzej. *A History of Russian Thought from the Enlightenment to Marxism.* Stanford: Stanford University Press, 1979.

Wegs, James Robert "Austrian Economic Mobilization During World War I: With Particular Emphasis on Heavy Industry," Ph.D. diss., University of Illinois, Urbana, 1970.

Westwood, J. N. *Russian Naval Construction 1905–1945.* London: Macmillan Press Ltd., 1994.

Zav'ialov, S. *Istoriia Izhorskogo zavoda.* Moskva: Ogiz Gos. Izdat., 1934.

Zelnik, Reginald. *Labor and Society in Tsarist Russia: The Factory Workers of St. Petersburg, 1855–1870.* Stanford: Stanford University Press, 1971.

INDEX